D0712361

ENDING THE MANAGEMENT ILLUSION

ELIMINATE THE MENTAL TRAPS THAT THREATEN YOUR ORGANIZATION'S SUCCESS

Hersh Shefrin

New York   Chicago   San Francisco   Lisbon   London
Madrid   Mexico City   Milan   Montreal   New Delhi
San Juan   Seoul   Singapore   Sydney   Toronto

1 2 3 4 5 6 7 8 9 0   DOC/DOC   0 9 8

ISBN: 978-0-07-149473-1
MHID: 0-07-149473-1

This publication is designed to provide accurate and authoritative information in regard to the subject matter covered. It is sold with the understanding that the publisher is not engaged in rendering legal, accounting, or other professional service. If legal advice or other expert assistance is required, the services of a competent professional person should be sought.
—*From a Declaration of Principles Jointly Adopted by a Committee of the American Bar Association and a Committee of Publishers and Associations*

McGraw-Hill books are available at special quantity discounts to use as premiums and sales promotions, or for use in corporate training programs. To contact a representative, please visit the Contact Us pages at www.mhprofessional.com.

This book is printed on acid-free paper.

For Leo, my laptop companion.

CONTENTS

PREFACE

I have lived with the illusion of management all my life. I witnessed it as a small boy, running around our family business. I witnessed it in the businesses run by my friends' parents. I imagined that things were different in big companies.

Many years later, I did consulting, as professors tend to do. I learned that the illusion of management is alive and well in big companies and also in government. But I kept hoping that the illusion would evaporate.

It never did. So, I finally decided to write this book.

I thank my editor, Jeanne Glasser, for the years she spent trying to convince me to write this book, for eventually persuading me, for supporting me during the writing process, and for making great suggestions that have made the book better than it would have been.

I thank many people for sharing their insights with me over the years. My biggest thanks go to Bill Palmer, CEO of Commercial Casework, for his great generosity. Bill has lectured on open book management to my classes, invited my classes to tour his company, provided me with data, and shared his insights into the realistic workings of an open book company. I thank Bo Burlingham for sharing wonderful stories and insights about open book management with my undergraduate students and with the MBA student body in the Leavey School of Business at Santa Clara University. I thank Jack Stack for helping me to understand open book management more deeply than I thought possible. I thank Rita Bailey for her penetrating observations about what makes Southwest Airlines a successful company. I thank Travis Peterson for taking the time to explain exactly how Southwest uses a simulation game in its training program.

Finally, I thank my wife, Arna, for her encouragement, comments, and patience in connection with the writing of this book.

Hersh Shefrin
January 2008

CHAPTER 1

PSYCHOLOGY AND SUCCESS

Behavioral finance is in the process of transforming the world of business and finance. That is terrific. I say this not just because I have been personally working hard to make that transformation happen. It is terrific because behavioral finance offers incredibly important lessons that can help businesspeople the world over make better decisions.

Behavioral finance is the study of how psychology affects financial decision making. I have been studying the impact of psychology on financial and economic decisions for more than 30 years. Back in the 1970s, my professional colleagues' reaction to the application of behavioral ideas lay somewhere between rejection and outright hostility. I remember more than one shouting match. Ah, those were the days. Over time, I am happy to report, the resistance began to melt away. And today, the whole financial paradigm is going behavioral!

A decade ago, I felt that behavioral finance was like a secret: It was something important to be shared. Do you know the definition of a secret? It's something that you tell to one person—at a time. Well, I decided to write a book to share the secret with one reader at a time. That book was *Beyond Greed and Fear*, the first comprehensive treatment of behavioral finance and also the first book on the topic written explicitly for financial practitioners.

I am happy to report that *Beyond Greed and Fear* is doing its job of getting the word out to financial decision makers about behavioral finance. I don't know if the book is read in Antarctica, but I can testify that it is used on all the other continents.

The subtitle of *Beyond Greed and Fear* is *Understanding Behavioral Finance and the Psychology of Investing*. Truth be told, the target readers of *Beyond Greed and Fear* are investors rather than corporate managers. I have written this book to speak directly to corporate managers about the value proposition that behavioral finance offers them. This value proposition has at its heart the running of a psychologically smart business. Human psychology has both pluses and minuses. Psychologically smart companies learn how to manage both the pluses and the minuses. In fact, psychologically smart companies invest in the development of processes to manage both.

If you open an introductory textbook on psychology, chances are you will find a discussion about illusions. Most of these are optical illusions. A famous optical illusion is that the Gateway Arch in St. Louis appears taller than it is wide. In fact, the arch is as tall as it is wide. Psychologists have extended their study of illusions from the optical variety to broader categories.

Psychologist Daniel Kahneman, who received the 2002 Nobel Prize for Economics, has pioneered the study of biases as illusions in perception. His work with the late

Amos Tversky provides the psychological underpinning to behavioral finance. In this book, you will read about many of the ideas Kahneman and Tversky introduced, concepts such as availability bias and anchoring bias.

Some behavioral biases actually have the word *illusion* in their names. Examples are "the illusion of control" and the "the illusion of effectiveness." In this book, I will tell you about a whole series of biases that impact the managers of companies. I call this series "the illusions of management."

Biases can have both pluses and minuses. People who are optimistic and confident can work wonders. Optimism and confidence are generally good qualities. But you can have too much of a good thing. People can be unrealistically optimistic and overconfident. And managers are people. Managers who are unrealistically optimistic and overconfident are prone to creating disasters. I will share a few disaster stories with you in this book. Unrealistic optimism and overconfidence are "behavioral biases." Basically, a behavioral bias is a predisposition toward making a mistake. What corporate managers need to know is how to create a psychologically smart business that faces up to biases head-on—and deals with them.

The act of reducing bias is called *debiasing*. I feel quite confident in saying that debiasing is a new word for most readers. If you are wondering whether I am not just confident but overconfident, then you are off to a good start with this book. Debiasing is a very important word. It lies at the heart of behavioral business intelligence, which is to say running a business in a way that is psychologically smart. The secrets I will share with you in this book are secrets for debiasing. Do what it takes to commit the word *debiasing* to memory. Say it aloud five times pausing for ten seconds between repetitions. Write it down on a piece of paper. Use it in a sentence the next time you speak to somebody. Let it become your mantra!

I've done enough consulting in my career to see firsthand how pernicious psychological biases are. In my experience, most companies recognize the problems that biases pose but have no idea about how to address them. The cost of failing to address biases is inferior execution. Or put differently, the path to improved execution goes through debiasing!

To be successful, a business, like a sports team, must excel at execution. In sports, dropped balls, turnovers, and unnecessary penalties are obstacles to winning. In business, faulty products, late deliveries, and excessive cost are obstacles to succeeding. Keeping mistakes to a minimum is a huge challenge that is easier said than done. What you will find in the pages of this book are practical steps that business leaders can take to meet the debiasing challenge. I'll also provide you with lots of examples.

Nortel: Too Much of a Good Thing

If I describe biases to you in abstract terms, you will get the general idea of what the concept means and how it affects decisions adversely. If I give you an example, you will get an even better idea. What about firsthand experience? Well, witnessing a bias at work in your own environment can be a double-edged sword. On the one hand, direct observation can offer the deepest learning. On the other hand, there is all that pain ...

Here is an example to feature biased decision making. On January 2, 2007, *The Wall Street Journal* ran a front-page story about Michael Zafirovsky, the chief executive officer of telecommunications firm Nortel Networks.

By way of background, Nortel is a Canadian firm headquartered in Toronto. In August 2000, its market capitalization peaked at $242.8 billion and dominated the value of the

Toronto Stock Exchange Index. However, in the wake of the collapse of the technology bubble, its market cap declined dramatically, bottoming at $2.1 billion in September 2002. In 2004, the company was hit with an accounting scandal, when it was found to have manipulated its financial statements to deceive investors and trigger large, unwarranted bonuses for its executives.

Michael Zafirovsky took over the reins at Nortel in November 2005, when its market capitalization had rebounded to $13.9 billion. *The Wall Street Journal* described him as both optimistic and confident. The article pointed out that he was a believer in "forceful optimism," that he was very optimistic about the company's future prospects, and that he was confident he could lead the company to that better future.

People who exhibit unrealistic optimism tend to experience disappointment more frequently than they had anticipated. People who exhibit overconfidence tend to experience surprises more frequently than they had anticipated. During his first year at the helm of Nortel, Zafirovsky experienced a series of disappointments and surprises. A key disappointment was Nortel's operating profit margin, which Zafirovsky had forecast would improve in 2006. Instead, increased competition caused the margin to decline during the first three quarters of the year. A key surprise was that Nortel would have to restate its financial results after 2003 because of weak internal financial controls. The market reaction was not favorable. In 2006, when the S&P 500 returned 15.2 percent, Nortel's stock returned –12.6 percent.

Disappointments and surprises are the hallmarks of unrealistic optimism and overconfidence. As it happens, when the press describes a particular CEO as optimistic and confident, the odds are excellent that the CEO is unrealistically optimistic and overconfident. This is not to say that

CEOs lack intelligence. Most are highly intelligent. It is just that an overconfident CEO is not as intelligent as he or she imagines.

Michael Zafirovsky's disappointment at not being able to turn Nortel around as quickly as he had planned surprised him, although it did not surprise Nortel's board. The combination of disappointment and surprise affected him personally in that he wound up sleeping less and worrying more. In his first year as CEO, he slept about four restless worry-filled hours per night, and his work-week ballooned to 100 hours. He found himself sending more e-mails between midnight and 6 a.m. than was his custom. He spent less time with his family, and when he did vacation with them, he was surprised to find that he would spend half of that time on the phone dealing with work-related crises.

General Psychological Traits

Unrealistic optimism, overconfidence, and poor accounting, which feature strongly in the saga of Nortel, are core issues in this book. The first two are psychological traits, whereas accounting is a business function. I will have a lot to say about accounting in later chapters. Here, I want to offer some additional remarks about psychological traits.

Human beings are generally prone to unrealistic optimism and overconfidence. These traits are especially important when it comes to planning. In fact, people tend to have so much difficulty planning that psychologists have given the phenomenon a special name: the *planning fallacy*. What makes the planning fallacy fallacious is more than poor planning. It is the fact that most people recognize that in the past they have planned poorly but come to believe that in the future they will plan successfully.

Overconfidence is pernicious and can be fed by other psychological traits that often color, or bias, our judgments. One such bias is called *confirmation bias*.

People who exhibit confirmation bias attach too much importance to information that confirms their views and too little importance to information that runs counter to their views. Call them stubborn, if you like, or worse. However, there are lots of people who demonstrate confirmation bias, and some are quite successful.

Another trait that feeds overconfidence is the "illusion of control." People who suffer from the illusion of control imagine that they exert more control than they actually do. The outcome of most situations involves a combination of luck and skill. Some people can exercise a great deal of skill but end up unlucky. Others can exercise little skill but end up lucky. Think of the phrase "beginner's luck."

People who suffer from both confirmation bias and the illusion of control tend to be especially overconfident. Think about the rate at which teen drivers have accidents. Did you know that per mile driven, drivers between the ages of 16 and 19 are four times more likely to have an accident than are older drivers? Did you know that the number-one cause of U.S. teen fatalities is traffic accidents?

What do you think explains these statistics? Is it a lack of experience behind the wheel? Or is it more likely that teen drivers are overconfident, believing themselves to be more in control than is actually the case?

For the answer, I suggest that you ask any parent of a teenage driver. At one time, the main contributing factor to teen automobile accidents was alcohol consumption. However, according to the National Highway Traffic Safety Administration, teen drinking has decreased dramatically in recent years. Today, it is not drunk driving but cell driving that causes most teen car crashes. (Cell driving is speaking on a cell phone while driving.)

The key issue is distraction. Talking on a cell phone while driving is distracting. Teens are also known to drive at the same time as they play handheld games, listen to music on their iPods, and send text messages. Having other teen passengers is also distracting and increases the likelihood of a fatal accident by a factor of two (with a single passenger) or five (with two or more passengers). Do you think teen drivers are apt to be more confident when they are part of a pack? For the answer, ask any parent of a teen driver.

Confirmation bias and the illusion of control combine forces to provide an ego boost. When events turn out poorly, people tend to attribute the outcome to bad luck rather than a deficiency in their own skill. When events turn out well, they attribute the result to their own skill rather than good luck. This combination also has a name: *fundamental attribution error*.

Bad Psychology, Disastrous Decisions

Mistakes can be very expensive. The dot-com boom and bust of the 1990s and early 2000s were largely due to unrealistic optimism and overconfidence. The acquisition by AOL of Time Warner has come to be regarded as one of the worst in history, and it destroyed about $200 billion in shareholder value. In July 2006, on the television program *Charlie Rose*, AOL's CEO and cofounder Steve Case apologized for having made the acquisition, saying, "I'm sorry I did it."

Don't think that executives alone suffer from unrealistic optimism, overconfidence, confirmation bias, and the illusion of control or that executives alone succumb to the planning fallacy and fundamental attribution error. We are all vulnerable. Even people who write books about these issues are vulnerable ... even politicians. Presidents of great nations and their cabinet secretaries are vulnerable.

Robert Woodward's book *State of Denial*, published in 2006, describes the serious mistakes that President George W. Bush and his secretary of defense, Donald Rumsfeld, made in their management of the war in Iraq. The phrase "state of denial" is, of course, a pun because *state* refers both to nation-state and psychological state. Psychologically, being in a state of denial corresponds to confirmation bias, the tendency to discount or ignore evidence that does not confirm one's beliefs.

And it's not only Republican presidents who are susceptible to having their judgment clouded by psychological phenomena. In *Beyond Greed and Fear*, I documented how Democratic President Bill Clinton and first lady Hillary Rodham Clinton made important errors in judgment in the series of events that came to be known as Whitewater. Their problems stemmed from a psychological phenomenon called "aversion to a sure loss." Being averse to a sure loss means being willing to make bad high-risk bets. These bets involve the likelihood of an even deeper loss but offer a slim chance of beating the odds and avoiding a sure loss.

In the case of the Clintons, the sure loss stemmed from a failed real estate investment in a property development known as Whitewater. When Whitewater began to fail, the Clintons had to face the serious prospect that they would lose money. The Clintons were offered an opportunity to limit that loss by selling their position. Doing so meant having to come to terms with a sure loss. Instead, they refused, hoping to break even if not to earn the returns they originally expected. That was a bad bet, which resulted in an even larger loss for the Clintons.

From that point on, the losses deepened. The Clintons lost more money and lost a friend to suicide, Vincent Foster, whom they had assigned the responsibility of looking after the financial records associated with Whitewater. The investigation of that suicide led to the appointment of an independent counsel, Kenneth Starr, who investigated not only Whitewater but also Bill Clinton's relationships with Paula Jones and Monica Lewinsky.

Paula Jones sued President Clinton for sexual harassment that she alleged occurred during the time he was governor of Arkansas. Bill Clinton considered, and at Hillary's urging rejected, an out-of-court settlement with Paula Jones. A settlement would have entailed a sure loss, to which both were averse. During the deposition phase of that suit, he was questioned, under oath, about his relationship with Monica Lewinsky, with whom he had a relationship that featured sexual contact. At that point, he had a choice either to accept a sure loss and admit to the relationship or to make a bad, high-risk bet, hoping to avert a sure loss but exposing himself to a much deeper loss. Being averse to sure loss, he tried to beat the odds. In the end, he lost the bet and wound up being impeached by Congress. Although he was not forced to resign from the presidency, he paid a high price in terms of embarrassment before the world, the diversion of his time, legal costs, and very strained relations with the first lady.

Aversion to a sure loss also goes by the name "escalation of commitment." This term was applied to President Lyndon Johnson in connection with his handling of the Vietnam War during the 1960s. Even though the American military had advised President Johnson that the Vietnam War was not winnable and that the United States should reduce its commitment to that war, the president could not accept the associated sure loss and instead escalated U.S. commitment by increasing the size of the U.S. force.

History has a way of repeating itself. Let us fast-forward from the 1960s to 2006. In the November 2006 midterm election, the American public expressed its displeasure with the manner in which the war in Iraq was being managed, or should I say mismanaged. Immediately after the election,

Donald Rumsfeld resigned as secretary of defense. President Bush promised to develop a new strategy for fighting the war. And he did, announcing in January 2007 that he would escalate America's commitment of troops to Iraq by 20,000 in a program that came to be called "the surge." A few of those who escalate commitment wind up lucky and manage to beat the odds. But they really need luck on their side, for skill it is not. As for the surge, time will tell as to the extent luck will play out favorably for the president's strategy.

The Biggest Rogue Trading Loss in Banking History

In January 2008 rogue trader Jérôme Kerviel caused Société Générale SA to lose €4.9 billion, the equivalent of $7.3 billion. Never before had a rogue trader caused a bank to lose so much money. And what lay at the heart of Société Générale's disaster? Bad psychology.

Before the disaster Société Générale prided itself on its trading reputation. Indeed, the bank recruits its best traders from France's top-tier colleges, looking for "quants," individuals with exceptionally strong mathematical skills. At Société Générale, quants constitute an elite groups and are responsible for the trading of sophisticated derivatives.

Kerviel was no quant, a fact that lay at the heart of the disaster. Instead, he studied accounting at second-tier colleges, learning how to become a back-office controller. His qualifications landed him a job in Société Générale's back-office. However, he dreamed of becoming a trader!

In 2005 Kerviel's dream partly came true when the bank promoted him from its back office to one of its trading floors. That part was good news. However, the bank did not assign him to the elite quant group, but to a much less prestigious group. Kerviel's group was charged with making simple low-risk hedged trades on the direction of the markets, not sophisticated trades involving the use of high-powered derivatives.

Psychologically, Kerviel perceived himself to be operating in the domain of losses. His main loss related not to his financial position, but to his ambition. Kerviel viewed himself as being on the same level as the quants. Remember, people who perceive themselves to be operating in the domain of losses are prone to accept high-risk bets in an effort to avert a sure loss.

As I mentioned earlier, aversion to a sure loss got President Clinton into serious trouble. Indeed, the same psychological phenomenon drove Nicholas Leeson, who held the previous rogue trading record. Leeson could not accept sure losses in his trades at Barings Bank, and his high-risk attempts to avert those losses caused Barings to collapse.

Kerviel might have accepted his lot in life at Société Générale, continuing to engage in low-risk trading. But this meant accepting the sure loss of frustrated ambition. Instead he chose the high-risk route. He found an unauthorized way to establish large unhedged positions. In doing so, he hoped somehow to break out of his typecast mold.

Kerviel actually achieved a measure of success in his unhedged trading positions. That success emboldened him to ask for a bonus of over €600,000—an extraordinary amount, given his modest base salary of about €55,000. Alas, his trading profits did not provide him with the recognition he so desperately sought. But it did increase his confidence, emboldening him to take even larger positions.

Using the knowledge he gained while working in the back office, Kerviel found clever ways to hide his true positions from the bank. Those positions registered a mix of wild ups and downs. At one point in 2006, his positions were up €1.6 billion, about a third of the bank's net profit for the year! At another point, in the spring of 2007, his position was down €2.2 billion. A few months later, his position was up again, by €500 million.

Being up a large amount was a double-edged sword. Kerviel experienced the associated pride, but he could not disclose the size of the profit for fear of revealing his unauthorized strategy. In effect, he was now trading large positions to feed his psychological need for self-worth, the pride of outperforming the quants.

It took Société Générale until January 2008 to discover what Kerviel had been up to. When they did figure it out, they learned that Kerviel's positions exposed the bank to a loss of about €50 billion, more than the bank's net worth! At that time, the value of his position was down €1.5 billion. To reduce the bank's risk exposure, Société Générale's executives decided to liquidate Kerviel's entire position as quickly as possible. Unfortunately for them, market conditions for doing so were less than ideal. Société Générale sustained a loss of €4.9 billion.

Bad psychology did not just drive Kerviel's behavior. It also drove the behavior of Société Générale's executives and managers. They typecast Kerviel as a trader who lacked the skill to manage sophisticated positions. He did not fit their stereotype of a sophisticated trader, but did fit their sterotype of an unsophisticated trader. Psychologists use the term "representativeness" to describe overreliance on stereotypes. In this regard, the bank executives reacted with absolute disbelief when they received the initial news about Kerviel's positions, asking how it could be possible.

After the story broke, Kerviel indicated that his superiors had turned a blind eye to the amount of money he placed at risk. He effectively charged them with confirmation bias. Why? Because they had to have realized he could not report substantial trading profits from small, hedged positions.

Indeed, the bank's risk-management system had sounded several alarms about Kerviel's trading positions. But Kerviel was always able to provide explanations that discouraged further inquiry. He also claimed to have broken a cardinal internal control rule by taking very little vacation. In particular, he took very few holidays in 2007, thereby preventing his superiors from taking a close look at his books. He justified his behavior by explaining that work helped him deal with the pain of his father's recent death, and his superiors accepted his explanation.

Société Générale's executives appeared to display overconfidence. In 2005 they boasted that their bank was well positioned to outperform the industry. In particular, they emphasized the high quality of their risk-management system. They pointed out that in the previous 15 years they had experienced no major incident in trading equity derivatives. After the Kerviel story broke, the bank's chairman and co-chief executive, Daniel Bouton, came under fire to resign. But the bank's board expressed confidence in his leadership.

A month after discovering the extent of Kerviel's trading activities, Société Générale issued a preliminary report detailing the breakdown in its risk controls. The report documents that between July 2006 and September 2007, Kerviel's trades triggered no less than 24 alarms. However, controllers investigating these alarms dropped their inquiries when they failed to understand his explanations. The report criticizes the risk control unit for not being sufficiently thorough. In this regard, the unit apparently attributed the alarms to frequent difficulties associated with the entry of operations data into the bank's computer systems. Talk about confirmation bias!

The report contains an especially intriguing assessment of the employees working in the back office. The report indicates that the back office staff performed their functions in accordance with their job descriptions. Therefore, the report concludes that back office staff were not at fault, even though they possessed enough information to have raised additional alarms. This incident teaches an important lesson about the psychological concept of "narrow framing" and the importance of addressing narrow framing by helping a company's entire workforce to see the big picture.

Psychology and Environmental Degradation

Do not think that American presidents, CEOs, and teen drivers are the only people whose judgments are biased by human psychology. So let me move right along to a topic that will lead me to get on my soapbox for a few pages.

Global warming arguably represents the most important environmental threat to our planet in this century. And a lot of smart people have underestimated the threat. Why? The short answer is psychological bias.

This is serious. These biases might well spell our doom. If we don't muster the collective will to control the amount of carbon dioxide in our planet's atmosphere, we will suffer more than headaches and coughing spells. If we were to convert all our known coal and petroleum reserves into energy, there is very good science to suggest that we won't be able to breathe air without suffering serious brain damage. As one of my university colleagues is fond of saying, we will run out of healthy air before we run out of energy. Now that is a sobering thought.

Environmental issues figure prominently in this book not only because they have played a part in past policy debates but because they will become even more important as private sector firms seek solutions to environmental challenges. In this regard, I sincerely hope that managers working in companies that seek environmental solutions will read this book. They represent our hope. But they are also vulnerable to psychological biases. We will all benefit if they learn to run psychologically smart businesses.

In later chapters, I will describe how psychological issues impact the execution of environmental strategies. Here in this chapter, I want to help you understand the role that these biases have played in past debates—with the hope that maybe, just maybe, we can learn from the past and do some serious debiasing in the future. I am going to go on a bit about global warming not because I want to go overboard but because the issue is so very important.

During the 1970s, a series of scientific studies strongly suggested that chlorofluorocarbons were destroying Earth's ozone layer. Because the ozone layer absorbs ultraviolet radiation, the destruction of ozone was thought to increase the incidence of skin cancer in humans as well as adversely impacting plant and animal life. Scientific studies also suggested that carbon dioxide and other gases, such as methane, tend to absorb low-energy radiation, thereby trapping heat at the surface of the Earth. The warming of Earth's atmosphere came to be called "global warming." Because the trapping of heat by atmospheric gases is akin to the trapping of heat by a greenhouse, the effect came to be called the "greenhouse effect" and the associated gases "greenhouse gases."

When serious evidence about polar holes in the ozone layer began to surface, international political forces came to the fore with the intent of addressing the threat posed by chlorofluorocarbon emissions. At a 1987 United Nations conference held in Montreal, a treaty to ban chlorofluorocarbon emissions was signed. With the successful passage of this treaty, hope was sparked that the world community would turn its attention to addressing the greenhouse effect.

At the time, I read with interest the editorial positions that appeared in *The Wall Street Journal*, and for sake of illustration, I am going to focus on positions taken on its editorial pages. The summer of 1988 was particularly warm. At the time, some environmentalists suggested that the warm summer might be an indication of the greenhouse effect. However, in an editorial entitled "Political Irradiation" that appeared on July 25, 1988, the editors of the *Journal* suggested that there was "probably nothing to" the greenhouse effect.

Scientists around the world eventually concluded that the warm summer of 1988 was not a manifestation of the greenhouse effect. Nevertheless, this conclusion does not imply that there is nothing to the greenhouse effect. Indeed, the editorial's position generated a series of strong responses.

On August 8, 1988, a letter to the editor from the president of the World Resources Institute, Gus Speth, challenged the *Journal*'s position. He pointed out that during the twentieth century, the combination of fossil fuel combustion and deforestation had increased the atmospheric concentration of carbon dioxide by 25 percent. Speth then stated that every scientific body that was studying global warming had concluded that it needed to be taken very seriously.

Other letters to the editor followed. On August 17, 1988, Ken Bossong, director of the Critical Mass Energy Project, described the *Journal*'s editorial position as "nothing short of incredible." The editorial position was nothing if not bold. Some might say it reflected overconfidence. However, in view of the mounting evidence to which Gus Speth referred, overconfidence alone does not cover it. The issue is confirmation bias, the discounting of information that runs counter to one's views.

By October 1988, the Environmental Protection Agency began to weigh in officially on global warming. The U.S. government agency issued a report which predicted that global warming stemming from fossil fuel consumption would cause major ecological changes with serious economic consequences. In the next month, the Department of Energy issued a report stating that if the government mandated particular energy conservation improvements, U.S. carbon dioxide emissions by the year 2010 could be lower by 38 percent than they otherwise might be.

In line with confirmation bias, these government reports did not appear to change the editorial position articulated in *The Wall Street Journal*. On November 8, 1989, the *Journal*'s editors opined that environmentalists were strongly motivated, not so much by addressing the threat posed by global warming, as by the opportunity to attend lush conferences appealing for funds to feather their own nests, in the sense of promoting their own "careers, perquisites and politics."

On February 6, 1990, the editors suggested that the threat of global warming was akin to the threat from asbestos—overblown. On January 11, 1991, the *Journal*'s editors effectively accused environmentalists in public broadcasting with confirmation bias because they refused to air a documentary by producer Hilary Lawson, which suggested the evidence was mounting that global warming is untrue.

On June 1, 1992, the editors challenged the pessimistic conclusions of a long-term global warming study done for the Environmental Protection Agency by scientists at Oxford University and the Goddard Institute for Space Studies. In their challenge, the *Journal*'s editors called environmentalists "elitist" and suggested that increased carbon dioxide would lead to greater plant growth and therefore more food for a rising human population.

The presidential administrations of Ronald Reagan and George H. W. Bush, which covered the period 1980 through 1992, did not support reductions in greenhouse gas emissions. To be fair, though, George H. W. Bush did increase the budget for the Environmental Protection Agency and was viewed favorably by agency staff.

White House sentiment changed in 1993 with the election of the Clinton–Gore ticket. Al Gore, in particular, proved to be a champion of the effort to combat greenhouse gas emissions.

On December 10, 1997, a *Journal* editorial was highly critical of the administration's support of international negotiations taking place in Kyoto, Japan, which aimed to reduce greenhouse gas emissions. The *Journal*'s editors questioned the scientific basis of the greenhouse effect. They suggested that human-generated emissions of carbon dioxide are but a small proportion of the carbon dioxide in the atmosphere. They argued that there was too much uncertainty about the benefits of reducing greenhouse gas emissions to justify the cost in forgone production. They opined that the Clinton administration had a hidden agenda—namely, the generation of additional revenue from the taxation of energy. Finally, the *Journal*'s editors flatly stated that none of the predictions of temperature increases attributed to greenhouse gas emissions approached catastrophic proportions.

In 1997, Al Gore returned from Kyoto hoping to persuade the U.S. Senate to ratify the Kyoto treaty. In this goal, he would prove unsuccessful. His presidential bid in 2000 also proved unsuccessful. Nevertheless, Gore continued his efforts to address global warming. These efforts led him to create a successful film and associated book, which he titled *An Inconvenient Truth*. In these works, Gore documents the rise of temperatures worldwide, the melting of polar ice with already visible dramatic unfavorable consequences for Antarctic penguins and Arctic polar bears, and the increase in tropical storm activity, such as Hurricane Katrina that devastated New Orleans.

An Inconvenient Truth argued that continuing the recent rate of greenhouse gas emissions will create major catastrophes for our planet in the foreseeable future. What makes the truth inconvenient is that once it is acknowledged, the next step is to take action!

In January 2007, a highly respected United Nations scientific panel, known for being cautious, issued a series of predictions about rising temperatures and sea levels for the next several centuries. Notably, the Intergovernmental Panel on Climate Change (IPCC) concluded that the chief contributor to global warming, or at least some of its effects, is human-made emissions of greenhouse gases as opposed to natural causes. Among the effects in question are more killer heat waves, heavy flooding, devastating droughts, and more severe and frequent hurricanes. The panel emphasized that they predict significant increases in temperatures and sea levels even if greenhouse gas emissions are brought under control immediately. Therefore, failing to bring emissions under control will make matters that much worse.

I suggest to you that the concept *inconvenient truth* is psychological. Confirmation bias looms large. Its cousin, *cognitive dissonance*, looms large. The *dissonance* in cognitive dissonance involves a conflict between what people think they should do and what they feel they want to do. One way of resolving the conflict is to create a story that supports what people feel they want to do, thereby dispelling the dissonance.

People who do not wish to take actions against the emissions of greenhouse gases might combat cognitive dissonance by creating explanations suggesting that there is too much uncertainty about the effects of global warming to reduce greenhouse gas emissions, that proponents of reductions in greenhouse gas emissions have ulterior motives, or that the consequences associated with greenhouse gas emissions are relatively minor. As you might have noticed, the editors of *The Wall Street Journal* have made use of all these explanations.

In 2001, George W. Bush assumed the presidency. His administration did not support the greenhouse gas emission reductions called for by the Kyoto treaty, a point that Al

Gore emphasizes in *An Inconvenient Truth*. The *Journal*'s editors, true to their traditions, continued to criticize policies aimed at reducing greenhouse gas emissions in the United States. For example, on December 9, 2002, the editors described recent cold weather and suggested that such cold spells constituted counterexamples to the positions taken by those concerned about global warming. Confirmation bias and cognitive dissonance continued.

George W. Bush's Russian counterpart, Vladimir Putin, also appeared to take an unfavorable position toward the Kyoto treaty. In 2003, he appeared to argue that, on balance, complying with the treaty's accords would crimp Russia's ability to double its economy in the next 10 years. He used many of the same arguments favored by *The Wall Street Journal* editors. He also added a new one, suggesting that global warming would be a good thing for Siberia. Gasp! Happily, this view did not carry the day, and Russia ratified the treaty in 2004.

A key benefit to Russia from ratifying the Kyoto treaty stems from the "cap and trade system." The *cap* in cap and trade is the placement of an aggregate limit on greenhouse gas emissions. The *trade* in cap and trade is the trading of "licenses to emit greenhouse gases."

Cap and trade is a mixed public sector–private sector system for addressing pollution. The idea is that companies or countries own licenses allowing the bearer to emit pollutants into the environment. The holder of such a license can either use it or sell it on the open market. Under the Kyoto treaty, Russia's emissions rate during the 1990s places it in a position whereby it is able to sell many such licenses, thereby generating considerable revenues for itself.

U.S. industry has been ahead of the George W. Bush administration in pushing for a cap and trade system for carbon dioxide emissions. Among the most prominent of the industrial leaders urging action were the CEOs of General Electric, DuPont, and Duke Energy. In February 2007, even leading electricity producers, which rely on greenhouse gas emitting coal-fired plants, began to voice their support for federal government action aimed at limiting greenhouse gases.

In December 2007, Al Gore and the IPCC were co-awarded the Nobel Peace Prize for their efforts to raise awareness about global warming. Coincidentally, in mid-December 2007, a major international conference on global warming was taking place in Bali, Indonesia. The conference featured high drama as the United States was strongly resisting the European Union's proposal that by 2020, industrialized nations reduce emissions by 25 percent to 40 percent.

In defending its original position, American delegates pointed out that since 2001 the United States had spent $37 billion, more than any other country, to combat climate change. They provided a series of examples such as investments in low-emission coal-fired electrical generation and low-emission automobiles.

The argument did not persuade environmentalists. Using his Nobel Peace Prize pulpit, Gore publicly criticized his own country's position, stating: "My own country, the United States, is principally responsible for obstructing progress here in Bali." Facing relentless pressure from the global community, the United States reversed its position at the last minute.

Although this is not a book about environmental policy, I have woven an environmental thread throughout it. I have done this for three reasons. First, I consider global warming to constitute a huge threat to maintaining a favorable climate on our planet. Second, the private sector has the potential to address the threat. Third, psychological obstacles stand in the way of reacting to this threat sensibly.

The cover story in the August 2006 issue of *Bloomberg* magazine sounded an alarm about venture capital and the start-up of environmental firms. The alarm is that firms in the search for new environmental technologies will repeat the history of the dot-coms, with its frenzy of activity, over-valuation bubble, and subsequent burst.

Debiasing Games

An important reason for the overvaluation dot-com bubble in the late 1990s stems from the reliance by both investors and managers on psychology-based valuation instead of fun-damentals-based valuation. Simply put, most investors and corporate managers are not very skilled at valuation. For this reason, I am including valuation techniques as part of the tools associated with good business execution. This is not to say that investors and managers are not smart. Many are. Still, people can be smart and yet suffer from unrealistic optimism and overconfidence.

Is there anything that people can do to help themselves reduce their susceptibility to biases such as confirmation bias and unrealistic optimism? The short answer is yes. But that answer is too short. A better answer is yes, but it's not easy. The purpose of this book is to describe practical, proven steps that corporate leaders can take to limit their organizations' susceptibility to error and bias, even though it's not easy.

Past success often leads people to overconfidence. Think again about Mike Zafirovsky. Before he became CEO of Nortel Networks, Zafirovsky had been a successful execu-tive, first at Jack Welch's General Electric and then at Motorola, where his rank was number two, behind CEO Chris Galvin. In addition, *The Wall Street Journal* described him as highly competitive, stating that he had run more than seven marathons and completed the Ironman Triathlon.

Although people learn to be overconfident, they can also learn to mitigate their vulnerabilities to unrealistic optimism and overconfidence. They can play debiasing games. During his first year at Nortel, Zafirovsky began to play debiasing games with himself. He frequently posed the following kinds of questions to himself: Are my decisions correct, or are they misguided? Am I receiving information that I need to hear, or am I only receiving information that people think I want to hear? Am I being unrealistically optimistic? Am I ignoring important warning signals?

People commit errors when acting as individuals and also when acting as members of groups. In organizations, groups make most major decisions. What kind of debiasing games can organizations set in motion?

The starting point for instituting organizational debiasing games is the recognition that psychologically induced mistakes are akin to addictive diseases. What behaviorally induced mistakes and addictive behaviors share is habituation. Psychologically induced mistakes, like addictions to alcohol, food, illicit drugs, nicotine, and compulsive gambling, become ingrained habits. And habits are difficult to break.

We know something about how to treat addictive diseases. We know that 12-step programs are group programs that have truly helped many people combat their addictions. Indeed, step one is to acknowledge the problem, which in the case of psychologically induced mistakes means acknowledging our susceptibility to phenomena such as confirmation bias and unrealistic optimism. Step two involves acknowledging that we are not top dog when it comes to power. Such acknowledgment serves to combat overconfidence. To be sure, debiasing does not require the full application of all traditional 12 steps. However, many of the principles that work for addictive diseases also work when it comes to debiasing.

There is a growing academic literature on debiasing. The contributors to this literature are chipping away at what it takes for people to reduce their vulnerabilities to behavioral biases. These academic studies not only send the message that progress is possible, but they provide concrete suggestions for debiasing.[1]

The Illusions of Management

I am going to get back on my soapbox for a few pages. I am a big believer in behavioral corporate finance, the application of psychology to corporate financial decisions. In addition,

---

[1]Because this book is written for corporate executives, I do not provide an extensive literature survey. However, readers who are interested in this literature will find many useful insights in the following:

Feng, Lei, and Mark Seasholes, 2005. "Do Investor Sophistication and Trading Experience Eliminate Behavioral Biases in Finance Markets?" *Review of Finance* 9, no. 3, 305–351.

Kaustia, Markku, Eeva Alho, and Vesa Puttonen, 2007. "How Much Does Expertise Reduce Behavioral Biases? The Case of Anchoring Effects in Stock Return Estimates." Forthcoming in *Financial Management*.

Kraya, Laura, and Adam D. Galinsky, 2003. "The Debiasing Effect of Counterfactual Mind-Sets: Increasing the Search for Disconfirmatory Information in Group Decisions," *Organizational Behavior and Human Decision Processes* 91, 69–81.

Lovallo, D., and D., Kahneman, 2003. "Delusions of Success," *Harvard Business Review*, 56–60.

Russo, J. Edward, and Paul Schoemaker, *Winning Decisions*, 2002, Doubleday-Currency.

Srivastava, Joydeep, and Priya Raghubir, 2002. "Debiasing Using Decomposition: The Case of Memory-Based Credit Card Expense Estimates," *Journal of Consumer Psychology*, 12(3), 253–264.

Soman, Dilip, and Wenjing Liu, 2006. "Debiasing and Rebiasing: The Illusion of Delayed Incentives," working paper, Rotman School, University of Toronto.

I hold the position that psychologically smart companies make use of behavioral corporate finance. There is a good reason for this.

Business managers need to know how to keep score, just as players on a sports team need to know how to keep score. If you don't keep score, you cannot tell if you are winning or losing, if you are succeeding or failing. If you don't keep score, you will suffer from the illusions of management. In the world of business, finance and accounting provide methods for keeping score.

I might be subject to some bias of my own. In the last few years, I have written both an article and a textbook with the title *Behavioral Corporate Finance*. You will not be surprised to learn that I have drawn on both these works for this book. At the same time, these works were aimed at different audiences from the target readers of this book. The article was aimed at finance managers. The textbook was aimed at students in university business programs. This book is aimed at corporate managers who are interested in running psychologically smart companies.

How well do most employees understand the financial conditions of the firms for which they work? Not many, I suggest. How many firms create unbiased forecasts of future cash flows to serve as inputs into discounted cash flow analyses? Not many, I suggest. Yet financial knowledge and unbiased cash flow forecasts are critical aspects of sound business execution. When it comes to debiasing, there is much work to be done. And much of that work centers on making better use of corporate finance techniques.

If you want to build a psychologically smart company, you will have to face four key challenges. These challenges are associated with processes for predicting the financial future of the firm, focusing on key measures that drive performance, rewarding people for doing the right thing, and sharing information widely. In other words, the major challenges involve bias-free processes for accounting, planning, incentives, and information sharing.

To some readers, what I just said will sound trivial. After all, don't most companies already do those things? Well, yes, if you ignore the phrase "bias-free." In practice, biases serve as giant obstacles for conducting those four processes well.

Take accounting: In the wake of the Sarbanes-Oxley Act being passed, public companies have dramatically improved their financial controls. This has largely happened under pressure from section 404 of the act, which focuses on the adequacy of companies' internal controls, financial reports, and external audits. However, having good controls in place does not always mean that they are well used within the firm with respect to standards.

Most businesspeople outside accounting and finance are intimidated by accounting. This is unfortunate because accounting and finance keep score of how well a company is doing. Remember, if you don't keep score, you will suffer from the illusions of management. It will be hard to tell if you are winning or losing, succeeding or failing. People who want to lose weight are in trouble if they are reluctant to stand on the scales. In this respect, standards feature financial goals and targets against which to measure performance.

Take planning: Most people find doing it well to be an enormous challenge. Most people fail to plan their Christmas shopping properly and fail to allow enough time to complete household chores. Moreover, they recognize that this is so, yet fail to learn from past experiences. They suffer from the illusion that although they planned poorly in the past, they will plan well in the future! Most people carry over the same behavior patterns from their home lives to their work lives. If they succumb to the planning fallacy in their home lives, the same habits are often present in their work lives.

Notably, Nortel Networks' CEO Michael Zafirovsky was unrealistically optimistic in his plans for turning his new company around, having overemphasized the firm's global reach and intellectual-property portfolio. His plan had attached too little weight to Nortel's poor internal systems, inefficient bureaucracy, and junk-bond credit rating.

Take incentives: A key challenge for any corporation is to align the interests of its managers with those of its owners. Meeting this challenge requires that employees have the right incentives, incentives that induce them to think, feel, and act like owners.

Alas, when it comes to incentives, bias prevails. Putting effective incentive systems in place is no easy matter. Designing good bonus policies is very difficult work, as most who have ever done so will attest. At one point, many investors and boards operated under the illusion that granting stock options to executives and board members would serve to align their interests with those of shareholders.

The illusion was shattered in 2006. That year, *The Wall Street Journal* reported that hundreds of companies had engaged in options backdating. Backdating is the act of retroactively changing an option grant date to increase the value of the option. Rather than align the interests of executives and shareholders, backdating amounts to an out-and-out unwarranted wealth transfer from shareholders to executives. Call it stealing if you like.

Finally, take information sharing: Here, too, bias prevails. Corporate organizational structures tend not to encourage the effective sharing of information. The reasons are complex. Some reasons stem from self-interest; others are psychological and involve group dynamics. There are a lot of very costly examples of poor information sharing, which lead to a phenomenon called the "illusion of effectiveness."

An example I cover in a later chapter involves the aircraft manufacturer Airbus. When Airbus was developing its most advanced plane to date, the A380, the company experienced a large number of major difficulties. However, employees within the company failed to share information with each other about these difficulties. As a result, Airbus encountered major production delays and lost large sales to its competitor Boeing.

Room for Improvement

I'm still on my soapbox. The overarching management illusion is that there is little value in having a financially literate workforce, in engaging in unbiased planning, in structuring intelligent incentives, and in sharing information effectively.

Accounting, planning, incentives, and information sharing are bread-and-butter issues for most companies. To be sure, these topics are part of every major business school's curriculum. Yet, it seems to me that there are at least two places where there is significant room for improvement in the way companies carry out these activities.

The first place is integration. If you work in a corporate setting, you need to understand how to integrate four functions: accounting, planning, incentives, and information sharing. Think of your business as a stagecoach and the four functions as horses that drive the business along. You want to make these horses work together as a team. In a more modern metaphor, we would say we want the car to fire on all four cylinders.

Most businesses fall short when it comes to integrating the four functions. For that matter, most business schools fall short when it comes to teaching students how to integrate these functions. In this book, I describe a series of experiential-based techniques for developing integrated processes that enhance corporate value.

The second place for improvement involves explicit attention to debiasing. As in 12-step programs, if the members of an organization want to reduce their susceptibility to biases, they need to recognize their specific vulnerabilities and past mistakes. Pulling this off takes a deft hand and a supportive culture.

Corporate culture plays a critical role when it comes to debiasing. Minimizing the effect of psychological biases must be woven into the fabric of a corporation's culture. Otherwise, those biases will continue to thrive. The same remark applies to processes that integrate accounting, planning, incentives, and information sharing. Integration—connecting the dots—is a feature that must be woven into the culture of the corporation. The dots won't connect themselves!

The management illusion is that managers believe they can run a company successfully with a financially illiterate workforce that engages in ineffective planning, has little incentive to succeed, and doesn't get enough meaningful information. Simply put, the illusion is that managers think they run psychologically smart companies when they don't.

Sometimes people are lucky, and sometimes they are unlucky. One person can do the right thing and yet be unlucky in how things turn out. Another person can do the wrong thing and yet be lucky in way things turn out. Rational people try to do the right things and hope to be lucky. Except for death and taxes, there are no guarantees in the world.

In this book, I describe what you can do to build a psychologically smart business. Needless to say, I offer the promise of integrated processes for better decisions but no guarantees for success. But say it I must: The illusion of control is constantly looking for new victims.

CHAPTER 2

BEHAVIORAL INTELLIGENCE: BEST PRACTICES FOR RAISING AND SPENDING MONEY

Behavioral intelligence is the ability to run a psychologically smart company. Now, psychologically smart companies are made, not born. That is good news. It's good news because companies can learn to become behaviorally intelligent. And the path to behavioral intelligence is an eye-opening journey, which begins with a first step. That first step is to find some psychologically smart companies and copy their best practices.

Diamond in the Rough

A great resource for identifying corporate leaders and psychologically smart companies is *Inc.* magazine. *Inc.*'s readership mostly consists of small-business owners and entrepreneurs. *Inc.* was founded by publisher Bernie Goldhirsh and is headquartered in Boston. Its first issue appeared in April 1979. The magazine publishes one issue per month.

I want to tell you a fascinating story about the role *Inc.* has played in identifying the factors that underlie successful business execution.[1] It is a story about finding a diamond in the rough. The story begins in the early 1980s when *Inc.*'s executive editor was Bo Burlingham. At the time, Burlingham directed a corporate survey about executive compensation. *Inc.* would solicit responses from corporate executives and sift through the responses for those that seemed especially interesting. The executives who had provided the most interesting responses were then invited to Boston to participate in a roundtable on compensation. Their remarks provided the content for an article on compensation that would appear in the magazine.

Bo Burlingham assigned an intern to sift through the compensation survey responses. She was struck by one particular response. That response was from an executive named Jack Stack who was the CEO of Springfield Remanufacturing Corporation (now SRC Holdings), a small privately held firm in Springfield, Missouri, that rebuilt diesel engines.

In running his company, Stack made heavy use of bonuses not only for compensating executives but for the entire workforce. His survey response described a series of techniques involving games and targets that struck the *Inc.* intern as highly unusual.

There are two ways to go when one comes across a response that is highly unusual. The first is to discard it. The second is to embrace it. The intern embraced it with great enthusiasm. She sought to persuade Burlingham to

[1]Bo Burlingham, lecture at Santa Clara University, March 13, 2006.

include Jack Stack in the group of executives invited to Boston for the compensation roundtable. Fortunately, she succeeded.

When Jack Stack participated in that roundtable, he spoke about how structured incentives had helped SRC turn itself around after approaching the brink of insolvency. He also hinted at integrated processes for accounting, planning, incentives, and information sharing. But like a diamond in the rough, many people missed most of it. However, they did not miss the point about the effectiveness of well-structured bonuses and targets. Jack Stack had struck a chord.

The writers at *Inc.* were impressed, so impressed that they excluded Jack Stack and his remarks from the article that described their conference. Yes, you read correctly, excluded. Why? Because they thought his ideas were so interesting that they merited an article of their own.

Bo Burlingham dispatched two of his writers to SRC, charged with the task of gathering material for a story dedicated to Jack Stack and his company. What they observed struck them as utterly novel. They observed a gamelike atmosphere, with billboards in the cafeteria that flashed out labor utilization rates, and an engaged workforce. Stack likened the action at SRC to the action at Caesar's Palace casino in Las Vegas.

The two *Inc.* writers were amazed. However, they had different views about how to write up their observations and experiences at SRC. One writer believed their story should emphasize the gamelike features that they witnessed. The second writer believed it was inappropriate to write about business as if it were a game.

It fell to Burlingham, as executive editor, to strike a balance between these opposing views, which he did. The result was an article titled "The Turnaround" about Jack Stack and SRC that appeared in the August 1983 issue.

Normally, August is a dead month for business publications. Most regular readers are enjoying their vacations, not focused on business publications. It therefore came as a huge surprise when the article about SRC generated a record response for *Inc.*

Burlingham did not actually attend the roundtable that included Jack Stack. In fact, he didn't meet Stack until 1985. The meeting that eventually took place between the two occurred at an *Inc.*-sponsored conference. The meeting happened because Burlingham, curious as to how events had unfolded at SRC since the publication of the August 1983 issue, invited Stack to speak.

Stack's conference presentation took place in the morning and electrified his audience. As he spoke, the room in which he was speaking began to fill up to the point where people were standing in the aisles outside the doorway, straining to hear what he had to say.

The lunch that followed the morning conference presentations proved propitious. Bo Burlingham invited Jack Stack to join him at his table. Between them sat Harriet Rubin, a well-known and successful writer and publisher who in 1989 founded the firm Currency.

Burlingham and Stack conversed about "The Turnaround" and the reaction to it. Burlingham told Stack that the article had generated a huge response and that it was his favorite piece in *Inc.* He asked Stack whether SRC had experienced a similar response. Stack answered that it did, so much so that they could hardly run a staff meeting anymore because so many visitors had come to SRC trying to learn its methods.

At this point, Harriet Rubin turned to Burlingham and suggested that he write a book about SRC. Rubin had published the works of many leading executives, economists, and management consultants.

Burlingham's first reaction was to point out that he already had a full-time position as executive editor at *Inc.* However, the more he thought about the idea, the more he began to understand that what was taking place at SRC constituted a diamond in the rough. And there was value in polishing that diamond! He realized that Stack was special, that what he was doing at SRC was special, and that without some help, the approach being developed in Springfield, Missouri, would remain a purely local phenomenon and never make it past Springfield's city borders.

And so, Burlingham decided to step down from his position as executive editor at *Inc.* and collaborate with Stack on a book. The end product turned out to be a polished diamond, *The Great Game of Business*, by Jack Stack with Bo Burlingham, which Currency Doubleday published in 1992.

What made *The Great Game of Business* a polished diamond was its focus on developing that team of four horses: integrated processes for accounting, planning, incentives, and information sharing. Because of his emphasis on building games around being rewarded for achieving particular goals, Jack Stack called his approach "The Great Game."

Like an expert jeweler, Bo Burlingham had taken the rough Great Game approach developed by Jack Stack and polished it to clarity. Further polishing followed a decade later in a sequel by the same authors, *A Stake in the Outcome*.

In *The Great Game of Business* and *A Stake in the Outcome*, you will not find explicit discussions about the psychological underpinnings of the planning fallacy, unrealistic optimism, overconfidence, and aversion to a sure loss. These issues are all implicit. The point is that integrated processes for accounting, planning, incentives, and communication serve the cause of debiasing.

Jack Stack had built a better mousetrap, and some people were beating a path to his door. These people were not just his customers but executives running other companies. As interest in the SRC approach grew, Stack responded like a good capitalist. He set up a consulting division at SRC to make those other executives his customers. And once a critical mass developed of other firms using their version of the approach, SRC established an annual conference called The National Gathering of Games.

There are now many open book companies, large and small, private and public: Harley-Davidson, Whole Foods, Zingerman's Delicatessen, Commercial Casework, and Southwest Airlines. All of these companies provide valuable lessons about best practices.

Open Book Management

Inc. magazine has played a key role in spreading the word about SRC's approach. In the 1990s, the magazine's editors learned that other companies, not part of the Gathering of Games community, were following approaches that had much in common with that of SRC. Although the executives at these other companies were not using the language of games to describe what they did, Bo Burlingham discerned that there was a loosely structured movement that had taken root. He decided to document this movement in the pages of *Inc.*

A writer named John Case was assigned the task of documenting the movement. Case decided that the movement needed a name and chose the phrase "open book management." Case wrote up his findings for *Inc.* magazine, which became the business publication most closely associated with the movement. In addition, he wrote other pieces, including an article in the *Harvard Business Review*, and his own book.

The *book* in open book management refers to a firm's financial books, thereby emphasizing the importance of financial standards, the second element in accounting, planning, incentives, and information sharing. Lying at the heart of open book management is the idea that members of the workforce have the knowledge and information to base their workplace decisions on the firm's financial statements. Such knowledge and information enable the workforce to monitor costs and control expenses.

Financial Literacy: The Backbone of Financial Standards

What makes companies like SRC Holdings behaviorally intelligent? This is a big question. The answer begins with financial literacy.

Behaviorally intelligent companies train their workforces to be financially literate. A financially literate workforce is able to contribute effectively when it comes to developing financial plans that focus on key accounting measures, is rewarded based on how well the company performs according to those measures, and engages in continuous communication about current performance according to those measures.

In 1995, *Fortune* magazine ran an article describing the approach at SRC. The article singles out Craig Highbarger, a 32-year-old SRC machinist, and points out that he had been trained to understand the costs associated with the products he worked on, including allocated overhead. This training enabled him to make intelligent choices with the intent of maximizing the bottom line.

My experience tells me that Craig Highbarger is the exception rather than the rule. My experience tells me that finance and accounting actually intimidate most people. If you're not a financial manager or an accountant, I suspect that you might be one of those intimidated persons. Am I right?

Let me share a secret with you. Basic finance and accounting aren't rocket science. But a lot of businesspeople react to finance and accounting as if they were rocket science. Why? I think the problem is that finance and accounting lack a user-friendly interface.

Look, what is certainly true is that most people can be educated to understand and use finance and accounting. Think about Craig Highbarger, the SRC machinist. He told *Fortune* magazine that if he and his colleagues are handed an income statement with a few missing items, they know how to fill in the holes. It's not that difficult.

Traditional corporate finance is built around a series of concepts that sound quite technical: cash flow, valuation, risk and return, market efficiency, capital budgeting, capital structure, and payout policy. To explain these concepts intuitively, I'm going to take a specific company as an example and discuss the kinds of financial decisions it is called upon to make.

Some people think that finance is too specialized to be of interest to those concerned with general management. My view is that anyone who thinks he or she can be successful in business without being financially literate had better count on being lucky.

If you truly have financial expertise, you might consider skipping the rest of this chapter. But I think that would be a mistake. What you want to take away with you from this chapter are the basics of what financial literacy entails. This is especially important because the next chapter discusses the psychological obstacles that lead many organizations to be financially illiterate.

It's soapbox time, at least for a paragraph. Financial literacy entails focusing clearly on cash flows, where money comes from and where it gets spent. Financial literacy entails basing valuation on cash flows using present value techniques. Financial literacy entails understanding the returns a company's investors require to compensate them for risk. Financial literacy entails managers knowing when to trust market prices and when not to trust them. Financial literacy entails basing the decision to adopt a project on how much value the project adds to the wealth of the company's investors. Financial literacy entails finding the proper balance of debt and equity. Financial literacy entails catering payouts to the needs of investors.

There is a lot to know about financial literacy. Or put another way, there are a lot of ways financial illiteracy can lead to bad decisions. The more educated a company's workforce, the more behaviorally intelligent the company's processes and the more likely it is that the company will make the right decisions.

Financial literacy comes in degrees. Psychologically smart companies recognize that different people achieve different degrees of financial literacy. And they work with it. You don't have to remember everything you read here to be financially literate. But going through the rest of this chapter will help you appreciate the scope of financial issues that confront most companies. The base-level issues for financial literacy come first; they form the common denominator of financial knowledge in a behaviorally intelligent organization. The ones that come later are fine points that everyone can understand, but the CFO and CEO must understand.

Do you remember the line from the Watergate movie, *All the President's Men* (1976), about following the money? This chapter is about following the money and the decisions about where money comes from and where it goes. In the rest of this chapter, we'll use an example to illustrate how a financially literate workforce can follow its company's money.

R.R. Donnelley: A Story in Numbers

R.R. Donnelley is the largest commercial printing company in the United States, if not the world. Some of its divisions happen to be run along open book lines, which is the reason I have picked it to illustrate key ideas. I am going to take you on a tour of Donnelley's financial landscape to help you see the company through financially literate eyes.

Let's begin with a sketch of the company. R.R. Donnelley was founded more than 140 years ago. Based in Chicago, it employs 60,000 people and has 120 printing facilities in five countries. The items that Donnelley prints are everywhere and not just because Donnelley printed the *Harry Potter* book series. It also printed President Bill Clinton's book *My Life*, and it prints *The New York Times* magazine, *Sports Illustrated*, *Reader's Digest*, and *TV Guide*. My guess is that you are a consumer of at least one of Donnelley's products.

Donnelley has three different businesses segments. They are: (1) Publishing and Retail Services, (2) Integrated Print Communications and Global Solutions, and (3) Forms and Labels. The first two segments are roughly the same size and account for about 80 percent of Donnelley's sales. Together, the three business segments engage in financial printing, direct mail, labels, forms, online services, digital photography, and color services. Donnelley's main customers are businesses in the following industries: publishing, health care, advertising, retail, technology, and financial services.

Cash Flow: Doing It Right

Where does Donnelley raise money and spend money? A financially literate person knows how to figure out the answer to this question. As it happens, Donnelley raises most of its money from sales: all those *Harry Potter* books, issues of *Sports Illustrated*, and the printing of financial prospectuses. It spends money printing all of that material. There are 60,000 employees to pay. There is money spent on materials such as paper and ink. There are electric bills for running the printing presses.

To get an idea about how much Donnelley spends relative to its sales, take a look at Figure 2.1. This figure shows the time path of Donnelley's sales and its net income between 1988 and 2005.

In Figure 2.1, the black line at the top represents sales, and the dotted line at the bottom represents net income, otherwise known as earnings. As you can see, there is not

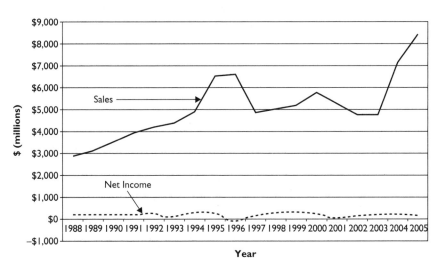

Figure 2.1 R.R. Donnelley Sales and Net Income, 1988–2005

a lot left over from sales by the time Donnelley meets its payroll and incurs all its other expenses.

Part of the reason there is so little left from its sales is that the printing industry is highly competitive. The industry is also fragmented in that Donnelley competes against a great many small printing firms, not just other large printing firms. For instance, in 2003, sales for the commercial-printing industry amounted to about $160 billion a year, but Donnelley's share was less than 5 percent.

A financially literate person knows the difference between net income and cash flow from operations. One of the first things Jack Stack teaches the employees at SRC is to understand the two most important activities in a company. Do you know what they are? Making money and generating cash. Making money is about net income. Generating cash is about cash flow from operations.

Net income is an average and does not actually measure how much money a company generated from its operations. Figure 2.2 contrasts the cash Donnelley generated from

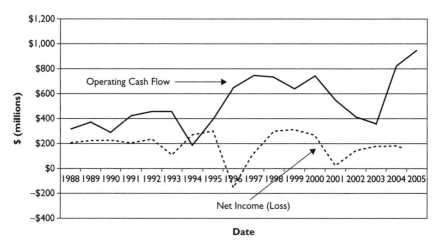

Figure 2.2 R.R. Donnelley Operating Cash Flows and Net Income, 1988–2005

its operations with its net income. As you can see from the figure, for most years Donnelley generated more cash than its net income suggests. An important reason is that net income is a mix of items, some of which have been carefully massaged. In 2005, Donnelley's operations generated just under $1 billion, not less than $200 million, as suggested by its earnings.

Besides paying for labor and materials, Donnelley spends money buying new equipment. It has also been spending a lot of money buying other companies. During the first quarter of 2007, Donnelley finalized three major acquisitions, which cost the company approximately $1.9 billion. The three acquisitions were Banta Corp., Perry Judd's Holdings Inc., and Von Hoffmann from Visant Corp. Of these, Banta had the lion's share at $1.3 billion.

In 2005, Donnelley made a $990 million purchase of the British firm Astron Group with operations in printing, mail services, and marketing support. The total amount that Donnelley spent on acquisitions in 2005 was just under $1.2 billion. In 2003, Donnelley acquired Moore Wallace Inc. for $2.8 billion. The merger created an $8-billion-a-year printing conglomerate that ranked as the largest in North America. All these acquisitions cost money, unless they are paid for in stock, as was Moore Wallace.

Donnelley generates cash from its operations and spends cash on investments, meaning new capital equipment, acquisitions, and the like. Think about what remains from its operating cash flows after it has spent money on its investments. Figure 2.3 shows the time path for this remainder between 1988 and 2005.

Take a look at Figure 2.3. What you will notice is that over time, the remaining cash flow after investment went up and down, like operating cash flow. However, the remaining cash flow was sometimes negative, especially in 2005

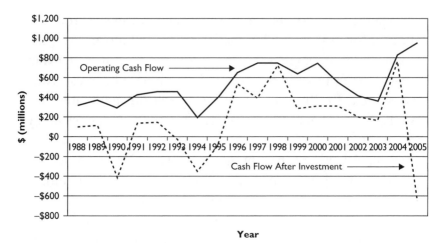

Figure 2.3 R.R. Donnelley Operating Cash Flow before and after Investment

when the firm was spending so much money making acquisitions. This negative amount is a deficit that needs to be covered with cash from somewhere. The question is where? Where does the money come from? A financially literate person knows the answer.

If your income and spending patterns were like those of Donnelley, where would you get cash in 2005 when you were spending more than you were receiving from your paycheck? You basically have three choices. First, if you saved some money in the past, you can spend some or all of those savings. Second, you can sell some of your possessions. Third, you can raise the money by, say, taking out a loan.

In 2005, Donnelley spent $655 million more than it took in from its operations. To meet this deficit, it spent $275.1 of its cash holdings and raised $379.9 in net new financing. It did not sell off any of its assets to raise cash.

Table 2.1 provides a capsule summary of the discussion about how much money Donnelley raised and how much it spent. The dollar amounts presented in the table are from 2005.

Table 2.1

R.R. Donnelley Cash Generated and Spent	2005
Cash generated from operations	$947.5
Cash spent on investment	$1,602.5
Deficit (surplus, if negative)	$655.0
Cash holdings used to address deficit	$275.1
Cash from sale of assets	$0.0
Cash raised through new financing	$379.9
Total cash raised to address deficit	$655.0

The information in Table 2.1 is communicated in the firm's Statement of Cash Flows, part of its financial statements. A condensed version of Donnelley's Statement of Cash Flows for 2005 is presented in Table 2.2.

Valuation: Doing It Right

Financially literacy involves knowing valuation. Here is a secret. A lot of people who sound like they are financially literate don't have a good grasp of what valuation entails.

Table 2.2

R.R. Donnelley Condensed Statement of Cash Flows	2005
Cash flow from operations	−$947.5
Cash flow from investment	−$1,602.5
Cash flow from financing	$379.9
Net cash flow	−$275.1

This is even true of a few open book gurus. Yes, it's true. I'm not exaggerating. And yes, I'm back on my soapbox! So, let me share a few boring details about valuation that can make the difference between making a few billion dollars and losing a few billion dollars.

Intrinsic valuation is based on cash flow. Cash flow from financing is about the amount of money raised from outside investors, meaning lenders, bondholders, and shareholders. In 2005, R.R. Donnelley raised about $380 million from outside investors. How do outside investors evaluate whether they are getting a good deal when they fork over $380 million of their own money to Donnelley? A financially literate investor uses valuation formulas that are based on cash flow.

Valuation is simple in principle and based on the concept of present value. The *present* in present value means "now." Present value is about what something is worth now. The intrinsic value of a deal is the present value of the cash you expect to receive from the deal. As simple as this statement might appear, it is easy to lose sight of the basic principle in a maze of financial numbers.

Consider three quick loan examples to get across the basics. In the first example, suppose Donnelley asked you for a one-year loan of $1,000 at an interest rate of 5 percent per year, and 5 percent is a competitive rate. Donnelley wants the $1,000 now, so the present value of the loan is $1,000. Because of the interest, you as the lender receive more than $1,000 in the future. In particular, you will receive $50 in interest because $50 is 5 percent of $1,000. Moreover, you will receive that interest at the end of a year, at the same time you receive back your principal of $1,000. In total, you will receive a check of $1,050 a year from now from Donnelley for having lent it $1,000 now.

I want you to understand that there is a crucial point to keep in focus. As an investor, the value you place on a transaction today is based on the cash flows you expect to receive in the future. This point sounds so innocuous, so simple, and so obvious. Yet, a lot of investors get into serious trouble because they lose sight of this point. In our example, the value to you the lender today of receiving $1,050 from Donnelley a year from now is the present value of that $1,050. At 5 percent, that present value is $1,000.

In a second example, suppose Donnelley asked you for a conventional two-year loan of $1,000 at 5 percent. In this case, you will receive two payments: $50 in interest at the end of a year and $1,050 at the end of two years. The present value of the loan is still $1,000, the amount that you lend to Donnelley now.

In a third example, suppose Donnelley asked you for a two-year zero coupon loan of $1,000 at 5 percent. The meaning of *zero coupon* is that Donnelley would like to avoid paying you $50 in interest at the end of the first year and wants to make only one payment at the end of two years. The question for you is how much to ask Donnelley to pay at that time? Answering the question involves a simple formula,

$$\text{Payment two years from now} = \$1,000 \times 1.05 \times 1.05$$
$$= \$1,102.50$$

The logic underlying the formula is simple. After one year at 5 percent, your $1,000 is worth $1,050, which is $1,000 × 1.05. The $1,050 itself earns 5 percent over the second year and grows to $1,102.50, which is $1,050 × 1.05.

In the first two examples, the return you earn on your $1,000 investment is the $50 per year that you receive in interest, the amount over and above the return of your $1,000 principal. In the third example involving the zero coupon, the return is still 5 percent, but it is embedded in the extra $102.50 that you receive when you receive back your principal of $1,000.

The task of valuation involves turning the concept of present value on its head. For example, suppose R.R. Donnelley offered to pay you $1,102.50 two years from now, and the competitive rate of interest was 5 percent. What is the value of Donnelley's offer? The answer is $1,000, the present value of the zero coupon loan, two years at 5 percent. The formula you would use to make the calculation is simply a rearrangement of the previous formula.

$$\text{Present value} = \frac{\$1,102.50}{1.05 \times 1.05}$$

As a general matter, to compute the present value of some amount to be received t years from now, divide the amount by $(1 + \text{competitive rate})^t$, meaning $(1 + \text{competitive rate})$ raised to the power t.

Here is a concept check question. For a two-year loan at 5 percent, what is the present value of the $1,000 return of principal? To get the answer, you would just use $1,000 instead of the $1,102.50 in the preceding formula. And the answer would turn out to be $907.03.

The longer you have to wait for the return of your principal, the lower the present value of that principal. If you had to wait 10 years, the present value would be $613.91. If you had to wait 100 years, the present value would be $7.60. For long-term loans, the return of principal fades in comparison to the interest payments.

Stock, misleadingly called equity, is like a very long-term loan where you wait a long time to receive back your

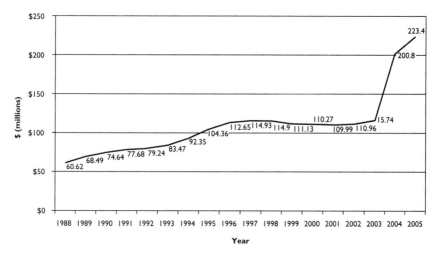

Figure 2.4 R.R. Donnelley Cash Dividends, 1988–2005

principal, so long that the present value of that principal is essentially worthless. Therefore, the entire value of the stock comes from its cash payouts, which are either dividends or share repurchases, adjusted for new share issues.

Figure 2.4 displays the dividend payments Donnelley made between 1988 and 2005. Notice that these payments followed a trajectory that was generally upward but hardly predictable. Dividend payments are less reliable than interest payments and therefore riskier. For this reason, investors tend to require higher rates of return to hold a company's stock than to hold its debt.

How would you begin to place a value on R.R. Donnelley's stock? The natural starting point is its dividend stream. What is the present value of that stream?

Suppose that at the end of 1987, shareholders had a pretty good idea about what Donnelley's future dividends were likely to be, meaning the numbers displayed in Figure 2.4. Suppose that shareholders viewed the competitive rate of return for holding Donnelley shares to be 12 percent. If "now" means December 1987, then the present value formula for Donnelley's future dividend stream, commencing in 1988, would be:

$$\frac{60.62}{1.12} + \frac{68.49}{1.12^2} + \frac{74.64}{1.12^3} + \frac{77.68}{1.12^4} + \ldots$$

As a general matter, I think it's unrealistic to assume that you can forecast all the ups and downs of future dividends depicted in Figure 2.4. Instead, textbooks focus on forecasting the future growth rate of dividends. Between 1985 and 2005, Donnelley's dividends grew by about 8 percent a year. Well-informed investors might have forecast that this was the case, which is more plausible than forecasting the exact shape of the actual stream.

Suppose that in 1987, investors forecast that, long term, Donnelley's dividends would grow at a rate of 8 percent. Suppose further that in 1987, they forecast that every dollar invested in Donnelley stock would generate 8 cents in capital gains per year, to match the forecasted dividend growth rate, and 3 cents in dividends. Taken together, the capital gains and dividends produce a total return of 11 percent, meaning 11 cents on every dollar invested in the stock.

The total rate of return (11 percent) is equal to the sum of the capital gains rate (8 percent) and the dividend yield (3 percent). The dividend yield is the ratio of total dividends to the value of the stock. If we use a little algebra in connection with the last two sentences, we get a simple valuation formula:

$$\frac{\text{Present value of}}{\text{future dividends}} = \frac{\text{Dividend payout next year}}{\text{Total return} - \text{dividend growth rate}}$$

To illustrate this formula for the end of 1987, take the actual dividend payout for 1988 ($60.62 million) and divide by 3 percent (11 percent – 8 percent) to arrive at about $2 billion. In words, the present value of Donnelley's future dividend stream is $2 billion. By way of contrast, Donnelley's actual market cap at the time was $2.5 billion, 20 percent more than the theoretical value.

Dividends are just a starting point to value stock. In the special case when Donnelley did not buy back any outstanding shares or issue any new shares, dividends would be the only cash flows that its shareholders would receive over time. However, Donnelley routinely did both. When a firm buys back shares, it pays cash to its shareholders in exchange for their shares. With a new share issue, the company receives cash from its shareholders.

To find out how much cash shareholders actually received, you would have to add the amount of the buyback and subtract the amount of the new share issue.[2] The total is called *net cash flow to equity*. In 1990, Donnelley both issued new shares and bought back shares. But it bought back more than it issued, so shareholders received $86 million in cash, more than the $74.64 million Donnelley paid in dividends. In the prior two years, 1988 and 1989, the reverse was true.

Net cash flow to debt is the cash that lenders and other debt holders receive. It consists of interest payments plus repayment of principal minus the amount of any new debt. The sum of net cash flow to equity and net cash flow to debt is called *net cash flow to investors*.

When net cash flow to investors is positive, investors receive cash from the company. When net cash flow is

[2]You would also have to adjust for other financing.

negative, investors contribute cash to the company. The value of the company, as opposed to just its shares or just its debt, is the present value of its expected net cash flow stream.

Free cash flow can be defined as net cash flow to investors plus the change in the company's cash position. Notice that this implies that the value of the firm is the present value of the firm's free cash flows minus the present value of the firm's change in cash. I hope you can see that the present value of the firm's change in cash flow over time should just be the negative of its initial cash position, assuming that the firm eventually pays out all its cash to investors. Therefore, the value of the firm is the present value of its free cash flow stream plus its initial holdings of cash.

Figure 2.5 displays Donnelley's net cash flow to investors and its free cash flows between 1988 and 2005. For most of the period, Donnelley's free cash flows were close to its net cash flows to investors. However, in 2004 and 2005, the

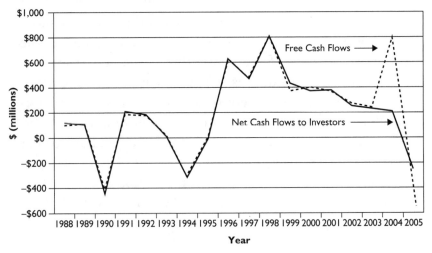

Figure 2.5 R.R. Donnelley Net Cash Flows to Investors and Free Cash Flows, 1988–2005

two series parted company. In 2004, Donnelley built up its cash position by $581 million. As a result, its free cash flows that year were higher than its net cash flows to investors by $581 million.

I should say that there are alternative ways to define free cash flows, and I discuss several alternatives in Chapter 3.

Some companies have high earnings but do not plan to pay dividends or repurchase shares for a long time. Doing valuation in this case is difficult in practice because it is hard to predict future large free cash flow amounts. One way to deal with this situation is to engage in some algebraic manipulation and compute what is known as *economic value added*. In the mid–1990s, Donnelley began to base valuations on economic value added.

Economic value added is a surplus. It measures the difference between actual profit and the profit that adequately rewards investors for bearing risk. Here is an illustrative example. In 1988, Donnelley's actual profit (after tax but before interest) was $225 million. This profit was used to pay both interest and dividends and therefore was jointly shared by Donnelley's debt holders and shareholders. In 1987, the book value of Donnelley's assets was $2.1 billion. To keep the arithmetic simple, suppose that in 1988, Donnelley's investors required a return of 10 percent to feel adequately rewarded for bearing the risk in Donnelley that they do. Then they would require 1988 profits to be $210 million, that being 10 percent of $2.1 billion. Economic value added in 1988 would be $15 million because actual profit of $225 exceeded required profit of $210 million by $15 million.

The valuation formula for the company's stock is a sum of two terms. The first term is the company's shareholders' equity at the time of the valuation. The second term is the present value of the stream of forecasted values for economic value added.

Risk and Return: Doing It Right

A financially literate person understands the relationship between risk and return. To tell you the truth, this is asking a lot of most people. But it's really important because if you don't understand it, you won't know when it makes sense to take risks and when it doesn't.

In the preceding example, shareholders were assumed to require a rate of return of 11 percent to feel adequately compensated for the risk of holding Donnelley stock. Suppose you purchased $1,000 of R.R. Donnelley stock in December 1987 and held that stock through December 2005. Over the 18 years, your $1,000 investment would have grown to $3,352. That amounted to a return of 6.95 percent per year, considerably less than the 11 percent you required. As a stockholder, you would have felt disappointed. However, bearing risk means that sometimes the outcome will be worse than you had expected. You might require 11 percent as your best guess of what would happen on average but recognize that risk means there is no guarantee.

Textbooks teach that the riskiness of a stock is measured in terms of its volatility. Figure 2.6 displays how the volatility of Donnelley stock and that of the S&P 500 changed between 1985 and 2005.[3] Can you spot the volatility spike that marks the 1987 crash?

Notice that Donnelley stock is more volatile than that of the S&P 500. However, the volatility pattern for Donnelley stock followed that of the S&P 500 for much of the time, though not all of the time. In fact, you could say that much of the risk of holding Donnelley stock appears to have been driven by the overall stock market as opposed to events

---

[3]Here, volatility is measured as a moving average return standard deviation.

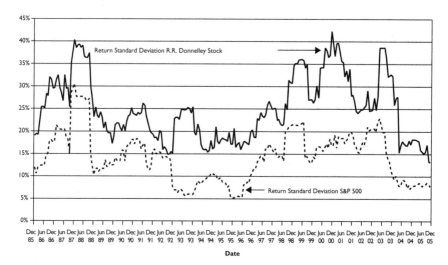

Figure 2.6 Volatility of R.R. Donnelley versus S&P 500, 1985–2005

specifically related to Donnelley itself. For example, when the economy was booming in the 1990s, Donnelley's catalog sales also boomed, as did the value of the S&P 500. In the recession of 2001–2002, Donnelley's sales declined as printing demand for new prospectuses declined, along with the value of the S&P 500.

The textbook measure of risk is a variable called *beta*. At the end of 2006, the beta of Donnelley stock was 1.5. This means that when the S&P 500 changes by 10 percent, on average Donnelley's stock changes by 15 percent.

Beta focuses only on volatility that is driven by the S&P 500. Beta ignores volatility that is driven by events unique to Donnelley. Textbooks argue that investors who hold Donnelley stock as part of a diversified portfolio can eliminate their exposure to unique events. However, diversification cannot eliminate their exposure to market-level risk, meaning beta risk.

Holding the S&P 500 involves taking a risk. Investors who do so could have held Treasury bills and faced virtually no risk. Suppose Treasury bills offered a rate of return of 3.5 percent. Investors who decide to hold the S&P 500 need to ask themselves how much more than 3.5 percent they require to bear the associated risk, as displayed in Figure 2.6. Suppose the answer is 5 percent, which is called the *market risk premium*.

How much should shareholders require for holding Donnelley stock in a diversified portfolio? The textbook technique for getting the answer is to recognize that a beta of 1.5 means that Donnelley stock is 50 percent riskier than the S&P 500. Therefore, if investors require a market risk premium of 5 percent, they should require a risk premium of 7.5 percent for holding Donnelley stock: 7.5 percent = 1.5 × 5 percent. And if the Treasury bill rate is 3.5 percent, then Donnelley shareholders would require 11 percent as a required return because 7.5 percent is the increment over and above 3.5 percent that investors require.

Donnelley's debt is less risky than its stock. For this reason, investors who held Donnelley's debt would require less than 11 percent. For example, Donnelley's debt holders might require 7 percent. Suppose 25 percent of Donnelley was financed with debt and 75 percent with stock. In this case, 25 percent of Donnelley's investors require a return of 7 percent and 75 percent require a return of 11 percent. Therefore, the average investor requires a rate of return of 10 percent because the weighted average of 7 percent and 11 percent is 10 percent, when the weights are 25 percent and 75 percent. The 10 percent is called Donnelley's *cost of capital*.

Donnelley's cost of capital reflects its underlying risk as measured by beta. To be fair, the beta of Donnelley's stock was not 1.5 throughout the period 1988–2005. Figure 2.7 shows that Donnelley's beta was below 1.5 for almost the entire period. Indeed, its beta was less than one for much of

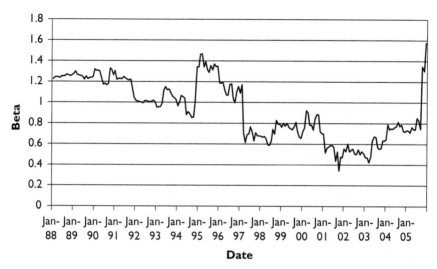

Figure 2.7 R.R. Donnelley Beta, 1988–2005

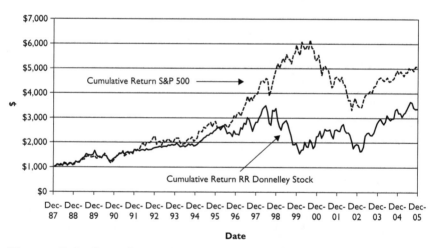

Figure 2.8 Cumulative Returns of R.R. Donnelley versus S&P 500, 1988–2005

the time. As a result, it might have been quite reasonable for the return to Donnelley stock to have been low.

A closer look at Donnelley's return pattern for the entire period provides some additional insight. Figure 2.8 displays the cumulative return to both Donnelley's stock and the S&P 500. Cumulative returns show how $1 invested in each would have grown over time. Notice that until 1995, Donnelley's stock performed as well as the S&P 500. However, after 1995, the stock consistently underperformed the S&P 500. Notably, this occurred during its low beta period.

Market Efficiency

Do you know what it means for a market to be efficient? Although this term appears a lot in popular financial publications, most people don't know what it means for a market to be efficient. And who can blame them? A lot of textbooks don't make the concept especially transparent. And there are several definitions.

Here is a working definition of market efficiency. When a market is efficient, market prices correctly measure fundamental value. In an efficient market, Donnelley's market cap would correctly measure the present value of its future expected free cash flows to equity. In an efficient market, corporate managers should trust market prices. In an efficient market, investors should also trust market prices, realizing that all securities are fairly priced.

Capex, Acquisitions, and Project Selection

In psychologically smart companies, managers make decisions on the basis of value creation. Doing this right requires enough financial literacy to know how to attach values to decision alternatives. One of the most important decisions companies make involves capex.

Capex is shorthand for capital expenditures, the amount spent to purchase new capital equipment. The term *acquisitions* refers to the value of what a firm spends to purchase other companies. In 2005, R.R. Donnelley spent 2.5 times more on its acquisitions than on its capital expenditures. Its acquisitions spree continued during 2006 and the early part of 2007.

Michael Corty is an analyst for Morningstar Inc. who follows R. R. Donnelley. In February 2007, he expressed some pessimism about Donnelley's acquisitions strategy. His pessimism was based on a comparison of Donnelley's return on invested capital to its cost of capital during the preceding five years. Corty pointed out that the actual return had been below the cost of capital in each of those years. Figure 2.9 tells the story.

What is the right way to analyze whether spending money on capital equipment, whether as part of capex or as an acquisition, makes sense for a company? For example, in November 2006, Donnelley announced its intention to spend $1.3 billion to acquire Banta Corporation. Banta is a provider of printing and digital-imaging solutions. What do traditional textbooks say about evaluating such deals?

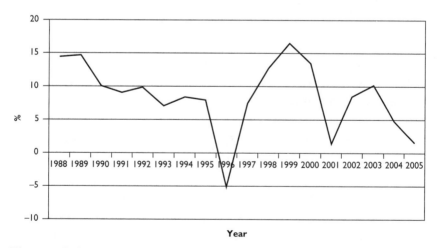

Figure 2.9 R.R. Donnelley Return on Invested Capital (%), 1988–2005

Traditional textbooks teach us that cash flows and valuation lie at the core of doing capex and acquisitions right. The traditional textbook approach calls for Donnelley's executives to ask themselves what difference acquiring Banta will make to the overall corporate cash flows of the company. For example, if Donnelley were to spend $1.3 billion at the end of 2006 to acquire Banta, then its cash flows from investment for 2006 would be $1.3 billion higher as a result. That $1.3 billion is an incremental cash outflow. To complete the analysis, Donnelley's executives would also need to forecast the difference that the Banta acquisition would make to its cash flow from operations in future years.

Here is a simple example to illustrate the key points. You can see that in 2006, cash flows from investment are –$1.3 billion, reflecting the $1.3 billion cash outflow that Donnelley spent to acquire Banta. Table 2.3 provides a hypothetical forecast that Donnelley's executives might have made for how acquiring Banta would have affected the company's cash flow between 2006 and 2012. The table shows that Donnelley's forecasted cash flow from operations in 2007 would be higher by $200 million (0.20 in the table) than would have been the case had Donnelley not acquired Banta. Moreover, incremental cash flow from operations subsequently grows by 15 percent through 2012. In addition, suppose Donnelley plans to spin Banta off at the end of 2012 for an estimated $2 billion.

The bottom line of Table 2.3 lists the incremental cash flows for the period 2006 to 2012, the years that Donnelley plans to own and operate Banta. The key questions that Donnelley's executives should ask when evaluating the acquisition of Banta in 2006 are the following: What is the impact on our investors' wealth now, in 2006, if we go ahead with the Banta deal? By how much would our investors' wealth change?

Table 2.3

R.R. Donnelley Incremental Cash Flows ($ billions)	2006	2007	2008	2009	2010	2011	2012
Cash flow from operations		0.20	0.23	0.26	0.30	0.35	0.40
Cash flow from investment	−1.30						2.00
Cash flow from financing							
Net cash flow	−1.30	0.20	0.23	0.26	0.30	0.35	2.40

To answer the questions, Donnelley's executives would have to use present value. Suppose the required return associated with Banta's incremental cash flows was the same as Donnelley's cost of capital, 10 percent. Then the value of the change to Donnelley's overall corporate cash flows resulting from the acquisition of Banta would be:

$$-1.30 + \frac{0.20}{1.1} + \frac{0.23}{1.1^2} + \frac{0.26}{1.1^3} + \frac{0.30}{1.1^4} + \frac{0.35}{1.1^5} + \frac{2.40}{1.1^6}$$

The resulting number from this calculation is $1.05 billion and is called *net present value* (NPV). This means that acquiring Banta increases the wealth of Donnelley's shareholders, at the end of 2006, by $1.05 billion. The $1.3 billion spent on Banta is more than compensated by the $2.35 value of the forecasted additional cash flows generated between 2007 and 2012.

Suppose Donnelley's executives were using NPV analysis to decide whether or not to acquire Banta. Then a positive NPV would indicate that making the acquisition is a good thing for its investors because it increases their wealth. If the NPV of acquiring Banta were a negative number, then Donnelley's executives would be advised to forego acquiring Banta so as not to lower the wealth of its investors.

Factoring NPV into the Value of the Company

By aggregating the NPV of all the firm's investments, you measure how much value its overall investment policy creates. A positive NPV company generates a return on its investments that exceeds the minimal expected return required by its investors to compensate them adequately for the risk they bear. Think back to the discussion about economic value added. Economic value added is positive when actual returns exceed required returns.[4]

A zero NPV investment is nothing to be ashamed of. A zero NPV investment does not merely break even. Rather, a zero NPV project is one that is expected to earn its required return, thereby producing zero economic value added.

A negative NPV does not necessarily mean losses in the future. It just means that a company's investors do not earn a competitive rate of return, which in the Donnelley example is 10 percent. This takes us back to the concern raised by Morningstar analyst Michael Corty about Donnelley's acquisitions: If the past is a prologue, the acquisitions will

---

[4]Assuming that book value of assets is positive.

not earn their required returns. In effect, Corty worries that Donnelley's acquisitions amount to negative NPV investments, thereby generating negative economic value added.

The intrinsic value of a company is the sum of its assets, as measured on its balance sheet, plus the present value of its expected economic value stream going forward. It is the present value of the economic value-added stream that captures the NPV of the company's investment policy. For example, on February 16, 2007, Donnelley's market cap was $8.34 billion, and its shareholders' equity was about $4.02 billion. The difference, $4.32 billion, serves as a rough approximation of the market's assessment of Donnelley's overall NPV. It is worth noting that the market does not appear to share Michael Corty's assessment that Donnelley's overall NPV at the time was negative.

Investments that earn higher returns generally produce faster-growing companies. Think about $1 of assets. Suppose that next year that dollar generates a return on investment of 20 percent, and the firm plows 75 percent of that return back into the company's assets. In that case, the $1 of assets will grow by 15 percent, that being the product of the 20 percent return and the 75 percent plowback. Therefore, the higher the return on investment, the higher the internally generated growth will be.

Faster-growing companies tend to be associated with higher valuations. To see why, think about the valuation formula described earlier, whereby the value of a company's stock is measured as the ratio of its expected dividend a year from now and the difference between required return and expected growth rate. Everything else being the same, a higher growth rate implies a higher valuation.

Think about a company that is expected to grow at a constant rate in the future. Suppose that the NPV of this company's overall investment policy is zero. The foregoing discussion implies that the intrinsic value of the company's stock will simply be the ratio of its expected earnings next year and the required return on its stock.

NPV is the value added over and above the zero NPV base case. Therefore, the value of a company's stock will be its NPV plus the ratio of its expected earnings next year and the required return on its stock.

Here is a quick illustrative calculation that pulls together many of the concepts discussed. Suppose we wanted to estimate the value of Donnelley's NPV in February 2007. On February 16, Donnelley's market cap stood at $8.34 billion. Analysts were forecasting that the company's earnings in 2007 would be about $600 million. If the market is efficient, then Donnelley's market cap of $8.34 billion provides the best estimate of the intrinsic value of Donnelley's market cap. To obtain the required return on Donnelley's stock at the time, we use its beta, the prevailing Treasury bill rate, and the market premium. At the time, the Treasury bill rate stood at 5.2 percent and Donnelley's beta was 1.5. Given a 5 percent market premium, this implies that the required return to Donnelley stock was 12.7 percent.[5]

We are now at the last stage of computing Donnelley's NPV. If we compute the ratio of Donnelley's earnings estimate by its required return, that ratio turns out to be $4.7 billion. Because the value of Donnelley's stock is the sum of this ratio and Donnelley's NPV, Donnelley's NPV must be $3.6 billion, the difference between $8.3 billion and $4.7 billion. Table 2.4 provides a capsule summary of the calculations.

[5]12.7 percent is the sum of 5.2 percent and 1.5×5 percent.

Table 2.4

R.R. Donnelley $ (billions)	February 16, 2007
Market capitalization	$8.3
Earnings estimate	$0.6
Treasury bill rate	5.2%
Market premium	5.0%
Beta	1.5
Required return	12.7%
Earnings estimate / required return	$4.7
Overall NPV	$3.7

Notice that the $3.6 billion estimate for Donnelley's NPV is close to the market's $4.32 billion assessment of the value of its future economic value-added stream.

Computing Forward P/E

Price-to-earnings, P/E, is a familiar concept. It seems so easy, almost trivial. But it is extremely deceptive, at least if you want to use it in a financially literate manner.

A forward P/E ratio is the ratio of forecasted earnings next year and the current value of the company's stock. Traditional finance textbooks teach that the forward P/E of a company's stock reflects the NPV of its investments. The higher the NPV of a company's investments, the higher the intrinsic forward P/E ratio of its stock will be.

The benchmark P/E for a firm occurs when the NPV of the company's investments is zero and the company's expected growth rate is constant. In this case, the firm's P/E ratio is the inverse of the required return on its stock. The reason is that the intrinsic value of the company's stock will simply be the ratio of its expected earnings next year and the required return on its stock.

When NPV is not zero, the P/E ratio reflects the ratio NPV divided by value of the stock. Call this ratio the "relative NPV contribution." A little algebra shows that the P/E ratio is the inverse of a product—the product of the required return on the stock and 1 minus the relative NPV contribution. If you think about it a bit, you will see that the higher NPV is, the higher relative NPV contribution is; and the higher relative NPV contribution is, the higher the intrinsic forward P/E ratio is.

Here is an example to make these concepts more concrete. On February 16, 2007, Donnelley's forward P/E was 14.09, the ratio of its market cap to analysts' average estimate of its earnings for 2007. Table 2.5 illustrates how the 14.09 number can be computed as the inverse product of required return and 1 minus the relative NPV contribution.

Table 2.5

R.R. Donnelley	February 16, 2007 Forward P/E Analysis
P/E = Market cap / Earnings estimate	14.09
Relative NPV contribution	44.1%
1 − relative NPV contribution	55.9%
Required return	12.7%
Product of last two terms	7.10%
Inverse of product	14.09

Capital Structure

Raising capital technically means raising money that does not have to be returned to investors before one year. A company's capital structure refers to its mix of long-term debt and equity financing.

How should a firm decide on the right mix of debt and equity? Traditional finance textbooks teach that the criterion for choosing the right mix is the same as the criterion for choosing capital projects—namely, to maximize the value of the company.

For the most part, the value of a company is based on its cash flows from operations and investment, not its cash flows from financing. Therefore, capital structure will be irrelevant unless it affects value.

A company's free cash flows technically belong to the company's investors. Those investors are typically a mix of debt holders and shareholders. For the most part, capital structure is an issue about how those cash flows get divided between debt holders and shareholders. Debt holders want their cash flows in the form of interest payments and return of principal. Shareholders want their cash flows in the form of dividends and stock repurchases. Both groups also provide funding when a company raises new money. Debt holders make new loans or buy newly issued bonds. Shareholders buy new issues of stock. New money is also part of free cash flow.

The form of financing can affect the value of a company. Interest payments are treated differently from dividends when it comes to corporate tax. Interest payments are tax deductible, whereas dividends are not. As a result, a company typically receives a tax benefit, known as a *tax shield*, when it uses debt financing instead of equity financing. Increased debt also raises the odds of a corporate bankruptcy, and bankruptcy is expensive. Bankruptcy costs reduce the value of a company. New financing also brings with it additional costs such as flotation costs, which are fees paid to investment bankers.

Textbooks in corporate finance suggest that companies should choose their capital structures by weighing the benefits and costs associated with different mixes, with the view of maximizing overall corporate value. Capital structure only affects the value of a company by the amount of the additional financing costs.

One point to keep in mind is that changing a company's capital structure automatically changes the beta of its stock. The higher a company's debt-to-equity ratio, the higher its beta will be. A company that carries no debt will have a stock beta that is lower than it would be if the company has debt. Of course, higher risk means higher required returns. A company that increases its debt-to-equity ratio by 10 percent will find that the required return on its stock will go up by the product of 10 percent and the company's risk premium. A company's risk premium is the difference between its cost of capital and the Treasury bill rate.

A higher debt-to-equity ratio also increases expected earnings per share (EPS). Traditional finance textbooks caution shareholders not to get overly excited by this fact. The higher EPS comes together with higher risk. The two together will only affect intrinsic value by the magnitude of the financing costs and nothing more.

Financing costs aside, what changing capital structure influences is the way that the value of a company is divided between debt holders and shareholders. It is about carving up a pie.

Here is a classic textbook question. Suppose a company that initially holds no debt decides to borrow money to repurchase 30 percent of its outstanding stock. If there were no tax effects about which to be concerned and the cost of financial distress was very small, what would happen to the intrinsic value of the outstanding shares that remained, both in total and on a per share basis?

The short answer is that the value of the remaining outstanding shares would decline by 30 percent, but the price per share would stay the same. The reason is that the intrinsic value of the company as a whole would stay the same because this bit of financial engineering would not change the future cash flows on which its intrinsic value depends. However, 30 percent of the value of those cash flows would belong to the new debt holders. After all, if these debt holders are rational, they will want back in value at least what they put in. And the shareholders will not agree to give them more than 30 percent.

The upshot is that the shareholders who do not sell back their shares end up holding 70 percent of the intrinsic value of the company. With the number of shares down to 70 percent of their former level, the resulting price per share would stay the same on an intrinsic basis.

How would the stock buyback story change if the cash to repurchase the shares came from the company instead of a loan? Well, now the company's assets would fall in value by 30 percent. The total value of the shares would fall by 30 percent. The number of shares would fall by 30 percent. And the price per share would stay the same.

Payout Policy

A company pays out cash to its shareholders in one of two forms: dividends and share repurchases. Traditional finance textbooks suggest that payout policy affects corporate value because of taxes, things that executives know which shareholders do not, and whether shareholders can trust executives.

If dividends are heavily taxed relative to capital gains, a company can do its shareholders a favor by not paying cash dividends. After all, what would be so terrible if a company waited a long time to pay cash out to its shareholders instead of paying them a steady stream of dividends now? The answer depends on whether the company could be expected to earn the same risk premium for shareholders by holding the cash instead of paying it out. If so, then textbooks suggest there is no penalty in avoiding dividend payouts.

A company with really great investment alternatives might be able to earn a higher return on investment than shareholders could earn if they received the cash and reinvested it. This suggests that it would be good not to pay dividends. However, that suggestion is a bit hasty. If a company has really good investment opportunities, it can raise the money to finance those opportunities externally and still pay out cash to its existing shareholders.

Suppose shareholders do not trust the executives of a company to maximize value but instead suspect them of using the company's cash to benefit themselves. In this case, shareholders might prefer to have the company's cash paid out to them as a dividend instead of being misappropriated by the executives. Of course, in this case, executives would be reluctant to pay those dividends, thereby forcing unhappy shareholders to dump the stock and thus drive down its price.

If a company is going to pay out dividends, then it needs to be aware that shareholders expect consistency in dividend policy. That consistency might be in terms of dividends per share, dividends per dollar of earnings, or dividend growth rate. Shareholders react positively to announcements of dividend increases, but they react extremely negatively to dividend decreases. Therefore, executives who consider increasing their company's dividends should feel very confident that doing so will not result in their having to backtrack.

When capital gains are taxed at a lower rate than dividends and a company's executives want to pay out cash, a share buyback might be a better way to go. In fact, since the 1970s, share buybacks have become a much more popular alternative for companies to pay out cash to their shareholders. The downside with buybacks is that they cannot be regular and consistent, as are dividends. The IRS views regular buybacks as dividends and treats them as such.

Culture, Process, and Corporate Finance

Finance is part science but also part art. Traditional textbooks teach the science. However, practice relies on a lot of art, and as a result, it is easy to lose sight of the science.

A key theme in this book is about building and fostering a corporate culture with processes for doing corporate finance well. Doing corporate finance well means laying out cash flows in a systematic and transparent manner. It means identifying the company's riskiness and associated required returns. It means basing valuation on future cash flows and required returns. It means basing decisions about capex and acquisitions on NPV. It means ascertaining the intrinsic P/E of a company's stock by linking it to the NPV of its investment opportunities. It means choosing capital structure to maximize the value of the company. It means choosing dividend policy from a forward-looking perspective with value maximization in mind.

In short, doing corporate finance well is part of being a behaviorally intelligent organization. And to be a behaviorally intelligent organization is to have behaviorally intelligent processes woven into the fabric of corporate culture. This can only happen in a company that promotes financial literacy for its workforce.

CHAPTER 3

BEHAVIORAL CORPORATE FINANCE: BIAS GREMLINS AT WORK

Bias gremlins are hard at work in every organization, diligently trying to mess things up. These gremlins operate by preying on people's susceptibility to psychological biases. That's why I refer to these gremlins as *bias gremlins*. They exist the way germs exist: They are everywhere, they are invisible, and they can inflict all kinds of damage—anything from minor discomfort to death.

Do you know the story of Louis Pasteur and Max von Pettenkofer? Louis Pasteur was the French scientist who identified germs as the cause of disease. Max von Pettenkofer was a German scientist who didn't believe that germs existed. To prove Pasteur wrong, von Pettenkofer asked Pasteur for a glass of water containing his vilest germs. Pasteur provided a glass full of cholera bacteria, which von Pettenkofer proceeded to gulp down. Von Pettenkofer was lucky, very lucky, to have survived his little experiment because by now we all know that germs exist, and cholera can be deadly.

Like von Pettenkofer, some organizations ignore bias gremlins and survive. Organizations can do the wrong things and still end up lucky. But psychologically smart companies don't want to count on luck to be successful.

Bias gremlins operate by introducing bias into the numbers, making the numbers appear to lie. Gremlins do whatever they can to keep managers focused on everything but the true numbers. Gremlins like distraction. They like drama. They like disagreement. They like disorder. They especially like the excitement of conflicting agendas. Gremlins have a motto: "So much value to destroy, so little time." If you let them, they will harm your business.

You need to think about beating gremlins the way you think about beating germs. You beat germs by living a healthy life. You cultivate positive habits for eating, drinking, exercising, staying away from things that are bad for you, and generally taking good care of yourself.

The analogy applies to companies. Companies need to cultivate good habits to beat bias gremlins. Do you know what good habits do? They help people debias! Remember what I told you in Chapter 1: Debiasing lies at the root of psychologically smart companies.

Citigroup: A Cost Czar?

Open book companies are up front about the fact that good numbers don't lie. They cultivate habits around the numbers. Closed book companies are exactly the opposite. Closed book companies provide fertile ground for bias gremlins to thrive.

There are plenty of examples of what happens to companies that don't keep open books. Typically, the managers of closed book companies get nasty shocks about the level of expenses. And keep reminding yourself about the key messages in Chapter 1: People who suffer from unrealistic optimism and overconfidence experience negative surprises more frequently than they anticipate.

Here is a story to illustrate the point about closed book companies and expenses. In December 2006, Citigroup installed a new chief operating officer with the unofficial title of "expense czar," or if you like cost czar. Now I ask you: Why did Citigroup suddenly need a cost czar?

Here's why. In 2006, Citigroup's operating expenses increased by 15.2 percent, whereas its revenues only increased by 7.1 percent. Investors paid attention to the numbers. They noticed. As a result, Citigroup's stock underperformed compared to the market averages. Between October 2003, when CEO Charles Prince took command of the firm, and December 2006, the bank's market value rose by 20 percent, much less than the 34 percent increase in the Dow Jones Wilshire U.S. Banks Index.

At least part of Citigroup's cost spike involved a drama that featured the use of corporate jets, extremely lush offices, and promotional activities that benefited some Citigroup executives personally but were difficult to justify in terms of the bottom line.

Presumably, the job of a cost czar is to monitor and prevent these types of expenses. Interestingly, the main culprit in this saga had once held the position of chief financial officer (CFO) of the firm.

It seems to me that until December 2006, Charles Prince was unrealistically optimistic and overconfident about Citigroup's expenses being under control. Indeed, it is a safe bet that Citigroup isn't run along open book lines. Why is it a safe bet? Here is the reason. In an open book culture, the whole workforce has the mentality of a cost czar.

In Chapter 2, I talked about Craig Highbarger, the machinist at SRC who had been trained to understand the costs associated with the products he worked on. Of course, such knowledge by itself does not guarantee that workers like Craig would want to make cost-minimizing choices. Indeed, it might be in Craig's best interests to work slowly and chat with his buddies instead of putting his nose to the proverbial grindstone. Right?

This is where two of our four horses, incentives and information sharing, come in. If Craig chooses the high-cost route, his bonus will be lower. Moreover, his high-cost actions will also lower the bonuses of his coworkers. And because information is widely shared at SRC through effective communication, before too long Craig will have to answer to others for his high-cost ways. Those others will be on the lookout, each with the mentality of a cost czar.

Twelve-Step Programs

Bias gremlins don't want companies to execute strategy successfully. That's not their mission. Their mission is to keep people ignorant about the numbers. So, what to do?

Remember, the way that you fight bias gremlins is by cultivating good organizational habits that promote debiasing. Well, that sounds a bit abstract because organizations consist of people. So a better way to make the point is to say the following: You fight bias gremlins by helping the people who make up the organization cultivate good collective habits that foster debiasing!

It's like a 12-step program. Twelve-step programs have a long history of helping people work in groups to develop healthy habits.

The first step of a 12-step program is to admit that there is a problem. There is no point in having people meet together to beat the gremlins if people won't acknowledge their gremlins. Yes, their gremlins!

Behavioral corporate finance tells us that gremlins are particularly adept at getting managers to make mistakes about all kinds of numbers: cash flows, valuations, net benefits from investments and acquisitions, and the financing mix. Lying at the root of these mistakes are the psychological concepts I introduced in Chapter 1. Remember that the top two are unrealistic optimism and overconfidence. These are joined by confirmation bias, the illusion of control, and aversion to a sure loss.

To be sure, there are other bias gremlins that are also hard at work, inducing people to make bad decisions. You will meet some of the new gremlins along the way. In any event, what you learn in the rest of this chapter is how these bias gremlins try to get the numbers to lie and what you can do to fight the bias.

Cash Flow Gremlins

Do you remember how free cash flow was defined in Chapter 2? Do you know any other definitions of free cash flow? Free cash flow is a tricky concept that confuses a lot of people. If you answered no to the first question, you are acknowledging that you don't remember how free cash flow was defined in Chapter 2. If so, thank you for your honesty.

If you answered yes to the second question, then you are basically saying that you have some previous experience with free cash flow and know how the term is defined. If so, do you know enough to compute free cash flow? If you think you do, here is a short self-test. Table 3.1 provides you with information drawn from Intel's 2005 Statement of Cash

Table 3.1

Intel Condensed Statement of Cash Flows $ (millions)	2005
Income, depreciation, and other nonworking capital items	$13,316.0
Change in operating net working capital (− signifies increase)	$1,507.0
Cash flow from operations	$14,823.0
Capex	$5,818.0
Noncapex cash flow from investment	$544.0
Cash flow from investment	$6,362.0
Cash flow from financing	−$9,544.0
Net cash flow = change in cash position	−$1,083.0
Interest paid	$27.0
Income taxes paid	$3,218.0

Flows. Can you use this information to compute Intel's free cash flows for 2005?

If you read about free cash flows in *Stock Diagnostics*, the Web site http://freecashflow.com, or a Deutsche Bank analyst report, you probably learned that free cash flow is cash flow from operations minus capex. If this is indeed the formula you applied, then you should have computed Intel's free cash flow for 2005 to be $9,005 million, the difference between $14,823 and $5,818. Indeed, this is the number that appears as Intel's 2005 free cash flow in Deutsche Bank's analyst reports.

It's pretty easy, right? You don't need all those numbers in Intel's Statement of Cash Flows. You only need two of them.

Table 3.2

R.R. Donnelley Condensed Statement of Cash Flows $ (millions)	2005
Income, depreciation, and other nonworking capital items	$966.3
Change in operating net working capital (− signifies increase)	−$18.8
Cash flow from operations	$947.5
Capex	$471.0
Noncapex cash flow from investment	$1,131.5
Cash flow from investment	$1,602.5
Cash flow from financing	$378.5
Net cash flow = change in cash position	−$275.1
Interest paid	$129.2
Income taxes paid	$162.7

The only problem is that the answer is wrong: Intel's 2005 free cash flows weren't $9,005 million, even if the Deutsche Bank analysts said they were. To see why, use Table 3.2 to do the same free cash flow computation for R.R. Donnelley that we just did for Intel.

Take the analogous items for Donnelley, cash flow from operations ($947.5) and capex ($471), subtract the second from the first, and what you get is $476.5 million. The only trouble is that this number does not equate to the 2005 Donnelley free cash flow number in Figure 2.5 from Chapter 2.

The numbers displayed in the figure are –$525.8 million for free cash flow and –$250.7 million for net cash flow to investors. In 2005, free cash flow was lower than net cash flow to investors because Donnelley used $275.1 million in cash.

Look, free cash flow of +$476.5 million is a far cry from free cash flow of –$525.8 million. The difference between the free cash flow number you would get using the Deutsche Bank formula and the amount of cash Donnelley's investors actually received in 2005 is more than $1 billion! This is hardly peanuts. And free cash flow is the basis for computing the fundamental value of R.R. Donnelley. We can't let the gremlins win!

What is the logic underlying the Deutsche Bank formula for free cash flow? A company generates cash flow from operations that is available to be paid out to its investors, at least in theory. However, it first has to spend money buying new capital equipment. Therefore, what remains from operating cash flow after paying for the equipment is then available to be paid to investors. The logic is so simple. It's virtually intuitive. The problem is that it's too simple. And as for it being intuitive, one of the big problems with intuition is that intuition masks bias gremlins.

It's time for our first debiasing game: correctly computing free cash flow. Here is what's wrong with the logic of using only cash flow from operations and capex to compute free cash flow.

Free cash flow is the sum of net cash flow to all investors, debt holders, and shareholders, plus the change in cash holdings. Now, cash flow from operations is cash flow that only pertains to shareholders, not debt holders. Therefore, you have to figure in interest paid. Next, you would want to take all investment expenditures into account, not just those in capex.

What can you do to debias? If you take cash flow from operations, add interest paid, and subtract cash flow from investment, you should obtain free cash flow. You can check this for R.R. Donnelley's 2005 free cash flows. If you add the sum of $947.5 and $129.2 and then subtract the sum of $1,602.5, you will get –$525.8, the right number.

That's it, the first debiasing game: pulling out three numbers from a table and knowing which ones to add and which ones to subtract. How hard is that?

The easy part is doing the arithmetic. The hard part is breaking old bad habits. One bad habit is using the wrong formula. Another bad habit is trusting what you read in the financial press. From *Kiplinger's Personal Finance Magazine*, you would have learned that free cash flow is net income plus noncash charges minus capital costs. From *CFO Australia*, you would have learned to use the formula cash flow from operations minus the sum of capital expenditure and working capital movements. From *Credit Investment News*, you would have learned that Donnelley's free cash flow for 2005 was +$250 million.

As I said earlier, step one of a twelve-step program is to acknowledge that there is a problem. You are avoiding the first of the 12 steps if you believe what *Kiplinger's Personal Finance Magazine* or *CFO Australia* states about how to define free cash flow, if you believe the number in *Credit Investment News*, or if you believe the Deutsche Bank analysts.

There are two psychological issues associated with cash flow gremlins. The first is called "framing transparency." Framing is synonymous with description. The first issue is that the description of what free cash flows represent lacks transparency. It lacks transparency because it focuses on cash generated by the company instead of cash received by investors. Without a clear sense of what is measured, it is easy to come up with multiple definitions, all of which appear equally plausible.

Here is a good way to help with the framing of free cash flows. If you subtract the company's change in cash from its free cash flow, you should get net cash flow to investors: the sum of dividends and interest net of new debt and new equity. In 2005, that number turned out to be –$250.7 for Donnelley. What this number means is that in 2005, Donnelley's investors didn't receive a nickel from the company. Instead, they paid $250.7 million to the company!

Remember, the value of a company is the present value of future expected net cash flows to investors. A –$250.7 million does not help generate value! So instead of getting snowed by all these competing definitions of free cash flow, keep your eye on net cash flow to investors (NCFI). You can then get free cash flow simply by adding the change in cash to NCFI!

The second bias gremlin is known as "availability bias." This concept means that undue weight gets attached to information that is readily available relative to information that is not as readily available. In this case, what are readily available are the erroneous notions of free cash flow described in the financial press.

Availability bias is pernicious. To appreciate how pernicious, consider the following question: What is your best estimate of how many people died worldwide in 2006 from shark attacks? Think about your answer before reading on. You might also want to give a low estimate and a high estimate so that you are 80 percent confident that the answer lies in your forecast range.

Shark attacks tend to be widely reported in the press, and so information about shark attacks is readily available. Therefore, you are vulnerable to availability bias when answering questions about the frequency of shark attacks. In terms of direction, the bias tends to produce a number that is too high. It turns out that four people died from shark attacks during 2006. How close were you? Did four lie between your low estimate and your high estimate? If not, then you are overconfident too.

Risk and Return Gremlins

Figuring out the right discount rate to use is a challenge. In theory, the rate at which to discount future cash flows depends on how risky those cash flows are.

An article that appeared in *CFO Australia* describes some of the major mistakes that companies make when using discount rates.[1] The article discusses the views of Tom Copeland, a finance professor at MIT. Copeland suggests that when executives use the beta formula described in Chapter 2, they keep the market risk premium the same over time, but in reality, it varies. In particular, he suggests that the premium has been declining over time. In Australia, there is great variation in the number attached to the market premium. Some use the historical value of 7 percent, and others use 4 percent.

The *CFO Australia* article also describes the views of Kevin Reeves, a corporate finance partner at PricewaterhouseCoopers. Reeves criticized corporate executives for using the same number for required return on equity year after year. In contrast, the textbook approach described in Chapter 2 involves changing the required return on equity to reflect changes in such key variables as the debt-to-equity ratio, interest rates, and inflationary expectations.

The bias gremlin here is known as "status quo bias." This bias corresponds to inertia. Often, people feel that they should make a change, but because they lack the courage of

[1]See Elizabeth Fry, "Hole Numbers," *CFO Australia*, September 1, 2005.

their convictions, they take no action for fear it will turn out to be the wrong thing to have done.

Valuation Gremlins

Valuation is based on discounted cash flow (DCF). Some financial executives make valuation mistakes because they rely on erroneous valuation formulas. Others make valuation mistakes because they form erroneous forecasts of free cash flow. Still others make valuation mistakes because they use erroneous discount rates.

If you use base valuation on discounted free cash flow numbers, you have to be careful about how you define free cash flows. Earlier, I pointed out that you can't just use capex and ignore the other components of cash flow from investment. Some analysts argue that for valuation purposes it's okay to focus only on capex because other investments, like those for acquisitions, don't reduce the value of the company. Arguments like these are nonsense. Valuation gremlins do indeed cause some managers to make acquisitions that reduce the value of the company.

Valuation gremlins are especially active in high-technology companies. Geoffrey Moore has written a number of excellent books about marketing strategy for high-technology firms. However, when it comes to issues of valuation, he makes important mistakes. The most egregious mistake is in his book *Living on the Fault Line*, where he argues that the value of a company's stock is the present value of its future earnings.

Do you know why Moore's stock valuation formula is wrong? It is wrong because earnings are not pure cash and are certainly not all paid out to investors. It is cash flows to equity, namely dividends, and repurchases net of new issues that are to be discounted, not earnings. Think about a company that holds no debt and does not plan to issue new shares or repurchase new shares in the future. Then the intrinsic value of its stock is the present value of its expected dividends. If the company plans to pay out as dividends 1 percent of its earnings and you value the company's stock using its earnings instead of its dividends, then you will overestimate the value of the company by a factor of 100.

Gremlins are also at work when executives use simple rules of thumb, called *heuristics*, to do valuation. The most popular rules of thumb involve price-to-earnings ratios. Here, earnings are defined either as net income or earnings before interest, tax, depreciation, and amortization (EBITDA). The heuristic is simple. Forecast earnings for next year. Determine what seems to be a suitable price-to-earnings ratio, and multiply the two to come up with value.

Here is an example. In spring 2006, Deutsche Bank forecasted that the price of Intel stock would increase from $20 to $30 over 12 to 18 months, an increase of about 50 percent. Its rationale was that Intel's P/E ratio had fallen to 17, a number below its historical value, and over the next 12 to 18 months would revert from a value of 17 to about 25, an increase of about 50 percent.

The chief difficulty with the P/E heuristic is that the price-to-earnings ratio tends to be selected cavalierly instead of based on considerations such as risk and NPV, which were described in Chapter 2. There is nothing in the Deutsche Bank report on Intel that talks about risk or NPV. For that matter, there is nothing in the Deutsche Bank report that computes value based on free cash flow, even though the report includes free cash flow numbers, improperly defined as they are.

Gremlins can also induce executives to generate erroneous cash flow forecasts. Tom Copeland contends that many financial executives routinely underestimate the capital expenditures their companies will need to support their future sales. Part of the issue, he claims, is that executives fail to forecast the whole balance sheet. He has a point. And that point also applies to defining free cash flow mistakenly as cash flow from operations minus capex. That definition leaves out cash flows from other investment items and interest paid.

There are all kinds of gremlins at work when it comes to using appropriate discount rates in valuation. Nobody can predict the future. Actual cash flows might be very different from predicted cash flows—sometimes more favorable and other times less favorable. Actual cash flows can also turn out to be less risky than predicted or riskier than predicted. Moreover, the degree of cash flow risk faced is often partly at the discretion of executives who have options as the future unfolds.

Because the degree of risk varies as the contingencies unfold, the underlying discount rate appropriate to discount cash flows also varies. As a result, you cannot just discount the predicted cash flows at a fixed discount rate. Instead, you have to use option valuation techniques to do it right. And that is a whole other story, which I would love to tell, but it would distract me from the main message of this book.

Capital Budgeting Gremlins

Capital budgeting gremlins are very active in the corporate world. Before delving into several examples, consider some of the standard tests for identifying these gremlins in the real world.

Duke University, in conjunction with *CFO* magazine, routinely surveys financial executives. The survey can be found at http://www.cfosurvey.org/. The survey consists of 10 questions plus some identifying information about the company. Table 3.3 contains an adaptation of question 10 from the survey. The actual question pertains to the future, whereas the modified question in the table refers to a period in the past. Please read the question in Table 3.3.

Notice that the question has two parts, a and b. In a, your task is to guess what the return for the S&P 500 was for the 10-year period 1956–1965. The idea is to do this without looking up the answer. Unless you have a great memory for

Table 3.3

On December 31, 1955 the annual yield on 10-year treasury bonds was 2.9 percent. Please complete the following:

---

a. Over the subsequent 10 years, 1956–1965, I would guess that the average annual S&P 500 return was:

Worst Case: There is a 1-in-10 chance the actual average return was less than:	*Best Guess:* I expect the return was:	*Best Case:* There is a 1-in-10 chance the actual average return was greater than:
%	%	%

b. During the next year, 1956, I expect the S&P 500 return was:

Worst Case: There is a 1-in-10 chance the actual average return was less than:	*Best Guess:* I expect the return was:	*Best Case:* There is a 1-in-10 chance the actual average return was greater than:
%	%	%

---

financial history, it is a not an easy question to nail. That is why you are asked for your worst case guess and your best case guess in addition to your best guess. It is very important that you choose your worst case guess and best case guess so that you feel there is a 1-in–10 chance that your worst case guess will be too high and a 1-in–10 chance that your best case guess will be too low.

Please go ahead and answer part a of the question by writing down three percentage numbers, one for your worst case, one for your best guess, and one for your best case.

In part b of the question, your task is to answer similarly, except that the time period is 1956 rather than the entire 10 years. Please answer part b. Once you have done so, repeat part b for 1957 instead of 1956. Then do the same for 1958 and repeat for 1959, 1960, ..., all the way through 1965.

If you have finished the task, then you should have written down 33 percentage numbers. The next task is to check how well you did. The historical answers to part b can be found in Figure 3.1.

The answer to part a is 7.35 percent. Check to see if 7.35 percent lies between your low guess and your high guess. If it does, give yourself a hit. Otherwise, give yourself a miss. You can also measure your accuracy by computing the difference between your best guess and 7.35 percent. For example, if you best guess was 10 percent, then your forecast error was 2.65 percent.

If your best guess was above 7.35 percent, you might be inclined toward unrealistic optimism. The annual rate of return to holding the S&P 500 between 1926 and 2006 was 6.2 percent. Between 1926 and 1955, the rate of return was 4.8 percent.

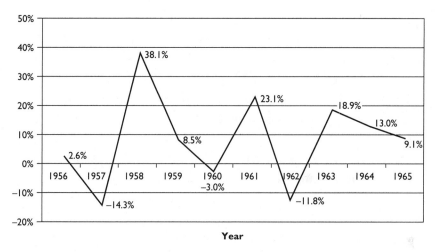

Figure 3.1 Return to S&P 500, 1956–1965

If you are well calibrated, you should have about 8 hits in part b. That is because, with your worst case and best case each being set with a 1-in–10 chance of missing, there is a 2-in–10 chance of missing for any year. Put another way, there is an 8-in–10 chance of getting a hit in any year. With 10 years of guesses, the expected number of hits is 8.

If you had many fewer than 8 hits, say under 5 hits, it is safe to say that you are overconfident. If you had 10 hits, you might be underconfident. Overconfident people set their guess ranges too narrowly. Underconfident people set their guess ranges too widely. Only well-calibrated people, as in the Goldilocks fairy tale, set their guess ranges just right.

The responses of the executives from the Duke-*CFO* magazine survey suggest that as a group they are unrealistically optimistic and overconfident. Their best guess returns were too high by about 3.8 percent. Their hit rate was

3.9 percent. The width of their guess ranges was so narrow as to imply that the stock market features very little risk.[2]

Being influenced by gremlins has its consequences. Unrealistic optimism leads executives to produce cash flow forecasts that are too rosy. Overconfidence leads executives to underestimate the risk attached to those cash flows. Taken together, unrealistic optimism and overconfidence induce executives to overestimate the NPV of their projects. As a result, the greater the degree of unrealistic optimism and overconfidence, the more inclined are executives to adopt projects and undertake acquisitions. And this isn't idle speculation. It is what the evidence shows.

Here is a concrete case that was described on the front page of *The Wall Street Journal*.[3] In April 2006, Larry Siegel was the CEO of Mills Corporation, a real estate investment trust (REIT) that developed and owned shopping malls.

Mills became a public company in 1994. Its malls were regarded as some of the most creative in the industry for the way they combined shopping and entertainment. Siegel's vision was to build malls that combined the best of two worlds: the world of the outlet mall that featured brand names sold at discount prices and the world of the full-service mall that offered a wide range of services, especially food and entertainment. At Mills's malls, shoppers found food courts, skateboard parks, massage parlors, glow-in-the-dark miniature golf, simulated NASCAR driving, and IMAX theaters.

Larry Siegel had been Mills's CEO for about a dozen years. Mills's investors characterized Siegel as a "salesman"

[2]See Itzhak Ben-David, John Graham, and Campbell Harvey, "Managerial Overconfidence and Corporate Policies," Duke University working paper, 2007.
[3]See Ryan Chittum and Jennifer S. Forsyth, "Market Decline: How a Glitzy Mall Developer Built Its Way into Big Trouble—Mills Corp. Courted Shoppers with Mini Golf, Massages; Now Banks Crack Down—'Larry, He Is a Salesman,'" *The Wall Street Journal*, April 14, 2006.

whose words needed to be appropriately discounted. Why would an investor want to discount Siegel's statements? The answer, in a word, is gremlins. CEOs have a knack of exhibiting unrealistic optimism and overconfidence.

Let's talk numbers. In 1995, Mills' return on equity (ROE) was 11 percent. Then, between 1996 and 2001, its ROE ranged between 22 percent and 78 percent, averaging 39 percent. Mills's malls were a big hit with shoppers. But in 2002, its ROE fell to 10 percent, and problems set in. Those problems had to do with its investment policy. Between 1995 and 2006, Mills constructed 13 new shopping malls and restructured another two malls to fit its new mold. By 2006, Mills had 42 malls both inside and outside the United States. Moreover, it expanded beyond its original vision based on outlet malls and began to compete in the space occupied by regional malls. It also invested internationally, with projects in Singapore, Madrid, and Scotland.

Figure 3.2 provides a quick trajectory of Mills's fortunes, displaying Mills's market cap between 1997 and 2006.

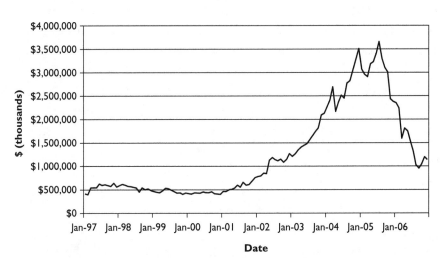

Figure 3.2 Mills Corp Market Cap, 1997–2006

As a general matter, unrealistic optimism and overconfidence lead executives to take on too many projects, spend too much money on those projects, and underestimate the future cash flows from those projects to the point where the projects have negative NPV. Mills's cash flow projections for the period 1995 to 2006 were overly optimistic by about 20 percent. Newer projects proved to be especially disappointing.

Unrealistically optimistic, overconfident executives underestimate risk. Mills even spent $120 million on a project named Xanadu in the New Jersey Meadowlands before winning the right to develop the site. As you can see, Mills had very busy gremlins at work.

Siegel's gremlins induced him to invest on an extremely large scale. While his competitors' malls were built on 1 million square feet, Mills's malls occupied 50 percent more space. Where were the cash flows needed to justify that size of investment supposed to come from? The answer is that Mills's malls would have to draw customers from beyond the 10- to 20-mile radius associated with most malls. Somehow the value proposition that Mills's malls offered customers meant that all the entertainment would compensate for the extra time and fuel spent going to a Mills mall instead of a closer alternative, such as an outlet mall.

Siegel believed that if he provided the entertainment, the customers would come in sufficient numbers and with sufficient dollars to spend. The only thing was that space for entertainment substituted for space that retailers could occupy. Moreover, customers did not find Mills's value proposition as attractive as Siegel had hoped. Fewer were willing to spend the extra time and gas to drive to a Mills mall. For these and other reasons, by 2004, annual sales per square foot in Mills's malls turned out to be below average for regional REITs. Particularly hard hit were Mills's more recent investments—those in regional malls. To add insult to injury, these disappointments occurred during an incredibly hot real estate market.

Ultimately, Mills's overly optimistic cash flow projections proved to be its undoing. In the end, the company wrote off about $655 million in losses from Xanadu, the New Jersey Meadowlands project, which it sold to a Los Angeles investment firm. Short of cash, in February 2007, Mills sold itself to a competitor, mall operator Simon Property Group, which together with its hedge fund partner, Farallon Capital Management, paid a total of $1.64 billion in cash.

Gremlins not only affect what unrealistically optimistic, overconfident executives spend. They also affect what they don't spend. Mills failed to invest enough in maintaining existing properties, instead diverting those funds to growth in new malls. This type of mistake can be extremely expensive, as the next example illustrates.

BP is a global oil company headquartered in London. It has American operations in both the Gulf of Mexico and at Prudhoe Bay in Alaska. The company's oil rigs suffered considerable damage during Hurricane Katrina, the storm that devastated New Orleans. There was little BP could have done to avert that disaster. Its Alaskan operations also suffered damage, but that damage was entirely avoidable. Keep in mind that Prudhoe Bay is the largest oil-producing field in the United States. By failing to invest sufficiently in maintaining its pipelines, BP cost itself a lot of money and caused a major disruption in U.S. oil supplies.

BP transports the oil it extracts at Prudhoe Bay to market through a pipeline. Pipelines build up sediment through time, and that buildup can eventually corrode the pipes, leading to leaks and spills. Oil companies check pipelines for sediment buildup and possible leaks using a technique called "pigging." Pigging involves the injection of a cylindrical droid into the line.

Some pigs are smarter than others. The industry actually uses the term *intelligent pig* for instruments that are loaded with sensors. Besides intelligent pigs, oil companies can run maintenance tests using other external testing devices such as ultrasound. Although not as effective as intelligent pigs, the external devices are more convenient to use and less expensive.

During 2002, BP had a dispute with the Alaskan Department of Environmental Conservation. In July of that year, the two parties were negotiating a settlement. To resolve the dispute, the department asked BP to use intelligent pigs to probe its pipelines for leaks, along with a list of other tasks, and to pay a fine of $150,000. However, a month later, BP wrote to the department to say that it had no evidence to suggest that its lines had anything more than minimal sediment buildup, and as a result, it saw no need to use intelligent pigs. Five days after receiving this communication, the department withdrew its requirement that BP pig its lines.

The use of intelligent pigs is standard in the industry. BP had last run an intelligent pig through its Alaskan pipelines 10 years earlier in 1992. In contrast to BP, Alyeska Pipeline Service probes its lines with an intelligent pig every three years. It also runs a cleaning pig at least twice a month. Alyeska operates and maintains the 800-mile Trans Alaska Pipeline System.

BP eventually ran an intelligent pig through its lines in August 2006, 14 years after its last such probe. In doing so, it shut the stable door after the proverbial horse had bolted. Severe pipeline corrosion together with a leak caused BP to shut down half of its output from Prudhoe Bay.

Using an intelligent pig every few years is a psychologically smart thing to do. Waiting 14 years to run an intelligent pig is a psychologically dumb thing to do. It is especially dumb when U.S. policy is seeking to reduce the country's dependence on foreign oil. It was especially dumb in 2005 after Hurricane Katrina caused a major disruption in U.S. domestic oil production in the Gulf of Mexico. Is the source of the problem that BP is a British company and therefore oblivious to U.S. foreign policy? Or is the source of the problem human psychology?

Unrealistic optimism and overconfidence figure prominently in the BP story. People who are unrealistically optimistic underestimate the probability that an unfavorable event will happen to them. Overconfident people underestimate risk. Overconfident people also discount the opinions of others. In 2003 and 2004, BP received correspondence from local oil workers or their representatives warning about the danger of failing to use intelligent pigs.

Availability bias also figures strongly. Do you know the phrase "out of sight, out of mind"? Well, the corrosion inside those pipes was certainly out of sight, and therefore not salient, at least not until 267,000 gallons of oil began to spill onto the ground.

The primary culprit at BP appears to have been one Richard Woollam, who was head of corrosion monitoring for BP at Prudhoe Bay. It's difficult to say for certain what his mindset was at the time. It was Woollam who led BP's efforts in August 2002 to have the requirement for intelligent pigging removed. In September 2006, Congress investigated events from the previous March, and Woollam took the fifth to avoid incriminating himself. The general opinion is that his focus was on cost cutting. Moreover, he appeared to have engaged in a series of tactics that were designed to intimidate BP employees into keeping contrary opinions to themselves.

Although Woollam was the primary culprit at BP, his behavior is not an isolated case. BP has a systemic problem with its culture that runs deep. Misdirected cost-cutting decisions at a Texas City BP facility resulted in a major explosion in 2005 that killed 15 people. A BP employee who worked at both Prudhoe Bay and Texas City indicated that the culture could be described by the slogan: "Can we cut costs by 10 percent?"

All else being equal, lower costs are preferable to higher costs. However, in the real world, all else is not equal. There can be consequences to cost cutting. If the consequences of cutting costs feature negative net present value, then cutting costs is dumb, not smart.

John Browne, formally Lord Browne of Madingley and CEO of BP, had spent a decade meticulously crafting an environmentally friendly image for his company. In doing so, he brought respect to both himself and his company, including respect from political figures who singled him out among oil industry leaders. All that respect went up in smoke after the Prudhoe Bay leak. What we learned was that the culture of BP was focused on cutting costs and improving margins but not value maximization in either the private sense or the social sense. Indeed, as far back as 1995, Lord Browne himself characterized cost cutting as a way of life.

As we have seen, bias gremlins can lead some executives to be foolish in the way they spend corporate money and others to be foolish in not spending corporate money when they should. Added to these two behavioral patterns are gremlins that induce executives to throw good money after bad by refusing to pull the plug on losing projects.

There are lots of examples of companies that were late pulling the plug. In 1998, Daimler's unrealistically optimistic, overconfident chairman Jürgen Schrempp paid $36 billion for Chrysler in a bid to turn his firm into a global carmaker. In 2007, after years of bleeding, Daimler was looking to sell Chrysler. In May of that year, it finally did for $7.4 billion to Cerberus Capital Management of

New York, a private equity firm that specializes in restructuring troubled companies.

Schrempp's global vision also led him into Asia. In 2000, Daimler spent about $3 billion to acquire a 34 percent stake in Mitsubishi Motors, which it later increased to 37 percent. In 2004, DaimlerChrysler AG announced that it would finally pull the plug on its investment in Mitsubishi Motors Corp.

In 2004, the media company Time Warner finally pulled the plug on CNNfn. Time Warner spent nine unsuccessful years trying to build a financial network, CNNfn, that would successfully compete with CNBC.

In November 2005, the steel company Alcoa announced that it was finally pulling the plug on Eastalco, a cost-ineffective smelter in Maryland. Eastalco had entered into a long-term contract with Allegheny Power and was paying 40 percent more for electricity than its competitors. Despite the high variable costs of production, Alcoa was reluctant to close the smelter down. When it finally did so, some viewed the event as the closing down of one of the most expensive smelters in history.

Some executives recognize their gremlins and play debiasing games trying to beat them back. Andy Grove, the legendary CEO who led Intel for many years, provided an excellent example in his influential book *Only the Paranoid Survive*. In the book, Grove recounts a conversation he had with his Intel colleague Gordon Moore, the executive associated with the phenomenon known as Moore's Law. Grove asked Moore what he thought would happen if Intel's board fired him and brought in a new CEO? Moore responded that he thought the new CEO would terminate Intel's involvement in the memory chip business.

Grove's next statement illustrates how a debiasing game works. He said, okay, in that case let me fire myself and do what my replacement would do. And that is what happened. Figuratively, he fired himself. Literally, he took Intel out of the highly competitive low-margin memory chip business and moved it into the less competitive high-margin microprocessor business.

Market Efficiency

Just to remind you, the tenet of market efficiency is that the price is right. This means that market prices provide the best measure of intrinsic value. If the market is efficient, there is no point in investors searching for mispriced securities to buy low and sell high. Investors cannot expect to beat the market except by being lucky. The only returns investors can expect to earn are the returns that reflect appropriate compensation for risk.

Traditional textbooks teach that the market is efficient. The behavioral view is actually a bit different. The behavioral view is that because investors have their own gremlins with which to contend, the market price is not always right. Systematic mispricing does take place in markets. There are opportunities to buy low and sell high. Smart investors are able to earn returns that more than compensate them for the fundamental risk they bear. And remember, I said *smart* investors: Beating the market requires considerable skill.

There are all kinds of systematic mispricing patterns. In the winner-loser effect, long-term losers outperform long-term winners. In the momentum effect, recent winners outperform recent losers. In the new issues effect, newly issued shares underperform in the long term. If the newly issued shares pertain to an initial public offering (IPO), there is often a price pop on the first day the shares trade; this effect is known as *initial underpricing*. In the repurchasing effect, companies that announce share buybacks, stating that they believe the shares are undervalued by the market, do indeed experience subsequent abnormally positive returns over time. These returns cannot be explained as compensation for risk. In the acquisition effect, the shares of companies that engage in acquisitions and whose executives simultaneously sell company stock do poorly after the acquisition.

Some mispricing patterns, such as the new issues effect, the repurchasing effect, and the acquisition effect, are particularly germane to corporate executives. Smart executives can buy low and sell high both in their corporate lives as well as in their personal investing lives. In other words, smart executives can engage in market timing.

Capital Structure Gremlins

Capital structure is about the nature of the promised returns that companies make to investors in exchange for receiving investors' money. The investors consist of debt holders and shareholders who supply the companies with cash in the form of loans and equity financing. In return, companies promise interest payments to debt holders. Likewise, companies promise dividends to shareholders. Over time, interest payments and dividends are paid from the cash generated by the companies' operations, as well as from the sale of company assets or the drawing down of its cash holdings.

If you think of a company's sources of cash as a pie, then capital structure is about how that pie is divided into a slice for debt holders, a slice for shareholders, and a slice for taxes. In an ideal world, executives make decisions about capital structure with a view to maximizing the value of their companies. In an ideal world, executives properly weigh the pros and cons of increased debt relative to equity.

Pros involve tax savings from higher debt, so-called tax shields. Cons involve increased risk from possible bankruptcy and the fees associated with loan origination and stock issuance.

Executives have a fiduciary responsibility to existing shareholders. Therefore, they need to be attentive to whether the debt and equity issued by their companies are priced correctly by the market. Executives who issue new shares that the market undervalues dilute the equity of the original shareholders. Executives who issue new shares that the market overvalues do the reverse.

How do gremlins figure into decisions about capital structure? In particular, how do unrealistic optimism and overconfidence interfere with making sound capital market decisions? There are at least two ways.

The first way that unrealistic optimism and overconfidence affect capital structure involves the fraction of a company's value that is debt financed. Think about unrealistically optimistic, overconfident managers seeking to balance the tax shield benefits of debt against the expected costs of financial distress, especially bankruptcy. They will be inclined to underestimate the likelihood of going into bankruptcy and therefore to underestimate the expected cost of bankruptcy. Thus, unrealistically optimistic, overconfident managers will be prone to take on more debt than is appropriate.

Think back to our discussion about Mills Corporation and its unrealistically optimistic, overconfident CEO Larry Siegel. Mills decided to open shopping centers in St. Louis and Pittsburgh despite the existing degree of competition in both regions and the absence of new customers. To finance those projects, Mills borrowed heavily. The debt ratio of the average regional mall REIT in 2006 was 53 percent, meaning 53 percent of the company's overall market value was debt financed. In contrast, Mills's debt ratio was 72 percent. Mills also secured funding by entering into joint ventures in which it gave its partners preferred returns.

There are other capital structure gremlins at work, causing mischief by preventing executives from seeing the whole for the parts. Do you remember how the intrinsic value of a company's shares is affected when the company uses some of its cash to repurchase 30 percent of its existing shares? The company's assets fall in value by 30 percent. The total value of the shares falls by 30 percent. The number of shares falls by 30 percent. And the price per share stays the same.

Capital structure gremlins can even affect executives like Jack Stack, who pride themselves on getting finance and accounting right.[4] Stack discusses how his company would boost its stock price by repurchasing and retiring shares. Here is the gremlin logic. Because the number of shares goes down by 30 percent but not the company's earnings, those earnings get spread over fewer shares. Therefore, earnings per share (EPS) is higher by 30 percent. As a result, the stock price goes up by 30 percent because the higher EPS is multiplied by the same P/E multiple.

The flaw in the gremlin's logic is that intrinsic value is determined by future cash flows, and those cash flows will decline if 30 percent of the company's original value is paid out in cash. Multiplying EPS by a P/E ratio is a back-of-the-envelope technique but not the basis for computing intrinsic value. The cash the company used to repurchase the shares might instead have been used to pay out future dividends or to fund future projects that would have themselves generated cash.

---

[4] See Jack Stack and Bo Burlingham, *A Stake in the Outcome* (New York: Currency Doubleday), pp. 246, 247, 252.

While we are on the subject of dividends, I should mention that companies whose projects have high NPV can do their shareholders a favor by keeping their dividend payouts low and using the cash to fund projects instead. After all, high NPV means that the company is able to generate higher expected returns through its projects than investors can earn if paid the cash instead. Unrealistically optimistic, overconfident managers tend to overestimate NPV. As a result, these biases incline them to choose lower-dividend payout ratios. For example, beginning in 2003, Mills began to reduce its dividend payout ratio by 20 percent a year.

The general evidence from the Duke-CFO magazine survey is that the greater the degree of unrealistic optimism and overconfidence on the part of executives, the more prone they are to take on excessive debt. In the Duke-*CFO* magazine survey, the average debt ratio was 23 percent.

Suppose we divide executives into 10 groups according to their overconfidence. Imagine that for each group we compute the average debt ratio of the company that the executive works for. The Duke-*CFO* magazine survey results indicate that as we migrate from the group having the lowest overconfidence to the group having the highest overconfidence, the debt ratio increases by 0.5 percent every time we move up to a new group.

In addition, overconfident executives tend to take out debt with longer maturities. The average maturity for the survey firms was 3.7 years. However, the group with the highest overconfidence rating took out longer loans than the group with the lowest overconfidence rating by about one year. The longer maturity leaves a company with less financial flexibility and more interest rate risk.

I should also point out that some executives suffer from the opposite problem: too little debt. Companies that hold insufficient debt pay more tax than necessary. The gremlins at work here are different from the gremlins that induce unrealistic optimism and overconfidence. These other gremlins generate a lot of anticipated pain associated with defaulting on debt. The psychological phenomenon is called *loss aversion*. Most people exhibit loss aversion because the specter of a loss looms about 2.5 times as great as a potential gain of the same magnitude.

The second way unrealistic optimism and overconfidence affect capital structure involves market timing—the attempt to buy low and sell high. Unrealistically optimistic, overconfident executives are especially prone to issue new shares when they believe their company's stock is overvalued, to buy back shares when they believe their company's stock is undervalued, and to take on debt when they believe the market underestimates the probability of default.

In 2006, there was a frenzy of acquisition activity, much of which was funded by debt. In these leveraged buyouts, acquirers borrowed money from investors to buy the stock of companies they took over and then left the target firm to repay the debt. The point is that most of this debt was high yield, or junk as it is often called. The perception at the time was that debt holders were unrealistically optimistic about future defaults because the recent default rate had been low. As a result, they projected the past onto the future and continued to expect low default rates.

What's Next?

In the first three chapters of this book, I have focused on the role of psychological biases in corporate financial decision making. At this point, you should have a good sense of what bias gremlins are and how they affect corporate decisions. You should also have a sense that there are companies that have been successful in battling these gremlins.

The next five chapters develop a program for structuring debiasing processes to battle gremlins.

CHAPTER 4

ACCOUNTING: BUILDING A FINANCIALLY LITERATE WORKFORCE THAT KEEPS SCORE

Financial illiteracy is a fertile breeding ground for bias gremlins. The reason is simple. In business, managers and investors use finance and accounting to keep score. Finance and accounting provide measurable goals and indicators that tell managers how well their businesses are doing. Without those goals, bias gremlins will run the company.

Managing a company is like flying a plane using a combination of instruments and visual cues. The visual cues can help a bit, but it's the instruments that serve as the main devices that pilots use to make their decisions. It's the instruments that tell them how they are doing. If you take away the instruments, you take away discipline and replace it with intuition and emotion. The gremlins love it.

Financial literacy is the basis for keeping managers focused on the right performance gauges and managing those gauges. Financial literacy is the basis for keeping on the front burner what needs to be on the front burner and not letting less relevant items from the back burner push their way to the front. Financial illiteracy is a big problem that costs companies dearly. And except for open book companies, it seems to be a problem that few are willing to face up to, let alone address.

United Airlines: A Financially Illiterate Walk Off a Cliff

If employees don't pay attention to the accounting numbers, they can let their companies go down the tubes. United Airlines is a case in point. To see why, I'm going to present some business history, beginning with United's earnings trajectory. Take a look at Figure 4.1. What kind of pattern do you see in the numbers? Down, up, down, up, and then off the cliff, right? Okay, so let's talk about the story underlying those numbers.

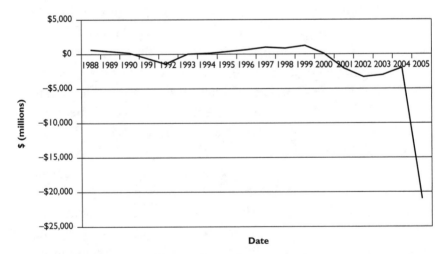

Figure 4.1 Net Income (Loss) of United Airlines, 1988–2005

United was once a proud airline. It has the distinction of being the first airline to fly in all 50 U.S. states. The year was 1984. But a year later, a labor negotiations impasse between United's pilots and management resulted in a strike. Management sought to break the strike by replacing the pilots with trainees. The pilots ultimately won the strike but were so stunned by management's aggressive actions that they decided to try to obtain a controlling interest in the company in an attempt to prevent a recurrence.

United had an employee stock ownership program (ESOP). In the late 1980s, United's workforce began to purchase company stock with the intent of converting United into an employee-controlled company. In this respect, they traded wages and work-rule concessions for stock in the company and by 1995 had purchased 55 percent of the company's outstanding shares. Those lower wages took the form of concessions in the five years from 1995 to 2000.

In those five years, United's wages were below the industry average. As a result, its earnings grew at a healthy pace, a trend you can discern in Figure 4.1. After a period featuring high volatility, its stock became strong, as can be seen in Figure 4.2. *Fortune* magazine runs an annual survey about America's most admired companies. United made the top 10. One of the questions in the associated *Fortune* survey asks participants to rate company stock for long-term investment value. On this criterion, United also ranked in the top 10.

In early 1998, United's stock price peaked and began to decline. Although United's pilots owned a large chunk of the company, they negotiated a very lucrative contract. Airline travel fell with the collapse of the dot-com bubble and subsequent recession that began in early 2001. Then September 11 happened. Take a look at Figure 4.1 to see what happened to United's earnings after 2000. The red ink piled up. United

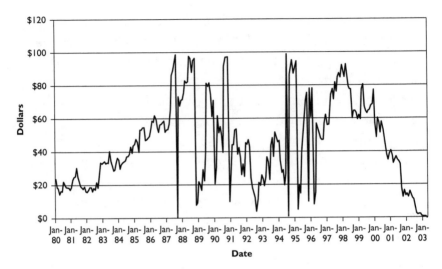

Figure 4.2 Stock Price, United Airlines, 1980–2002

petitioned the Air Transportation Stabilization Board for a $1.8 billion loan guarantee, but its petition was rejected. It sought concessions from its employee owners. In particular, it asked its mechanics to accept a 7 percent reduction in pay that would save the firm $700 million. The mechanics/owners refused. In December 2002, United declared bankruptcy, the largest airline bankruptcy in U.S. history, and the mechanics' shares became worthless. The company would not emerge from bankruptcy until 2006.

After the bankruptcy, United's financial fortunes improved for a while but then plummeted. Figure 4.1 shows how badly. A key part of the problem was its cost structure. Its labor costs per seat mile were $4.60, about 60 percent higher than those of rival Southwest Airlines and 30 percent higher than those of Continental Airlines. This is it, folks. You can ignore the underlying accounting issues, but you can't escape them! Either you squarely face up to the issues and respond sensibly, or you sink.

Take another look at Figure 4.2. You can follow United's stock price trajectory, especially after 2000 when the period of wage concessions came to an end. Remember, United was 55 percent employee owned, and its stock was plummeting. Not surprisingly, employee morale plummeted along with its stock price. Employees' trust in management declined as the board switched executive teams three times in an eight-month period.

United is not an open book company. In an open book company, every employee knows the company's critical numbers. If United were an open book company, everyone in the organization would know that $4.60 per seat mile is too high a cost to be sustainable. Everyone in United's organization would understand what would have to be done to change the company's cost structure to become competitive in the long run. In fact, everyone in its organization would have understood the issue long before the point of crisis was reached and moved to do something about it.

Accounting Bias

Except for managers who work in finance and accounting, I think businesses have a bias against accounting. I think managers will do almost anything to avoid accounting and prefer to leave accounting to the accountants. The bias gremlins really have the upper hand here. If you view business as a game, then the financial statements are the scoreboard. Yet a great many managers do not understand financial statements. To the extent that financial illiteracy is a disease, it's an epidemic.

Epidemics are hard to tackle, especially if people have learned to live with them. People with problems who have plenty of company don't always make a big effort to solve those problems. It's easy for people to throw up their hands and ignore a problem, hoping it will go away. Dealing with problems like financial illiteracy takes collective willpower and patience. We don't solve these kinds of problems overnight.

In many ways, financial illiteracy is like smoking. Deep down, we know it's a problem. We've known it for years. And it's been difficult to act. We have known for years that heart disease is the number-one killer of Americans. The American Heart Association Statistical Update for 2006 tells us that with one exception, heart disease has been the number-one killer in the United States every year for more than a century. The one exception is the 1918 flu pandemic. Do you know what the most important risk factors are when it comes to heart disease? The answer is high cholesterol, high blood pressure, current smoking, and total diabetes. Of these, which one is actually controllable? Smoking, of course.

There is also the issue of secondhand smoke. The Center for Disease Control and Prevention, U.S. Department of Health and Human Services, tells us that every year, approximately 35,000 nonsmokers die from heart disease caused by secondhand smoke, and 3,000 nonsmokers die from lung cancer caused by secondhand smoke.

Slowly but surely, America is facing up to the problems created by smoking. Smoking bans are spreading across the country. Smoking bans are being enacted in many workplaces, restaurants, hospitals, government buildings, museums, schools, airplanes, and theaters.

I think it's time we faced up to the problem of financial illiteracy in business. I think we need to face up to the problem and address it squarely. Open book companies have shown that it's possible and provided us with examples of how to do it. Back in 1994, SRC—a manufacturing company, I remind you—spent six times more training its employees in financial statements than it spent in upgrading their production skills. If we have mustered the will to overcome inertia and tackle the problems with smoking, surely the business world can muster the will and stamp out financial illiteracy.

Fear and Will

Part of the problem with financial illiteracy is fear. Here is a story from Bob Saldich, who between 1990 and 1995 was president and CEO of Raychem Corporation. Raychem used the tools of radiation chemistry to create entirely new products, primarily for specialized military applications. Saldich joined the company in 1964 as manager of finance and personnel. At that time, the firm's revenues were $10 million. In 1999, when its annual revenues had grown to $1.8 billion, Tyco International Corporation acquired the company.

Raychem was primarily a company of engineers. Saldich says that the engineers in his company weren't just afraid of accounting. They were intimidated by accounting. When Saldich told me this, he chuckled, saying that accounting mostly consists of addition and subtraction. He chuckled because engineers use sophisticated, complex mathematics that goes well beyond addition and subtraction. It might sound funny, but Saldich has a point. Accounting is intimidating to most people, not just the engineers at Raychem. It's intimidating because it's opaque rather than transparent.

I take the position that making accounting transparent isn't that hard. And beginning with this chapter, I'm going to share some secrets with you about how to do it. The way to stamp out financial illiteracy is to institute great training programs for employees and then place accounting at center stage in processes for planning, incentives, and information sharing.

In this chapter, I describe what I think employees should learn about accounting in training programs and how they should learn it. I think the way to make accounting transparent is to combine numbers with a good story and use lots of English, especially questions for which accounting numbers are the answer.

After presenting accounting basics, I will describe how to structure decision rules for acting on accounting information. This discussion deals with the concepts of financial standards and heuristics. Financial standards are goals to shoot for. Heuristics are decision rules about how to take actions on the basis of how well a company does relative to its standards.

The core ideas in this chapter are about fighting accounting bias and therefore financial illiteracy. Debiasing involves training employees how to frame accounting issues transparently, so they not only understand the numbers but use them sensibly!

Environmental Thread

When it comes to training a workforce in financial literacy, SRC has led the way. To teach employees basic financial statements, SRC developed a program around a fictitious company that makes yo-yos. They used yo-yos to tell a story. It worked for them and for a lot of other open book companies that copied SRC's best practices. It also works for business school students. I know this firsthand, having applied some of SRC's techniques in my classes.

In the rest of the book, I'm going to use the fictitious company technique to illustrate training issues. Unlike

SRC, I won't use a yo-yo company. Instead, I'll use an environmental company and tell an environmental story.

There are a couple of reasons I have chosen an environmental story. The first reason is general environmental awareness so that I can get on my soapbox. The second reason is because environmental issues are moving to center stage in the world economy; we will all be better served if environmental companies learn to beat back their gremlins. It's soapbox time. I am going to go on a bit of an environmental diversion to set the stage for the accounting examples that come later in the chapter. But the diversion will involve numbers. And these numbers don't lie.

Global warming is beginning to make its presence felt around the world. Our planet's climate is really changing. The National Oceanic and Atmospheric Administration (NOAA) reported that between December 2006 and February 2007, the combined global land and ocean surface temperature reached a new high. This made it the warmest winter on record since the agency began tracking temperatures in 1880.

According to the National Climatic Data Center, 2006 was the warmest year on record in the lower 48 United States. The temperature was 2.2 degrees warmer than average and 0.07 degrees warmer than the previous warmest year on record, 1998. The winter of 2007 was the world's warmest since recordkeeping began more than a century ago, the U.S. government agency that tracks weather reported in March 2007.

In April 2007, the United Nations Intergovernmental Panel on Climate Change issued a report that can only be described as near apocalyptic. The United Nations panel comprised more than 2,500 scientists worldwide who relied on peer-reviewed research. Their report predicts that during the twenty-first century, extreme shortages of food and water in some parts of the world and massive flooding in others will severely affect the lives of more than a billion people. The report also predicts that millions of species will become extinct. A report released at the same time by a prestigious group of retired U.S. military officers predicts that climatic changes will cause major political destabilization, with wars over natural resources, especially water, and increased global terrorism.

Alternative energies of the future will be operating against the background of the science that underlies global warming. The essence of that science is not especially difficult to understand and involves infrared radiation. We experience infrared radiation directly when the glow of a campfire keeps us warm at night. That glow is infrared radiation.

When sunlight warms the Earth, infrared radiation is produced, and this radiation gets reflected back toward space. Some of this infrared radiation is absorbed by the atmosphere, a natural phenomenon that keeps our planet from being mostly a frozen wasteland. Greenhouse gases in the atmosphere, such as carbon dioxide and methane, are largely responsible for this beneficial absorption of infrared radiation.

Since the Industrial Revolution began in around 1750, carbon dioxide levels in the atmosphere have been increasing, from below 280 parts per million to about 360 parts per million. This change was abrupt relative to the slow decline in carbon dioxide concentrations over the preceding 130,000 years, when levels gradually fell from about 300 to just above 175. Columbia University scholar James Hansen forecasts that if current policies continue, carbon dioxide levels will reach 600 by the end of the twenty-first century.

If you've lost sight of my message in this chapter, it's that we need financially literate workforces who understand basic accounting numbers. In terms of global warming, parts per million of carbon dioxide in the atmosphere is a critical number!

Many in the scientific community consider a level of 450 to be a real danger point. What we now call global warming is simply too much of a good thing, with the higher temperatures causing major changes in climate that have devastating effects for the entire environment: melting glaciers, melting polar caps, increased ocean temperatures and sea levels, and fertile regions quickly becoming deserts. Moreover, these effects are happening much sooner than scientists had predicted. You can really see it in the Arctic, where the ice is thinning at a rapid rate.

A large share of the increased carbon dioxide emissions stems from burning coal. As of 2004, the International Energy Agency reported that 25 percent of the world's electricity production used coal. Oil and gas account for 55 percent. Nuclear energy accounts for about 7 percent. Alternative or renewable sources account for about 13 percent.

As population increases around the world and countries industrialize, there will be increased pressures to meet new demands for electricity by turning to coal. Why? Because it is cheap and plentiful; cheap, that is, if you don't figure in the environmental costs. Increased reliance on coal by both developed countries and emerging countries conceivably represents the greatest contributor to runaway global warming.

New alternative energy firms will be seeking ways to produce electricity that avoid large emissions of greenhouse gases into the atmosphere. The traditional renewables are wind, solar energy, biomass, geothermal energy, and biofuels. Of these, biomass is the largest source of renewable electricity in the United States, producing more energy than wind, solar, and geothermal energy combined.

Venture capital is investing heavily in renewable energies. According to research firm Cleantech Venture Network LLC, in 2005, venture capitalists invested $739 million in the sector, a record amount that represented a 36 percent increase from the prior year. The trend is encouraging. At the same time, the sector is risky, and people's psychology can blind them to many of the key risks, as happened in the dot-com boom of the 1990s. For that reason, using a fictitious environmental firm as an example might serve both to highlight the general issues and to help environmental firms improve their performance, which would help all of us in the future.

Introducing EnviroStuff, Inc.

In the rest of the chapter, and indeed the book, I will trace the story of the fictitious company EnviroStuff, Inc. I am going to concentrate on the first two years of EnviroStuff's existence, using its experiences as a vehicle to explain financial statements.

The first step in demystifying accounting numbers is to tell a story that underlies the numbers. People relate to stories. Here is EnviroStuff's story. I'm keeping the numbers modest to facilitate exposition.

Imagine that the year is 2010. EnviroStuff is a start-up with five entrepreneurs: Eve, Francine, Mike, Oscar, and Henry. The names correspond to positions. For example, Eve is CEO and Francine is CFO.

Working in a small facility in a low-rent industrial district, the entrepreneurs develop a new, clean, superefficient enviro-generator. Armed with a great idea and a rudimentary business plan but no cash, Eve and Francine set out to attract venture capital support for their start-up. Imagine that they seek at least $3 million in an initial round of funding.

The entrepreneurs make presentations to a series of venture capitalists. In their presentation, Eve and Francine describe their initial target market as local municipalities and golf courses that generate a lot of plant waste in the form of cut grass and tree branches. They point out that although their segment of the market, which was currently tiny, is dominated by local municipalities, they can see it growing to between $5 and $10 billion within the next five years. Moreover, as far as they can tell, nobody else has yet developed a comparable technology.

Eve and Francine manage to impress one particular venture capital group, VC Partners. VC Partners express interest in the technology but want to know what fraction of ownership in their firm the entrepreneurs are willing to exchange for funding. Eve and Francine respond by indicating that they are willing to give up 20 percent of their firm in exchange for $3 million of funding.

Here's a question for you: What value do Eve and Francine attach to their whole firm if 20 percent is worth $3 million? Well, they are saying that they think their whole firm is worth $15 million and that they are proposing to keep 80 percent, or $12 million in value.

VC Partners don't buy the valuation of $15 million. They counter that $15 million is unrealistic and go on to say that they require more than 20 percent ownership in exchange for funding. After some negotiation, VC Partners agree to provide $3 million in an initial round of funding and to receive 40 percent ownership in exchange. Put somewhat differently, the two parties compromise on a valuation of $7.5 million: 40 percent of $7.5 million is $3 million. Both founders and investors anticipate an additional round of funding, if required, after the first year.

EnviroStuff issues a total of 3 million shares. The five entrepreneurs receive 1.8 million shares of common stock.

VC Partners receive 1.2 million shares of preferred stock, which is convertible into common stock at a later date. VC Partners want preferred stock because it has priority over common stock in case the start-up fails and has to be liquidated. If that happens, VC Partners are first in line to recover any of the value that remains should the firm be dissolved. Preferred stock also offers some additional advantages in respect to governance.

At the end of 2010, EnviroStuff completes its financing and uses a portion of the funds to acquire fixed assets. The entrepreneurs spend $225,000 to purchase a parcel of land that offered space for future expansion. They then engage a contractor who erects two buildings, one for their administrative headquarters and a second for their operations plant. The cost of the headquarters building is $100,000, and the cost of the operations plant is $250,000, which together total $350,000. EnviroStuff pays for all of these items in cash.

EnviroStuff's entrepreneurs plan to manufacture enviro-generators by purchasing and converting standard machines called enviro-manufacturers. These machines are easily obtained from suppliers and easily adapted to accommodate the entrepreneurs' proprietary technology. Each enviro-manufacturer costs $50,000. The company purchases two enviro-manufacturers and pays $100,000 for them in cash. The normal lifetime of an enviro-manufacturer is two years.

In addition to manufacturing, EnviroStuff's entrepreneurs intend to engage in extensive research and development (R&D). They plan to devote their research efforts to developing future generations of their product. They plan to spend their development efforts on improving the productivity of their existing manufacturing operations, with the goal of reducing manufacturing costs. For this reason, they set aside a section of their operations plant for R&D efforts and purchased a research laboratory. A single laboratory costs $150,000, has a normal lifetime of two years, and occupies one-sixth of an operating plant. The entrepreneurs spent $150,000 for one R&D lab, which they pay for in full at the end of the year.

What remains of the original $3 million after EnviroStuff's entrepreneurs have spent money on land, plant, and equipment? The answer is $2,175,000. This amount was parked in cash (a checking account at the bank) and marketable securities (short-term securities that paid interest).

Balance Sheet at the End of 2010

Making accounting transparent involves telling a good story to explain the numbers and using questions posed in plain English for which accounting numbers are the answers.

A balance sheet is essentially a table that answers -two main questions. The first question is this: Over time, how much money did investors invest in the company? The second question is: How has that money been used to purchase assets?

Each of these questions is answered in two parts of the balance sheet. The liabilities part provides details that answer the first question, and the assets part provides details that answer the second.

A good training program will take employees through the balance sheet layout. For example, a trainer might ask employees to look at EnviroStuff's balance sheet at the end of year 2010 beginning with the liabilities. This is a springboard for the trainer to explain that the liabilities part of the balance sheet records the value of different monies provided by different investors. Investors come in many forms. Some lend money to the company as short-term debt, meaning they expect their money back, with interest, within 12 months or less. Others lend money to the company for longer than a year. And some investors are shareholders, who provide money to the company in exchange for a share of ownership, meaning an equity stake. The liabilities part of the balance sheet shows how much money the firm has received from its current investors.

Remember, questions are in plain English, and accounting numbers are the answers. To help demystify the balance sheet, Table 4.1 provides a simple balance sheet with the balance sheet item in the left column and associated questions to describe what these items mean.

You won't learn accounting by just sitting and listening. You need to think. A great thinking exercise is to answer the questions in Table 4.1 by leafing back through EnviroStuff's story for the answers. If you like, you can try your hand at this. That is the best way to really understand the information conveyed by the balance sheet.

Let's talk about answers. EnviroStuff did not borrow any money at all. Therefore, short-term loans are zero. Long-term loans due in one year are zero. And the company paid all of its bills. So, its Accounts Payable is zero. In fact, all items are zero until the line for Preferred Stock. And the answer to the question associated with Preferred Stock is $3 million

Some people encounter difficulty with the line item Common Stock and get the wrong answer. I think mistakes are wonderful learning opportunities. I congratulate people who come up with sensible answers, even if the answers are wrong. It's okay to get wrong answers, especially when you're learning accounting.

Table 4.1

Balance Sheet Liabilities

Notes Payable	How much money has the company borrowed short term that it still has to pay back?
Long-Term Debt Due within One Year	How much money has the company borrowed long term with principal that is due to be paid back within the next 12 months?
Accounts Payable	How much money did the company owe its suppliers for items it purchased but has not yet paid for?
Total Current Liabilities	What is the subtotal of the above three items?
Long-Term Debt	How much money has the company borrowed long term that it does not have to pay back within the next 12 months?
Other Liabilities	What is the value of any liabilities in the company's possession that are not current liabilities, long-term debt, or equity?
Preferred Stock	What is the value of money received in the past from investors who purchased the company's preferred stock?
Common Stock	What is the value of money received in the past from investors who purchased the company's common stock?
Retained Earnings	What is the running total of past net income that the company kept instead of paying out the money to shareholders as dividends?
Shareholders' Equity	What is the subtotal of the above three terms?
Total Liabilities and Shareholders' Equity	What is the sum of the company's Total Current Liabilities, Long-Term Debt and Other Liabilities, and Shareholders' Equity?

The answer to the Common Stock question is zero. It's zero because EnviroStuff did not receive any money for the common stock it issued to its entrepreneurs. That is not to say that the entrepreneurs' shares are worthless. Their shares are indeed worth something. Indeed, the venture capitalists and entrepreneurs have both settled on a total valuation of $7.5 million for the company, of which the entrepreneurs' share is $4.5 million. But the balance sheet does not record how much the shares are worth, only how much money the investors paid the company to acquire the shares.

Because the company has no past operations, its Retained Earnings are also zero. Therefore, the bottom line of the balance sheet is $3 million, the amount of money raised from the venture capitalists. Table 4.2 summarizes the discussion.

Table 4.2

Balance Sheet Liabilities	2010
Notes Payable	$0
Long-Term Debt Due within One Year	$0
Accounts Payable	$0
Total Current Liabilities	$0
Long-Term Debt	$0
Other Liabilities	$0
Preferred Stock	$3,000,000
Common Stock	$0
Retained Earnings	$0
Shareholders' Equity	$3,000,000
Total Liabilities and Shareholders' Equity	$3,000,000

Now, turn to the assets part of the balance sheet. Table 4.3 lists the line items and associated questions that define the line items. There is a bit more to fill out in the assets part than in the liabilities part. If you like, see if you can locate the answers to the questions.

The assets part of the balance sheet describes the amount of money EnviroStuff spent to purchase the assets it currently holds, minus any charges for depreciation, plus the value of any other assets it holds that consist of cash or items that can easily be sold to obtain cash.

The answer to the question associated with the first item is $2,175,000, this being the amount of money the firm holds after having spent money acquiring land, plant, and equipment. The answers to the next two questions are zero because the firm has not sold anything yet to customers and therefore has nothing remaining to collect from them, nor does it have anything in inventory.

The question associated with the item for Property, Plant, and Equipment refers to the headquarters building, operations plant, two enviro-manufacturing machines, and one R&D laboratory unit. The company spent a total of $600,000 for these items: $350,000 for the building and plant and $250,000 for the equipment. That is the answer to the associated question. The answer to the question that follows about Accumulated Depreciation is zero, as the equipment was installed at the end of the year, and no depreciation was charged.

The answer to the question associated with Land and Improvements is $225,000, the value of the land. There were no other assets, so Other Assets is zero. Put this information together in the table, and what you get is the assets part of EnviroStuff's balance sheet as displayed in Table 4.4.

Table 4.3

Balance Sheet: Assets

Cash and Marketable Securities	What was the value of the cash and cashlike investments that the company held at the end of the year?
Accounts Receivable	How much money did the company's customers still owe the company for items they purchased but had not yet paid for?
Inventory	What was the value of raw materials, work in process, and final product in the company's possession but not yet sold?
Total Current Assets	What is the subtotal of the above three items?
Property, Plant, and Equipment	How much did the company spend in the past to acquire plant and equipment?
Accumulated Depreciation	From the time the plant and equipment was first purchased, how much of the original expenditure has the company taken as a depreciation charge?
Plant and Equipment (Net)	What is the difference between the first two items?
Land and Improve-ments (Net)	How much has the company spent to purchase land and make improvements on that land?
Total Fixed Assets	What is the sum of the Plant and Equipment (Net) and Land and Improvements (Net)?
Other Assets	What is the value of any assets in the company's possession that are neither current assets nor fixed assets?
Total Assets	What is the sum of the company's Current Assets, Fixed Assets, and Other Assets?

Table 4.4

Balance Sheet Assets	2010
Cash and Marketable Securities	$2,175,000
Accounts Receivable	$0
Inventory	$0
Total Current Assets	$2,175,000
Property, Plant, and Equipment	$600,000
Accumulated Depreciation	$0
Plant and Equipment (Net)	$600,000
Land and Improvements (Net)	$225,000
Total Fixed Assets	$825,000
Other Assets	$0
Total Assets	$3,000,000

Balance Sheet Liabilities	2010
Notes Payable	$0
Long-term Debt Due Within One year	$0
Accounts Payable	$0
Total Current Liabilities	$0
Long-term Debt	$0
Other Liabilities	$0
Preferred Stock	$3,000,000
Common Stock	$0
Retained Earnings	$0
Shareholders' Equity	$3,000,000
Total Liabilities and Shareholders' Equity	$3,000,000

If you looked at EnviroStuff's balance sheet but did not know its story, how much could you figure out? You could certainly figure out that it did not take out any loans and relied exclusively on the sale of $3 million of preferred stock. You could also tell that it used the $3 million to purchase $875,000 of fixed assets (property, plant, equipment, and land) and parked the remainder in cash.

The Story behind the Income Statement for Year 2011

Our story about EnviroStuff continues into 2011 and provides the information that will go into preparing the company's income statement. At the beginning of 2011, EnviroStuff hires a workforce and begins operations. Doing so involves a recruiting expense of $105,863.

Mike assumes the position of chief marketing officer. Under his direction, EnviroStuff spends $50,000 at the beginning of the year to promote their enviro-generation product. This effort turns out to be fruitful, and they receive a series of inquiries from potential customers expressing interest. Almost all of the inquiries come from customers that EnviroStuff describes as innovators. Innovators are independent minded and highly focused on product quality.

Henry heads up human resources. Encouraged by the response from customers, he quickly hires two salespeople, two engineers to work on R&D, ten employees to manufacture enviro-generators, and two people to handle customer support. Total payroll for the year amounts to $1,758,630. Of this, manufacturing workers receive $577,435, the salespeople receive $200,498, the engineers receive $160,399, and the customer support people receive $120,299. In their capacity as upper management, the five entrepreneurs receive a total of $700,000 in salary.

Oscar is chief operating officer. During 2011, his manufacturing team produces 224 enviro-generators, and the sales force successfully sells 220 of these at a price of $2,200 each. Unsold units are stored in finished goods inventory.

EnviroStuff needs raw material to produce enviro-generators. To keep things simple, suppose there is only one type of raw material. (In practice, several raw materials might be required, such as water and a variety of different metals and plastics.) During 2011, the price of raw material is $100 per unit. The manufacturing team purchases 300 units of raw material, which they initially store in inventory. During the year, the manufacturing team draws 280 units of raw material from inventory for use in production. As a result, the firm ends the year with 20 units of raw material in inventory.

EnviroStuff needs to maintain its machines. It also has to pay utility bills. The company spends $8,721 to maintain its enviro-manufacturers and $2,907 to maintain its R&D unit. These machines have a normal lifetime of two years, as do R&D units. Utility bills are $20,000, of which $10,000 is for the headquarters building and $10,000 is for the operating plant.

At the end of 2011, EnviroStuff builds one more operating plant and purchases four additional enviro-manufacturers and two new R&D units. They pay the same price for these assets as they paid a year earlier.

During 2011, EnviroStuff takes out a three-year loan for $300,000. They do not pay out any dividends. They use straight-line depreciation and face a corporate tax rate of 35 percent. At the end of the year, they maintain a balance of cash and marketable securities amounting to $533,340. Of this amount, $25,000 is held in cash, with the remainder in marketable securities. During 2011, EnviroStuff earns $340,379 in interest on the marketable securities in its possession.

That's it for EnviroStuff in 2011. The next step is to display how these activities are reflected in its income statement.

The Income Statement for Year 2011

The income statement refers to activity during a period of time, such as a year. The balance sheet, you will recall, refers to levels as of a particular date, such as the last day of the year. Following the same line of discussion as for the balance sheet, Table 4.5 describes the questions associated with each line item in the annual income statement.

Consider Sales, the dollar value of items that the company sold and delivered to its customers. The company sold 220 enviro-generators at $2,200 each, for a total of $484,000. Just to be clear, $484,000 is the value of what EnviroStuff's customers purchased during the year. During 2011, they might not have actually paid EnviroStuff in full for those purchases.

The second line item in the income statement is Cost of Goods Sold, the value of the items sold and delivered to customers, as recorded in inventory. If I were leading a training program, at this stage I would ask employees to figure out the inventory value of the 220 units that EnviroStuff actually sold.

Training programs help employees understand that the value of finished goods items in inventory is based on costs of manufacturing activities but not nonmanufacturing activities such as promotion, sales force salaries, and so on. Manufacturing costs entail the wages paid to manufacturing workers, the cost of raw materials used in production, the portion of the utility bill for the operating plant associated with manufacturing, and maintenance costs for enviro- manufacturers.

A good way to develop costs is to go from total costs to costs per unit. The total amount spent on manufacturing labor was $577,435, all of which was used to produce enviro-generators. The total spent on raw materials was $30,000 for 300 raw material units, of which 280 were used in

Table 4.5

Income Statement

Sales	What was the dollar value of items that the company sold and delivered to its customers?
Cost of Goods Sold	What was the value of the items sold and delivered to customers, as recorded in inventory?
Gross Profit	How much was left from sales after paying the Cost of Goods Sold?
Research and Development	How much did the company spend on Research and Development?
Sales and General Administration	How much did the company spend on activities related to Sales and General Administration?
Depreciation	How much did the company take as a depreciation charge that was not already captured in Cost of Goods Sold or Research and Development?
Earnings from Operations (EBIT)	How much was left from Gross Profit after paying for Research and Development, Sales and General Administration, and Depreciation?
Interest Expense	How much did the company pay in interest?
Other Income	How much did the company earn from other sources of income?
Pretax Earnings	How much was left from operating earnings after paying interest and receiving other income?
Less: Provision for Taxes (35%)	How much is the tax rate multiplied by Pretax Earnings?
Net Income	How much was left from Pretax Earnings after subtracting the Provision for Taxes?

production. Therefore, the total value of the raw materials used in production was $28,000. To obtain costs per enviro-generator produced, simply divide the above dollar costs by 228, the total number of enviro-generators produced. On a per enviro-generator basis, the labor cost amounted to $2,577.83, and the materials cost amounted to $125.

Keep in mind that not all the enviro-generators that were produced got sold. Of the 224 units produced, 220 were sold, and the rest remained in inventory. Inventory records total value per unit produced multiplied by number of units in inventory. Cost of Goods Sold records total value per unit produced multiplied by number of units sold. Therefore, the cost of labor associated with the 220 units sold is $567,123, the product of $2,577.83 and 220. Similarly, the cost of materials associated with the 220 units sold is $27,500.

Labor and materials are called *direct costs* because they are traced directly to production levels. The other costs of production are indirect and constitute manufacturing overhead: utility expenses for the operating plant, maintenance costs, and depreciation on manufacturing plant and equipment. The best procedure is to figure out what these costs amount to in total and then convert to a per unit basis for enviro-generators.

The utility bill for the operating plant was $10,000. Manufacturing maintenance costs were $8,721. Depreciation on the enviro-generator manufacturing machines was $50,000, based on the two machines purchased at the end of 2010 for $100,000. These were depreciated using the straight-line method assuming a lifetime of two years, and so half of the original $100,000 spent is depreciated in 2011.

The operating plant was built for $250,000. It has a 25-year expected lifetime, and so the amount of depreciation taken per year under the straight-line method is $10,000. Keep in mind that not all of the operating plant is devoted to manufacturing. Some of it is used for R&D. Therefore, not all of the depreciation on the operating plant might apply to production. For the sake of argument, suppose that 75 percent of the operating plant was used for production, and 25 percent was used for R&D. In that case, the amount of operating plant depreciation that would apply to production would be $7,500. For the same reason, $7,500 of the $10,000 utility bill associated with the operating plant is for manufacturing activities, and $2,500 is for R&D activities.

Total manufacturing overhead is the sum of the $7,500 depreciation for the operating plant, $50,000 depreciation for the enviro-manufacturers, $7,500 for utilities, and $8,721 for maintenance. The total for these amounts comes to $73,721. On a per unit produced basis, manufacturing overhead is $329.11. The amount associated with the 220 units sold is the product of $329.11 and 220, which is $72,405.

What was the value of the items sold and delivered to customers as recorded in Inventory? This is the question to which the answer is the Cost of Goods Sold. The number is the sum of the direct cost of labor and materials ($567,123 and $27,500) and the indirect costs ($72,405). The grand total for Cost of Goods Sold comes to $667,028. Gross Profit is what remains from Sales after incurring the Cost of Goods Sold. The difference between $484,000 of sales and $667,028 is a negative $183,028. Already, we know that 2011 was not a profitable year for EnviroStuff.

The next item to compute is R&D. The direct cost of R&D involves the engineering salaries of $160,399. The indirect costs involve the portion of the depreciation on the operating plant associated with R&D activity ($2,500), the associated utility bill ($2,500), the depreciation on the R&D unit ($75,000), and maintenance on the R&D unit ($2,907). Indirect costs amount to $82,907, and the total direct plus indirect amounts for R&D come to $243,306.

Sales, General, and Administrative (SG&A) involves all other regular nonfinancial expenses associated with running the business. Sales expenses involve the salaries of the sales force ($200,498) and promotional expenses ($50,000). General expenses involve the salaries of customer support staff ($120,299). Administrative expenses include amounts spent on recruiting ($105,863), the utility bill for the headquarters building ($10,000), and the salaries for upper management ($700,000). Taken together, SG&A comes to $1,186,660.

The line item for Depreciation is for any depreciation item not already included in any of the previous items. The one item not yet accounted for is depreciation on the headquarters building, which would be $4,000 based a $100,000 expenditure and a 25-year expected lifetime. The next item in the income statement is Earnings Before Interest and Tax (EBIT), or Earnings from Operations. Its value is –$1,616,993, obtained by subtracting R&D, SG&A, and Depreciation from Gross Profit. Because EnviroStuff had no debt during 2011, except for the very end of the year, it paid no interest. It did receive $64,500 in interest from the marketable securities it held. Therefore, its net interest paid was –$64,500. Typically, interest paid would be recorded as this net amount. There are no items that would qualify as Other Income.

The remainder of the income statement is straightforward. Pretax Earnings is EBIT minus Interest Expense and Other Income, which comes to –$1,552,493. Net Income is Pretax Earnings minus tax, which turns out to be –$1,009,121.

Corporate tax (Provision for Taxes) is 35 percent of Pretax Earnings, which in this example is a negative number, –$543,373. Of course, the company does not pay negative tax: The Internal Revenue Service (IRS) did not mail EnviroStuff a check because it incurred a loss in 2011. Actual tax paid would be zero. However, because EnviroStuff might be able to carry the loss forward and offset some of its future tax liabilities once it becomes profitable, the income statement reported to investors might actually reflect the negative amount.

The way this works involves an as-if story. On the income statement, it looks like the IRS did send EnviroStuff not a check for $543,373, but a tax voucher whose value is $543,373. The voucher is like a gift certificate at a store, which can be redeemed at a future time for something valuable. The amount of the voucher is entered into the Provision for Taxes item as a negative number, which in turn serves to increase EnviroStuff's Net Income by $543,373. The value of the voucher is an asset for the company, something of value that it holds, like cash or inventory. At a future time, when the company is profitable and faces a tax liability, it can redeem all or part of the voucher for cash.

When all the questions defining the income statement are answered, the income statement for 2011 will have the numbers shown in Table 4.6.

Table 4.6

Income Statement	2011
Sales	$484,000
Cost of Goods Sold	$667,028
Gross Profit	($183,028)
R&D	$243,306
SG&A	$1,186,660
Depreciation	$4,000
Earnings from Operations (EBIT)	($1,616,993)
Interest Expense	($64,500)
Other Income	$0
Pretax Earnings	($1,552,493)
Less Provision for Taxes (35%)	($543,373)
Net Income	($1,009,121)

Balance Sheet for 2011

The principles for preparing the balance sheet for 2011 are the same ones used to prepare the balance sheet in 2010. Table 4.7 displays the balance sheet for 2011. This balance sheet tells some of the story described earlier and provides additional information.

Some of the questions that the balance sheet for 2011 enables employees to answer, which rely on information not provided earlier, are:

- What was the value of the cash and cashlike investments that the company held at the end of the year?
- How much money did the company's customers still owe the company for items they purchased but had not yet paid for?
- What was the value of raw materials, work-in-process, and unsold final product in the company's possession?
- How much money has the company borrowed long term where the principal is due to be paid back within the next 12 months?
- How much money did the company owe its suppliers for items it purchased but had not yet paid for?
- What is the sum of the company's total current liabilities, long-term debt and other liabilities, and shareholders' equity?

Heuristics and Standards

The reason to give employees training in accounting is to help them make better decisions. Accounting provides information that employees can act on. Most people rely on

Table 4.7

Balance Sheet Assets	2011
Cash and Marketable Securities	$60,379
Accounts Receivable	$242,000
Inventory	$14,128
Total Current Assets	$316,507
Property, Plant, and Equipment	$1,350,000
Accumulated Depreciation	$139,000
Plant and Equipment (Net)	$1,211,000
Land and Improvements (Net)	$225,000
Total Fixed Assets	$1,436,000
Other Assets	$543,373
Total Assets	$2,295,879

Balance Sheet Liabilities	2011
Notes Payable	$0
Long-Term Debt Due within One Year	$0
Accounts Payable	$5,000
Total Current Liabilities	$5,000
Long-Term Debt	$300,000
Other Liabilities	$0
Preferred Stock	$3,000,000
Common Stock	$0
Retained Earnings	($1,009,121)
Shareholders' Equity	$1,990,879
Total Liabilities and Shareholders' Equity	$2,295,879

decision heuristics to decide what to do. The term *heuristic* is an important term in behavioral finance and generally means "a rule of thumb."

There are two ways to look at heuristics. The first way is that heuristics are mental shortcuts that can predispose us to all kinds of bias. This way is identified with a school of thought that goes by the term "heuristics and biases." The second way is that heuristics are mental shortcuts that help us navigate a complex and uncertain world. This way is identified with a school of thought that goes by the term "fast and frugal heuristics." One way of looking at heuristics is as a glass half empty. The other is as a glass half full.

In a sense, both are true. The world is so complex that people need heuristics to focus on what is important in the swirl of events that surround them. As a species, human beings are smart, but they are not so smart as to make sense of all the information at their disposal and use that information optimally to make decisions. Many heuristics work well in some circumstances but not in others. Indeed, what distinguishes experts from nonexperts is that experts are better able to separate really important stuff from less important stuff. That is, what qualifies many experts as experts is that they have better heuristics than the rest of us.

In *Blink* (Back Bay Books, 2007), Malcolm Gladwell describes the work of scholar John Gottman, who studies the factors that determine whether a marriage will succeed or fail. Gottman identified and analyzed the manner in which a series of emotions and behavior patterns make the difference between successful and unsuccessful marriages.

Gladwell reports that although he, himself, put in a fair amount of effort to study Gottman's work, in practice he was overwhelmed by the complexity of the task. On the other hand, Gottman is able to boil down a huge array of emotions and behavior patterns into four key factors, which he calls contempt, criticism, defensiveness, and stonewalling. Gottman refers to them as akin to the four horsemen of the apocalypse. Moreover, based on just a few minutes of observation, Gottman can use the four horsemen to form a very accurate assessment of how healthy a couple's relationship is.

What John Gottman has managed to develop with the four horsemen are the cues for a fast and frugal heuristic. Cues are the basis for making a judgment or decision. The heuristic is the rule for how to act on the cues. Depending on which cues Gottman observes, he can tailor an intervention to help a couple improve their relationship.

Fast and frugal heuristics are the focus of study at the Max Planck Institute in Berlin. The institute's approach is documented in a book titled *Simple Heuristics That Make Us Smart* by Gerd Gigerenzer, Peter M. Todd, and the ABC Research Group.[1] This book describes how to develop straightforward effective rules for identifying cues and making decisions that result in high performance.

Excellent examples for understanding fast and frugal heuristics in a business setting can be found in the book *The Great Game of Business* by Jack Stack with Bo Burlingham. I mentioned this book in Chapter 2. In their book, Stack and Burlingham document the key lessons Jack Stack learned when he took his company from the brink of bankruptcy to financial health.

Heuristics and cues are among the many lessons Stack learned. Many of the cues he uses involve simple questions. Here are two examples. How profitable is the company? How much cash is the company generating? The answers to both questions can be found in the company's financial

[1]Gerd Gigerenzer, Peter M. Todd, and the ABC Research Group, *Simple Heuristics That Make Us Smart* (Oxford University Press, 1999).

statements. Information about profitability is found in the income statement. Information about cash is found in the balance sheet. The two questions are different. Being profitable and generating cash are different. For example, in the hypothetical EnviroStuff example described earlier, the company lost $1,009,121 in 2011, its first year of operations. However, its operations did not burn up $1,009,121 in cash, but $1,664,121 instead. The reason for the difference is that the income statement treats depreciation as an expense, which it is; however, depreciation is not a cash expense that the company pays out to anybody. In addition, the company did not receive cash for all of the sales it made during the year, it did not pay for all the raw materials it received, and it did not receive a tax voucher from the IRS. The point is that Net Income includes both cash and noncash items and therefore is not a measure of cash generation.

Income statement measures of profitability are more like time averages that are intended to smooth out lumps and bumps. For example, capital expenditures are usually lump sum purchases, which are not directly reported in the income statement, even though they often involve large cash outlays. Instead, capital expenditures are divided into a stream of smaller amounts, called *depreciation charges*, which are entered as expenses in future years, even though the cash might have already been paid out in the past.

Similarly, the cash outlays associated with Cost of Goods Sold might have been made at a point in the past, not the period in which the amount enters the income statement. The principle of matching Cost of Goods Sold to Sales in the time period the sales were made is called the *matching principle*. The principle is designed to provide a clearer view of the company's profitability by rearranging its cash flows in this way. In a sense, the income statement is structured along heuristic lines.

Here is another question that forms the cues for Jack Stack's heuristics. Is there some variable in your business that keeps you awake at night worrying? That question is designed to ferret out the best cues for your fast and frugal heuristics. These cues are the counterparts of John Gottman's four horsemen.

A pillar of the effective heuristics that Stack pioneered at SRC is that the major cues stem from the financial statements and are tied to both profitability and cash generation. These cues are called *financial standards*. They take the form of critical numbers, standard costs, and financial ratios. Of course, acting on cues only works if employees understand what the cues mean. That is the point of a company's workforce having a working understanding of accounting.

Financial Ratios

Financial ratios are cues that provide an opportunity to render some of the information embedded within a company's financial statements more salient. In this section, I describe what I think a good training program would cover about financial ratios.

First comes structure. Financial ratios are often divided into five categories:

- liquidity
- leverage
- efficiency
- profitability
- market valuation

The ratio best known for assessing a company's liquidity is its *current ratio*, the ratio of its current assets to its current liabilities. The higher the value of this ratio, the more protected are the company's short-term creditors. Why? Current assets are more liquid than fixed assets. It is easier to sell current assets for cash than to sell fixed assets. Hence, if the company needs to pay off short-term liabilities, it can secure the cash to do so more easily from its current assets than from its fixed assets. In the case of EnviroStuff, its current ratio at the end of 2011 was about 63. On the face of it, 63 is a very high value; however, the reason is that EnviroStuff had very little in the way of current liabilities, just its accounts payable.

For a start-up like EnviroStuff, a more appropriate liquidity ratio is the interval measure. The interval measure indicates how many days the company has cash to operate at its current burn rate, assuming customers pay their bills, without receiving a cash infusion from some source other than its current holdings. The formula for the interval measure is to divide the sum of cash, marketable securities, and accounts receivable by daily expenditures from operations as measured by the company's costs. For EnviroStuff, this number is 57 days.

At the end of 2011, EnviroStuff took on $300,000 of long-term debt. How do we measure whether this is a large amount? A company's leverage can be measured in several ways. A company's *total capitalization* is defined as the company's long-term liabilities, meaning the sum of its long-term debt and shareholders' equity. The fraction of a company's total capitalization comprising debt is its *debt-to-capital ratio*. For EnviroStuff, the debt-to-capital ratio was about 13 percent at the end of 2011. A related measure is *D/E*, the ratio of a company's long-term debt to shareholders' equity, which was about 15 percent.

The ratio known as *times interest earned* measures the number of times over that a company's EBIT and depreciation cover its interest payments. In this respect, the sum of EBIT plus depreciation represents the amount of cash thrown off by operations that is available to pay interest and taxes, with the residual belonging to shareholders. Notably, interest stands at the top of the line in this regard.

Efficiency refers to the usage of assets. Think of a wheel whose size represents the company's assets. Suppose that sales are generated by spinning the wheel, where each turn of the wheel generates a level of sales equal to the amount of the company's assets. One measure of asset efficiency is how many times per year the company can spin or turn the asset wheel to generate sales. Higher turnover corresponds to greater efficiency. The associated efficiency variable is called the *asset turnover ratio*. During 2011, EnviroStuff's asset turnover ratio was about 18 percent. Given that the company ran a loss in 2011, the asset turnover ratio might serve as a useful cue for gauging improved performance.

An analogous concept applies to inventory. The *inventory turnover ratio* can be thought of as the number of times per year that an item is pulled off the inventory shelf for use in production. A related measure is the number of days an item spends in inventory.

There is an analogous ratio for collections, the *receivables collection period*, also known as *days sales outstanding* (DSO). This ratio can be quite informative. For example, there are at least five reasons a company's DSO may have risen: (1) delayed payment by customers, owing to dissatisfaction because of poor quality; (2) end-loading of sales close to the end of a quarter; (3) a new policy offering extended credit terms; (4) the percentage of customers unable to pay their bills has increased; and (5) poor collection processes. During 2011, EnviroStuff's DSO was about 91 days, meaning that it waits about three months for its customers to pay their bills.

When a company invests in inventory and waits for its customers to pay their bills, its cash is tied up. Were it to pay for its raw materials on the day it took delivery of the raw materials, then its cash would be tied up by the sum of the days sales in inventory and the receivables collection period. However, a company might not pay its bills immediately. There is an analogous measure to the receivables collection period called the payables period, which measures how long the company takes to pay its bills. The *cash conversion cycle* is the sum of the receivables collection period and days sales in inventory minus the payables period. For example, consider a company that holds inventory for 65 days and takes 30 days to pay its invoices. This company will have its cash tied up for at least 35 days, the difference between 65 and 30. However, if its average collection period is 40 days, then its cash will be tied up for a total of 75 days, $75 = 35 + 40$.

Profitability can be measured in several ways. Notice that the amount of money the company has received from its shareholders is given by Shareholders' Equity in the balance sheet. Shareholders' equity is the amount of money that the company acquired from shareholders when it issued new shares or when it retained earnings that belonged to shareholders. From the perspective of the financial statements, shareholders receive net income (earnings) as the return on their direct investment. The ratio of net income to shareholders' equity is the return per dollar to shareholders on shareholders' dollars held by the company. This is the company's *return on equity*. An analogous ratio applies to all the company's investors, not just its shareholders. The analogous ratio is *return on assets*.

Because of the loss that EnviroStuff ran in 2011, its return on equity and return on assets were both negative.

Other measures of profitability also reflect the loss. Net profit margin is the ratio of net income to sales. Gross profit margin is the ratio of gross profit to sales. Operating margin is the ratio of operating profit to sales.

Because EnviroStuff's gross margin is negative, it is a good variable to target. For EnviroStuff to be profitable long term, it will have to find a way to reduce its costs of production, charge a higher price for its enviro-generators, or both.

There are several ratios used in connection with market valuation. The price-earnings ratio is among the best known. Another ratio is price-to-book, the market value of the company's stock divided by shareholders' equity. Both have little meaning for EnviroStuff in 2011, as it is a private company. However, it is worth noting that based on the discussion in Chapter 2, the value-to-book ratio is determined by the present value of the company's future economic value-added stream.

Training

Companies that run along open book management lines invest heavily in training, especially training in financial literacy. SRC places heavy emphasis on its workforce understanding basic financial statements, and it puts its training dollars where its mouth is.

My own experience with teaching financial statements is that the concepts are like Teflon: They don't easily stick, at least with most people. Getting financial statements to stick requires that people become emotionally engaged. The accounting numbers need to have meaning.

The most effective technique I have found for getting financial statements to stick is to embed them in a business simulation game. In fact, simulation games are among the best teaching tools I have. I describe simulation games in Chapter 8, including the classroom simulation game I use. This game is based on EnviroStuff and can be downloaded from my Web site, www.scu.edu/business/finance/faculty/shefrin.cfm.

Simulation games are becoming more popular because they place people in settings that are both hypothetical and realistic at the same time. This has a wonderful benefit. People can learn from their mistakes without having to pay the full cost of those mistakes.

My EnviroStuff simulation game asks players to prepare their own financial statements. Having to do this really sears the financial statement framework into their brains. The game also gets people to figure out what cues they want to use, induces them to set financial standards, and helps them structure decision heuristics.

Keep in mind that the core message of this book is that psychologically smart companies develop effective processes for accounting, planning, incentives, and information sharing. The present chapter covers accounting, and the next chapter covers planning. Chapters 6 and 7 cover incentives and information sharing, respectively. Simulation is the topic I cover in the last chapter of the book. What simulation does is teach people how to integrate the four processes into one whole ball of wax.

But in my excitement, I'm getting ahead of myself: On to planning.

CHAPTER 5

FINANCIAL PLANNING: TRANSLATING GENERAL STRATEGIC THINKING INTO CONCRETE FINANCIAL PLANS

Business planning is incredibly important and notoriously difficult.

To be sure, planning's important because an organization has a lot of moving parts, and it takes some forethought to get those parts to mesh in a dynamic business environment. But psychologically smart companies use planning to develop financial standards against which to benchmark actual performance. If you remember what I said in the last chapter, standards are the basis for cues, and cues are the indicators for decision heuristics.

Planning is difficult partly because the future is hard to predict and partly because our gremlins make it harder than it needs to be. The gremlins that drive our planning biases are robust and tough. You don't want to underestimate them.

To get us going in this chapter, I'm going to ask you some questions. I adapted these questions from some psychological studies on planning.

Consider four different types of tasks you undertook in the past for which you had deadlines.

1. Everyday tasks around the home
2. Holiday shopping
3. Completing income tax returns
4. School assignments, if you are a student or when you were a student

On average, how many hours before each deadline did you typically complete these types of tasks?

Once you have completed your answers to these questions, consider a similar question about the same four types of tasks. On average, how accurate are you in predicting when you will complete the four tasks described relative to your plans?

1. Much earlier than predicted
2. Earlier than predicted
3. As predicted
4. Later than predicted
5. Much later than predicted

There is a fair amount of dispersion in the way people answer these questions. However, there is a central tendency—a tendency to be routinely later than predicted.

The interesting psychological question is whether people take their own past tardiness into account when making predictions about how long it will take them to complete their future tasks. And here, the answer is generally that people act as if they ignore the past. Instead, they formulate their plans as if they will complete these tasks as predicted rather than later than predicted. Moreover, on average, they end up completing those tasks later than predicted, just as they had in the past.

This phenomenon of failing to learn the lessons of the past about planning times is called "the planning fallacy." There is a rich academic literature documenting the planning fallacy which shows the phenomenon to be remarkably resilient.

In the business world, a great many projects come in over budget, miss their deadlines, and fail to deliver on all promised features. Although most managers are aware of these general tendencies, they fail to adjust for these tendencies in preparing forecasts for future projects. The planning fallacy is alive and thriving in the business world.

In this chapter, I describe the nuts and bolts of financial planning in a psychologically smart company. The nuts-and-bolts part is pretty much standard fare. But the psychologically smart part is not standard fare at all. Being psychologically smart involves a lot: developing cues, structuring heuristics for how to react to cues, and instituting debiasing techniques to counter the planning fallacy.

My original idea was to cover the nuts and bolts of planning and then discuss the planning fallacy. That would seem to be the natural sequence, right? But I'm going to do it the other way around—that is, cover the planning fallacy before discussing the nuts and bolts of planning. I'll tell you why I want to do it this way. I think the way to teach the nuts and bolts of planning is to embed the debiasing techniques into the nuts-and-bolts procedures. Otherwise, debiasing techniques seem like an add-on instead of being central to the planning exercise, as they are in psychologically smart companies.

Understanding the Planning Fallacy

What does planning involve? Planning typically involves laying out a set of steps to complete a task. These steps often feature a planned scenario, or if you like, a story. Stories are important to people; we often think in narrative terms.

Here is what lies at the heart of the planning fallacy: the coincidence of optimistic planning predictions coupled with a more realistic general assessment of past behavior.

In a nutshell, people who succumb to the planning fallacy don't appreciate the vast number of ways in which the future might unfold. Instead, people get anchored on a story. Moreover, it's usually a story with a happy ending. And there's the rub. The typical planner establishes as his or her planned scenario an optimistic story in which very little or nothing goes wrong. In other words, the typical planner doesn't give enough attention to the ways his or her plans might fail.

Fail? Yikes! Thinking about failure isn't much fun. Yes, that's true. And it makes bias gremlins very happy. They feed on it.

Psychologists who study the planning fallacy tell us that the main culprit is that when people plan, they pay excessive attention to the narratives of their stories. If you like, they overweight the series of steps associated with their plans. After all, the steps associated with planned scenarios should terminate in success. Naturally, having a planned scenario terminate successfully is quite reasonable. Some might call this having vision. The difficulty is that the steps in the successful plan are psychologically salient, whereas the competing failure scenarios are less salient.

What debiasing technique can people use to mitigate their vulnerability to the planning fallacy? It turns out that there are at least three approaches to try. The first approach is to keep good records and make past planning history more salient so that the information is readily available.

The second approach is to develop explicit failure scenarios to go along with successful scenarios.

The third approach is to follow a process that explicitly takes into account past planning biases. Such a process explicitly requires that planners explain how their past experiences might be relevant to their current planning tasks.

Of the three approaches, the first two have had limited success. With the first approach, people seem inclined to downplay information about their past planning failures, implicitly saying, "Yes, but this time it will be different." With the second alternative, people are so unrealistically optimistic about their successful scenarios that the inclusion of failure scenarios still leaves the mix unrealistically optimistic.

The third approach is heavy-handed in that it forces planners to follow a process that incorporates their past histories. Heavy-handed though it may be, the third approach works pretty well.

One reason the third approach works well is that it forces a person to step outside him- or herself and take the position of an outside observer. Studies of how well outside observers predict the planning accuracy of others are especially insightful. Outside observers actually do tend to use past track records to predict completion times for others, which leads them to be more accurate. In this regard, they focus more on the personal characteristics of the person they are observing and are willing to attribute failure of timely completion to those characteristics. In contrast, those under observation are inclined to attribute their past failures to external events rather than to themselves. However, outside observers can take things a bit too far and become excessively pessimistic about the people they are observing.

Psychologists use the term "outside view" to refer to procedures in which planners adjust their forecasts to reflect biases in past forecasting tasks. In contrast, psychologists use the term "inside view" to refer to procedures that focus only on details specific to the forecasting task at hand. Taking an outside view essentially involves asking a person to step outside of him- or herself and take the position of an outside observer.

I think there is something else going on with the third debiasing technique, the heavy-handed outside view. It is very 12-steplike, as in 12-step process. In this regard, steps 4 through 7 of Alcoholics Anonymous read as follows:

4. Made a searching and fearless moral inventory of ourselves.
5. Admitted to G-d, to ourselves, and to another human being the exact nature of our wrongs.
6. Were entirely ready to have G-d remove all these defects of character.
7. Humbly asked G-d to remove our shortcomings.

Do you think these four steps are heavy-handed? They certainly require a mindset featuring humility. We have to take an inventory of our past faults. We have to admit our wrongs to another human being.

The 12-step process also involves a focus on morality and the perception of a higher power. I wonder about the extent to which this last feature affects overconfidence bias. New interesting research about the role of spiritual intelligence investigates the extent to which morality and the feelings about a higher power influence effectiveness in business organizations.[1]

The Airbus A380: The Fallacy of Planning for Perfection

Here is a business story to illustrate the planning fallacy. The letters EADS stand for European Aeronautic Defense & Space, the parent of aircraft manufacturer Airbus. In December 2000, EADS adopted a project for a new aircraft, the Airbus A380. The project was extremely ambitious in that Airbus had never built a plane as complex as the A380.

The new plane was to have many new and advanced features involving avionics and electrical and hydraulics systems, which were all to be state of the art. It was to be equipped with 100,000 different wires, totaling 330 miles in length, that were to perform 1,150 separate functions. In contrast, the next largest commercial jet made by Airbus featured only 60,000 different wires.

The development time associated with previous projects was between four and five years. With the planning fallacy in mind, let me ask you some questions. What do you think would be a prudent timeline to set for the development of a new plane that was to be much more advanced than anything the company had yet built? What do you think would be a prudent heuristic to use to develop an appropriate timeline? What would you think about a heuristic that takes the

---

[1]See Doug Lennick and Fred Kiel, *Moral Intelligence* (Philadelphia: Wharton School Publishing, 2005). Also see Yosi Amram and D. Christopher Dryer, "The Development and Preliminary Validation of the Integrated Spiritual Intelligence Scale (ISIS)," Institute of Transpersonal Psychology working paper, Palo Alto, CA.

development time for one of the A380's predecessors and multiplies that number by a factor X to reflect the increased complexity of the A380, the nature of the design process, and the resources allocated to do the job?

The executives at Airbus promised to begin delivering the Airbus 380 in early 2006, about five years after the launch of the project. This means that they settled on a value of X that was a little above 1.0, even though the A380 was far more challenging than prior projects.

This story has a predictable, albeit unhappy, ending. The planning fallacy infected EADS. The A380 was not ready to be delivered in early 2006 but in late 2007 instead. Something had gone wrong. That something involved the A380's 100,000 different wires that were to perform 1,150 separate functions.

In a nutshell, the cables that had been produced were too short. Somewhere along the line, somebody had made a series of calculation errors involving the routes that the wires would traverse in the plane. As a result, the wires installed in different sections of the plane were not long enough to connect with each other. All the wiring that was already manufactured and awaiting installation had to be completely scrapped. The resulting delays cost EADS about $6.6 billion in profit.

The delays were costly but nonfatal. The A380 eventually made it to the commercial skies. In late 2007 Singapore Airlines began to fly the A380 on its Sydney-to-Singapore route. Still, $6.6 billion is more than loose change.

In 2000, EADS executives did not go wrong by failing to predict that a major wiring miscalculation would delay the A380 project. They went wrong by relying on a scenario in which no major failure would occur!

Remember that the heavy-handed antidote to the planning fallacy is to force planners to follow a process that incorporates past history. As a general matter, actual costs for transportation infrastructure projects have been 28 percent higher than estimated costs. In addition, for nine of every ten projects, costs have been underestimated.[2] It is this kind of information that planning forecasts must properly reflect.

Behavioral Group Biases

When people form themselves into groups, they bring their own biases. Will the group's dynamics help to mitigate those biases? The answer is, it depends.

If a group has formed to tackle what psychologists call an intellectual task, then group dynamics typically mitigate the individual biases that the group's members carry with them.

An intellectual task has a clear right answer. For example, suppose you bring a large bowl of jellybeans into a room, put the bowl on a table, and ask group members to guess how many jellybeans are in the bowl. This task has a right answer. Typically, you will get a decent estimate of how many jellybeans are in the bowl by taking the average guess. This is because biases are self-canceling: One person's low guess (downward bias) will tend to counterbalance another person's high guess (upward bias). This principle is sometimes called "the wisdom of crowds" and is the subject of a fascinating 2004 book of that title by James Surowiecki.

If a group has formed to tackle what psychologists call a judgmental task, then group dynamics typically amplify the individual biases that the group's members carry with them.

[2]See B. Flyvbjerg, M. Skamris Holm, and S. Buhl, 2002. "Underestimating Costs in Public Works Projects: Error or Lie?" *Journal of the American Planning Association*, Summer 2002, pp. 279–295. Transportation infrastructure projects are as prone to cost underestimation as other types of large projects.

In other words, when it comes to judgmental tasks, group dynamics make things worse.

A judgmental task has no clear right answer. For example, deciding how much risk to accept is a judgmental task, at least before we know how the risk will play out.

The classic example of destructive group dynamics is *groupthink*, the tendency for groups to coalesce around a bad decision. Groupthink happens when group members are overly supportive of proposals placed on the table. This excessive support can happen because

- People inherently want to be supportive.
- People don't want to be unsupportive.
- People want to curry favor with the group's leader who has made a proposal.
- People are afraid to offer a position contrary to what the group's leader has proposed.

Think about what happens when a group's leader has a strong personality and is inclined to be a little more aggressive when it comes to taking on risk than are other members of the group. How aggressive toward risk will such a group tend to be? The answer is that the group will tend to be even more aggressive than the leader would be on his or her own. Psychologists refer to this phenomenon as *polarization*.

Do you know what accounts for polarization? It occurs because group members will tend to support their leader rather than countering his or her above-average appetite for risk.

And one other thing: After the group has concluded deliberations, people will tend to feel comfortable with the decision. Some psychologists call this tendency "the illusion of effectiveness."

EnviroStuff's Planning Session

In the remainder of this chapter, I want to discuss the nuts-and-bolts issues in financial planning. I have to be honest and tell you that describing the process of financial planning is a bit of a challenge because the subject matter is inherently as dry as dust. But in practice, it's not as dry as dust. If done well, it's pretty lively and dynamic.

Here is what I decided to do to get across the dynamic character of planning. I took the fictitious company EnviroStuff, Inc. from the previous chapter and built a planning story on top of it. To tell this story, I'm going to use dialogue. I'm not a frustrated playwright, so this isn't about my secret hopes of being discovered. But I need to convey a sense of how psychologically smart planning works in practice.

Lying at the heart of financial planning is the process of developing pro forma financial statements. These are not actual financial statements but "as-if" forecasted financial statements for future years that reflect how a company's strategy might play out. Typically, pro forma forecasts are developed as part of the annual budgeting cycle.

We pick up the EnviroStuff story from Chapter 4 at the end of 2011. At this stage, EnviroStuff's executives have sat down to develop a pro forma financial plan for 2012. Eve is CEO, Francine heads up finance and accounting, Mike leads marketing, Oscar is in charge of operations, and Henry heads up human resources. In case it's not obvious, the first letter of each name is intended to indicate the person's function.

Eve: Good morning, everyone. Today, we begin our planning process for 2012. I think we all agree that financial planning should be a comprehensive exercise, which needs to reflect the budget and a whole range of strategic decisions being made by the company. Francine and I will lead us through the task of preparing pro forma statements. One of the things I've learned about open book management is that the tone of a company and its corporate culture gets set at the top. As we begin our planning and budgeting process, I'd like to remind everyone that we are working to build a psychologically smart company. This means being attentive to how biases like unrealistic optimism and overconfidence make us vulnerable to the planning fallacy. So, as we move forward, let's try to be mindful about developing good habits, like taking the outside view, that can help us beat back our gremlins, Okay?! Francine is now going to get us going.

Francine: Thanks, Eve. Hi, everybody. I know this is new for some of you, so I'll try to go slowly. Financial planning is partly mechanical and partly judgmental. The mechanical part is heuristic based and involves a technique called *percent of sales* because many forecasted financial items are determined as a percentage of the sales forecast. In this respect, the sales forecast is the key driver of the forecast and the top line of the income statement. Let's begin with that top line and then move to Cost of Goods Sold, R&D, and SG&A.

Eve: Mike, you are our chief marketing officer and so have the primary responsibility for generating the sales forecast. Are you prepared to make an initial forecast for what EnviroStuff's sales will be in 2012?

Mike: Yes I am, and I welcome feedback from everyone else. Let me remind everyone that EnviroStuff's sales in 2011 amounted to $484,000, which I consider very respectable. Our company's two-person sales force managed to sell 220 enviro-generators at an average price of $2,200 to 15 municipal governments and three golf courses. Based on these positive results, I feel confident in predicting that our sales force can triple the sales number in 2012 to about $1.45 million. I think we are going to find 40 or so new customers, and each of those customers is going to order more units from us than the average customer did last year. Last year, the average customer bought about 12 enviro-generators from us. Next year, I predict that the average customer will buy about 17 enviro-generators.

Oscar: Mike, what about the price of $2,200? Do you see that price holding in 2012?

Mike: I hope so, Oscar. There appears to be a lot of demand for enviro-generators out there. And yes, we do have competition. But last year, we had no problem selling almost everything that we produced. My recommendation is that we hold steady on the price.

Eve: Mike, how do customers feel about the product?

Mike: As everyone knows, our first version did have some quality issues. But none were fatal. The product worked most of the time, although customers complained about the amount of time it took to learn how to use it. I feel optimistic that our engineers have solved the major quality problems and that the next version of the product is going to be much better.

Eve: Oscar, what is your sense of the quality issue? Have we solved the major quality issues?

Oscar: Based on what the sales force told us about customers' complaints, I think we have solved the major quality problems. Quality is going to be much higher in 2012 than it was in 2011.

Francine: Mike, I certainly hope that your sales projections turn out to be accurate. At the same time, I worry. I'm especially worried about the planning fallacy. You've outlined a rosy scenario whereby we find another 40 customers, with each customer buying 17 enviro-generators. But what could go wrong? What could make that prediction fail?

Mike: Look, no prediction is perfect. And forecasting future sales is not science. Maybe word about how good our product is won't travel as quickly as we would like. That could slow us down a bit. But our sales people have shown us that they are really good.

Eve: Oscar, what do you think? Can you play devil's advocate? Is Mike succumbing to any behavioral biases that we have to worry about? Nothing personal, Mike. I am sure you understand. All of us are vulnerable to these biases, including me. But we have to face up to them honestly if we are to deal with them.

Oscar: Of course, we are all vulnerable. Mike might be exhibiting anchoring bias. On the one hand, in developing his forecast for next year, he might be anchored on last year's sales. On the other hand, in responding to your question, Eve, about what could go wrong, Mike might be anchored on his forecast.

Francine: Mike, what do you think about Oscar's point that you might be anchored on your forecast? Is our only concern that word of mouth about our product is traveling too slowly? Aren't you concerned about one of our competitors racing ahead of us with a technological advance? What if there's a recession and the price of electricity falls? In that case, electricity from biomass becomes less profitable to produce. Shouldn't those possibilities be on our radar screen?

Mike: Good points, thanks; I agree, they should.

Oscar: We only recognize sales when we ship. A possible failure scenario is that something slips in our operations. Maybe our manufacturing equipment experiences a breakdown. Or we have a fire in the operations plant. Or we can't hire enough manufacturing workers.

Mike: Also good points, thanks.

Francine: Mike, how detailed is your marketing plan? Have you identified a specific list of prospects you plan to approach next year? You mentioned a target of 40 new customers. How many customers do you think the sales force needs to approach to sign up these 40 customers?

Mike: If this year was any indication, I think we
           would need to approach about 400 potential
           customers. And yes, we have a specific list.

Francine: Mike, I'd like to ask you to take an outside
           view. You've been doing sales forecasts for a
           few years now. As a general matter, do you
           tend to be too high with your forecasts?

Mike: I knew you were going to ask me that, and so
           I went back and had a look at my past record.
           Speaking honestly, my forecasts have tended
           to be high by between 10 and 15 percent.

Francine: And did you explicitly incorporate that past
           forecasting bias into your sales forecast for
           next year?

Mike: No, because the EnviroStuff market is so
           new, and my previous forecasts were for
           different markets.

Francine: Mike, what I'm about to say applies to all of
           us, including me. When true outsiders
           examine the forecasting skills of others, they
           focus on the personality traits of the
           forecasters. So although it might be true that
           your past forecasts were for different
           markets, your personality traits also figure in.
           It's really hard to look at our own traits.
           That's why we need to help each other spot
           our vulnerabilities. And our culture needs to
           offer a supportive environment so that we all
           help each other.

Eve: Thanks, Francine, that is so important. Mike,
           thanks for laying this out for us. It's a great
           starting point. I think the next step will be
           for you to do the next iteration of your sales

forecast based on our discussions today.
Please consider whether your projections are
realistic or whether they are unrealistically
optimistic as best guesses. I'm not saying we
might not achieve a tripling in our sales
because it might happen. But if it happens,
would it happen because we ran into some
good luck? Or would it happen because it was
reasonable to expect? Also, please consider
some reasonable failure scenarios in which
some things do go wrong. It might help us to
prepare for contingencies, mentally or
otherwise, if we have a sense of where the
surprises might come from. All of that
involves taking the inside view. So, when
you're finished with the inside view, do your
best to take the outside view, and think about
how the outside view would lead you to
modify the forecast that comes from your
inside view alone. Okay?

Mike: Okay, I'll get to work on that.

Eve: Great. For now, let's take your initial forecast
           as given and engage in some brainstorming to
           see what it would imply about what would
           take place in the rest of our company. The
           information that comes out of this discussion
           might also help you decide about whether to
           revise any of your previous thinking.

Francine: Oscar, as chief operating officer, can you
           share some of your thoughts about the impact
           on operations from tripling sales? For
           example, what about cost of goods sold,
           COGS? Last year, COGS amounted to $1.38
           for every $1 of sales. By how much can we

bring down that 138 percent ratio? If we applied the percent of sales heuristic directly, we would be forecasting costs of goods sold of over $2 million.

Oscar: As all of you know, our gross margin last year was negative, meaning that our cost of goods sold was higher than our sales. That's why the ratio was over 100 percent. A key reason for this was because we ran our operations very inefficiently. We were a little too ambitious in our hiring of manufacturing workers and could have made do with fewer people on the shop floor. But we learned a lot from our mistakes. And our engineering group made great strides in improving our production process. I don't think we are going to need to budget for any more manufacturing workers to triple the production level; in fact, we can actually lay off a few. If we plan to triple production, then we should budget for triple the raw materials. My best guess is that cost of goods sold will end up around $710,000 or so. If that happens and the sales number comes in around Mike's forecast, that cost ratio will drop from 138 percent to about 35 percent.

Francine: We definitely need that improvement to stem the cash outflow. What about the capital budget? What are you proposing that we need in terms of plant and equipment? How does that figure into COGS?

Oscar: The capital budgeting proposal for 2011 involved building a new operating plant and four additional manufacturing machines. The total amount you approved was $450,000. The impact on COGS in 2012 would be through manufacturing overhead, somewhere in the neighborhood of $175,000.

Francine: But the range you propose for COGS in 2012 is just a little more than its value in 2011. Are you being unrealistically optimistic in your COGS forecast? In fact, let me ask you another question. How much lower do you think COGS might actually turn out to be, given that we triple sales?

Oscar: I don't think we can reasonably expect to get COGS much lower unless raw material prices drop dramatically.

Eve: Could COGS turn out to be much higher than you expect?

Oscar: Yes, if we had a serious breakdown in our machines and had a huge repair bill. Or if we had a major quality issue and had to remake product.

Francine: Okay, so there's not much room below your COGS forecast for a superior outcome, but there is a fair amount of room above your COGS forecast for an inferior outcome. Do I have it right?

Oscar: Yes.

Eve: Mike, what do you think?

Mike: I think Oscar's COGS forecast might be unrealistically optimistic, and that it might only reflect the inside view. I'm chuckling now because I can also tell you that it's a lot

	easier for me to discuss the outside view when I'm on the outside rather than the inside.
Eve:	Oscar?
Oscar:	Yes, I see the point. But last year was our first year, and we didn't have any serious manufacturing problems. If something was going to go wrong, it was more likely to have happened last year. This year, we have a lot more experience. I think the odds of something serious going wrong with manufacturing are pretty remote.
Eve:	Okay, remember that overconfident managers downplay risks and end up more surprised than they expected to be. Why don't you think about whether your forecast for COGS needs to be revised and let us know later? Also, as Francine mentioned when we were going over Mike's forecast, all of us need to bring outside view thinking into our forecasts. For example, if in the past you tended to be unrealistically optimistic by 10 percent, you might want to bump up your inside view COGS forecast by 10 percent, in which case your forecast ratio might be 38.5 percent instead of 35 percent.
Oscar:	Yes, I understand. That makes sense to me. It's not something that I'm used to doing, but I see the merits of doing it.
Eve:	Great. What about R&D? What kind of a budget do you think we'll need for R&D?
Oscar:	I propose that we invest in another two R&D units. If we are going to be competitive in the long run, then we need to improve both

the quality of our product and the efficiency of our production line. Our engineers are pretty good. I think we can hold off hiring any more, as long as we give them new and better lab equipment to work with. If we do that, R&D on our income statement will show up as about $395,000.

Francine: How much value do you think that investment will create for EnviroStuff? Have you done an incremental cash flow analysis to estimate that?

Oscar: I do have something started, but I'm not quite done with the analysis. Can we talk about that later?

Francine: Sure. In that case, let's move to SG&A. Mike, what kind of a sales budget would you propose?

Mike: To triple our sales, it would be prudent to hire two more salespeople to bring our sales force up to four. That will cost about $225,000. And it wouldn't hurt to boost promotion spending by $50,000. We can hold steady on our customer support staff. So I propose an increase in our sales budget of $275,000.

Henry: Four salespeople to approach 400 customers? That's an average of two visits a week, which seems a pretty slow pace. What would happen if we didn't increase our sales force?

Mike: Our two current salespeople could approach four customers a week. But there's a lot of travel involved, a lot of downtime. They would be stretched and stressed. And if someone got sick, there is no bench we can turn to.

Henry: How busy were our customer support people last year?

Mike: They were busy because of the quality problem.

Henry: Suppose we didn't have a quality problem last year.

Mike: There wouldn't have been a whole lot needed in terms of customer support.

Henry: If we eliminated our customer support staff and hired one more salesperson, could the salespeople handle customer support in the absence of a major problem like the one we had with quality last year?

Mike: Yes.

Henry: Then okay, why don't we think about doing that to keep costs down in 2012? If Oscar thinks the quality problem is solved, perhaps the risk is small that we will really need to offer a lot of customer support at this stage. Does that make sense?

Mike: I think it does make sense from a cost point of view. But it will stress the sales force. But if we do it, the sales budget would come in at about $50,000 more than last year.

Francine: Let's pencil that in for now, but Mike, you can think about how much stress our sales force can handle and raise it again at the next meeting if you still feel strongly about it, okay? Henry, what about other SG&A items?

Henry: Those expenses should be down from last year by $90,000 because we paid recruiting costs to hire our manufacturing team. This coming year, we won't be hiring any more manufacturing workers. We are planning to hire a salesperson, so there will be some recruiting cost to pay.

Oscar: Eve, you always tell us how important it is that we play devil's advocate, so let me ask Henry the same question that you have been asking us. Is your cost estimate unrealistically optimistic? What might make those costs come out higher?

Henry: Thanks for the question. I appreciate it. Utility costs might soar. Or we might find that we have to hire more people than we expected and therefore pay recruiting costs. Or we might have to lay off some people and pay severance costs. Actually, now that I've said that, I realize I forgot to include severance costs associated with laying off the customer support staff. That means our G&A won't be as low as I suggested a few moments ago. Of course, our own salaries are also included in G&A. By agreement with our investors, those won't be going up in 2012. Okay, any other questions or comments?

Oscar: Not right now.

Mike: We can move on.

Francine: Thanks. So, let me summarize. We're putting together a financial plan to back up our general strategy of moving forward to supply enviro-generators to the market. At this

Table 5.1

Income Statement	2012
Sales	$1,452,000
Cost of Goods Sold	$710,619
Gross Profit	$741,381
R & D	$392,665
SG & A	$1,106,660
Depreciation	$4,000
Earnings from Operations (EBIT)	($761,944)

stage, we've taken a first stab at preparing a pro forma income statement for 2012. I've run a quick spreadsheet to show what we are looking at in terms of operations. The Depreciation number for 2012 will be the same as it was in 2011 (see Table 5.1).

As you can see, we are forecasting a positive Gross Profit for 2012 but a negative operating profit. Basically, we still have a lot of overhead to cover. If we didn't pay ourselves anything, EnviroStuff would almost break even in terms of EBIT, earnings before interest and tax.

Mike: Is that a subtle suggestion to us?

Francine: Ha ha. No, it's just a point of information. And I am confident that EnviroStuff will be a successful business that doesn't have to ask its executives to do without basic salaries. Moving right along . . .

Henry: Just before we move along, Francine, could we spend some time talking about that last point?

Francine: Of course.

Henry: Great. Eve keeps stressing that our corporate culture needs to reflect an awareness of groupthink. And the two of you always talk about the importance of respectful disagreement to counter groupthink, right?

Eve: Absolutely.

Henry: Okay, I'm not convinced that we can afford to pay ourselves what we are paying ourselves. We are forecasting that our SG&A will be almost as big as our sales!

Francine: You know what, Henry? You're right to bring up the issue. Thank you. It's a legitimate issue. I'll tell you what. Part of what we are doing here is assessing our financial strength going forward. So in this first round, how about proceeding under the assumption that we're going to keep our own pay the same and see where that takes us? Then in the next round of discussion, we can revisit the key expenditure categories, including this one. And to be sure that we do discuss the salary issue, can I ask you to raise it again during the second round?

Henry: I'd be happy to do that.

Francine: Great. So let me continue with the income statement. There are other income statement items below EBIT, basically interest and taxes. The only number that involves some judgment is the forecast for interest paid. I've gone ahead and used the number of $14,539. I got that number by computing how much interest we will pay on the $300,000 loan we are just about to take out and the interest I estimate we will receive on the marketable securities we will hold in 2012. The rest of the income statement is mechanical. Let's assume that Other Income will be zero, unless something comes up in our conversation that suggests the contrary. Earnings before tax is operating profit minus interest paid and other income. Multiply this number to get tax. Subtract tax from earnings before tax, and we get Net Income. So here's how the whole pro forma income statement for 2012 would look.

Table 5.2

Income Statement	2012
Sales	$1,452,000
Cost of Goods Sold	$710,619
Gross Profit	$741,381
R&D	$392,665
SG&A	$1,106,660
Depreciation	$4,000
Earnings from Operations (EBIT)	($761,944)
Interest Expense	$22,939
Other Income	$0
Pretax Earnings (EBT)	($784,883)
Less: Provision for Taxes (35%)	($274,709)
Net Income	($510,174)

Mike: Why do I keep hoping that Net Income is going to be positive?

Oscar: Because you're a marketing guy, Mike. Marketing guys always engage in wishful thinking, ha ha.

Francine: Right, Oscar. Just remember that old saying about people who live in glass houses.

Oscar: Just kidding, Mike.

Francine: Let's move on to the balance sheet items. We'll do the assets side of the balance sheet first, and I'll lead the discussion unless one of you would like to do that.

Oscar: Francine, I know you and Eve believe that everyone should be literate when it comes to our company's financials. So thanks for offering, but I'm happy for you to lead us here, and I see Mike nodding his head in agreement with me. We'll participate as actively as we can.

Francine: Great. Let's begin by focusing on current assets. Remember I mentioned that forecasting financial statements involves the use of a heuristic technique called percent of sales. The technique operates by assuming that many financial statement items will retain the same ratio to sales from year to year. Forecasting these variables is pretty easy if you follow the technique. Just compute the ratio to sales from last year and multiply by forecasted sales.

           For example, last year sales were $484,000, and accounts receivable were $242,000.

Hence, the ratio of accounts receivable to sales was 50 percent. So the heuristic for forecasting accounts receivable next year is to take 50 percent of $1,452,000. This comes out to $726,000. The idea here is that if our sales double, the percentage of those sales for which customers delay payment will stay the same, so the amount of money they owe us will also double. So, if we maintain our current policy for payment terms to customers, the percent of sales should stay the same.

Mike: How do we know our new customers will pay up like our old customers? What happens if one of our new customers is a local government that winds up with a tax shortfall and takes longer to pay us than we expected?

Francine: It could happen. Our forecast might be wrong. The question is whether we know enough to make a better prediction. In fact, our sales force should do enough research to assess how good each of our customers is at paying its bills. This is actually an issue you might want to develop and put some process around.

Mike: Okay, that makes sense.

Francine: The other asset on the balance sheet we would forecast using this heuristic is inventory. Again, the assumption is that our inventory policy stays constant and that our inventory of raw materials, work in progress, and finished goods varies in proportion with sales.

Oscar: Well, that might not be realistic. If we think that raw material prices are going to go through the roof or that there might be shortages in the supply chain, we might want to load up on raw materials early. Or if we are concerned about losing market share because we run out of stock when customers are expecting delivery, we might increase our inventory of finished goods as a hedge.

Francine: That is a very good point. Have you given any thought to those issues?

Oscar: Not really. Should I?

Francine: Well, inventory policy is part of our strategy. It's got an operations aspect, it's got a marketing and sales aspect, and it's got a finance aspect. We all need to be involved in figuring out what to do. We don't need to do that right now. For now, we can go with percent of sales as a first pass. But we should have a separate meeting to go over inventory policy and try not to get anchored by our first-pass analysis.

Mike: The other item in current assets is Cash and Marketable Securities. Do we use percent of sales to forecast that item as well?

Francine: I don't think it makes sense for us to use percent of sales to forecast cash. In fact, the exercise in which we are currently engaged should help us figure out what our cash policy will be. For now, let's assume that we are going to have to spend cash to grow and that we want to make sure we hold at least $25,000 in case of unforeseen events. We can

	revisit this assumption later. The next question is, what do we need to know to figure out how to forecast Property, Plant, and Equipment?
Oscar:	Didn't we already talk about our capital equipment purchases?
Francine:	Yes, we did go over your proposals for the 2011 capital budget but not for the 2012 budget. The 2011 capital outlays will figure into our balance sheet for 2011. And our 2012 capital budget will figure into our pro forma balance sheet for 2012. There is also another issue, and that is whether or not we plan to dispose of any property, plant, and equipment during the year.
Oscar:	Well, those enviro-generator manufacturing machines that we bought a year ago should last another year. But if we run them full throttle, they are going to be pretty useless by the end of the year. And then they'll just sit around unless we send them to the scrap yard. The same is true for the R&D units we bought a year ago. There is no point in those units sitting around taking up valuable space we could use to store inventory or house other equipment.
Francine:	One reason I like to do pro forma statements is to get us to think ahead this way. The balance sheet item for gross Property, Plant, and Equipment only records amounts that pertain to fixed assets we hold, not that we used to hold. So the balance sheet at the end of 2012 would not reflect machines and R&D

units we disposed of during the year. Can we assume that all the equipment we bought last year will get disposed of by the end of 2012?

Oscar: I think so.

Francine: Okay, so now there is the issue about the 2012 capital budget.

Oscar: Well, I thought you wanted to wait until the end of the year to see what our cash position would be before discussing capital spending.

Francine: You're right about that because a lot can happen before we commit, and if we can wait until we see how the year goes, then we should wait. Then we can see what our cash situation is like, what the market is like, and so on. That being said, keep in mind that we are planning right now. To forecast what our balance sheet will look like a year from now, we need to make an estimate of what our capital budget will be. So, Oscar, suppose 2012 turned out pretty much the way we are predicting. How much do you think we would need to spend on capital a year from now?

Oscar: Whatever you would let me spend Francine.

Francine: Well, at least you're honest. Suppose my answer was $200,000.

Oscar: Then I would complain that you're being short-sighted and that we should spend more. But if that's what you gave me, I'd purchase one new manufacturing machine and one new R&D unit. I think we need to spend heavily on R&D to improve our quality. We won't last long in this market if we sell inferior stuff. Our competitors will eat us alive.

Francine: I take your point. At the same time, let's use $200,000 for illustrative purposes and see how things play out, okay?

Oscar: Fine.

Francine: In that case, our gross Property, Plant, and Equipment would actually decline in 2012 from $1,350,000 to $1,300,000. That's because we would be retiring fixed assets we purchased for $250,000 and adding new fixed assets that cost us $200,000, making for a net reduction of $50,000.

Mike: I follow that. What happens to accumulated depreciation?

Oscar: Whatever happens, the $250,000 number that disappeared from Property, Plant, and Equipment when we retired those assets also has to disappear from accumulated depreciation, right?

Francine: Absolutely.

Mike: Why?

Francine: Well, the book value, meaning the net value, of the assets we retire is already zero because the assets will be fully depreciated. Because net is gross minus accumulated depreciation, if you remove $X from the gross number, you've got to do the same to the accumulated depreciation so that removing the asset does not change the net value on the balance sheet.

Mike: I'll take your word for it.

Francine: We don't have to belabor the point. You'll
           understand it before too long. Anyway,
           moving right along, our 2012 balance sheet
           number for land will be the same as our 2011
           number because we're not planning to buy or
           sell land in 2012, and land doesn't depreciate.

Oscar: Well, I see that the next to the last item on
           the balance sheet is Other Assets. Is that the
           tax deferred asset?

Francine: Indeed it is. This one records our tax-loss
           carryforwards, it's our future tax credit, or
           our gift certificate from the Internal Revenue
           Service. So at the end of this year, 2011, that
           number should turn out to be $445,373. Our
           2012 pro forma income statement shows a
           fictitious tax refund from the IRS of
           $173,769. So the forecast for our total credit
           at the end of 2012 should amount to the sum
           of these two numbers, $619,142.

Oscar: The concept seems straightforward enough.
           I wonder why we found it so difficult before.
           Maybe it's because the financial statements
           don't paint the true picture of what we pay
           in taxes.

Francine: Well, there is another set of books that we
           keep for tax purposes that presents the
           situation in a way that's clearer. But the way
           we are doing it here involves the typical
           presentation to investors. Anyway, here's
           what our first pass looks like for the assets
           side of the balance sheet (see Table 5.3).

Table 5.3

Balance Sheet	2012 Assets
Cash and Marketable Securities	$25,000
Accounts Receivable	$726,000
Inventory	$42,383
Total Current Assets	$793,383
Property, Plant, and Equipment	$1,300,000
Accumulated Depreciation	$288,000
Plant and Equipment (Net)	$1,012,000
Land and Improvements (Net)	$225,000
Total Fixed Assets	$1,237,000
Other Assets	$818,082
Total Assets	$2,848,465

Mike: I can follow all of that.

Francine: Great. How about you, Oscar?

Oscar: Me too. I've got it.

Francine: In that case, we can move on to the liabilities side of the balance sheet. Here is the way it works. The liabilities side shows how much money we have received from investors and suppliers. It basically displays the amount of principal we need to return to them. For loans, it really is the principal, not the interest. For stock, the analogy to interest is dividends, and dividends also are not a part of the balance sheet.

Mike: Thanks for reminding us. What about Accounts Payable? That item seems different.

Francine: Good question. Accounts Payable reflects our unpaid bills. The balance sheet shows what we owe our suppliers. That number is on the balance sheet because it is as if our suppliers have loaned us money to make those purchases.

Mike: Thanks.

Francine: You're welcome. Now, here is a question for you. Suppose we hope to get away without raising any new capital from investors in 2012. Could we do it, given the plan we have developed so far?

Oscar: Well, that depends on cash flow, right?

Francine: Right. What if we didn't need to turn to our investors for new funds or to banks for new short-term credit? What do you think the liabilities side of the balance sheet would look like for 2012?

Mike: Well, based on what you just reminded us about, that the balance sheet represents what we received from investors in the past, shouldn't those balance sheet numbers be the same as those in 2011?

Francine: Okay, which numbers?

Mike: The numbers for debt and equity.

Francine: You're partly right. Notes Payable is the line item for short-term debt, and it would stay the same. The item for Long-Term Debt would stay the same, and we have no long-term debt that will change in status because the principal will be due within a year. But how about Shareholders' Equity?

Mike: The same, too.

Francine: Well, that's true for the Preferred Stock and Common Stock line items. But is there anything else that you might be missing?

Mike: Oh, I see. I've missed Retained Earnings.

Francine: Right on. The Retained Earnings number on the balance sheet is a running total for all past Retained Earnings numbers. So we need to take the 2011 number and add to it the difference between 2012 net income and 2012 dividends. At this stage of our company, we have no intention of paying out dividends. So the number we add to 2011 Retained Earnings is the pro forma Net Income number for 2012. And that takes us to a value of –$322,714.

Mike: Is that it, then? Is Retained Earnings the only item that won't be the same?

Oscar: How about Accounts Payable? Shouldn't we use percent of sales for that, just like we did for Accounts Receivable?

Francine: Exactly correct. In fact, let me enter the formulas into my spreadsheet and display the results to everyone (see Table 5.4).

Oscar: Well, that's interesting, Francine. The balance sheet doesn't balance! Assets are more than liabilities.

Francine: That's right. Actually, it's liabilities and shareholders' equity.

Mike: Well, Oscar might be right, but having a balance sheet that doesn't balance surely can't be right.

Francine: You're right too, Mike.

Table 5.4

Balance Sheet	2012 Liabilities
Notes Payable	$0
Long-Term Debt due within One Year	$0
Accounts Payable	$15,000
Total Current Liabilities	$15,000
Long-Term Debt	$300,000
Other Liabilities	$0
Preferred Stock	$3,000,000
Common Stock	$0
Retained Earnings	($1,519,294)
Shareholders' Equity	$1,480,706
Total Liabilities and Shareholders' Equity	$1,795,706

Mike: Okay. Well, it's nice when all of us are right. But what about that difference? My quick calculation says that assets exceed liabilities and shareholders' equity by $1,052,759.

Francine: Well, clearly, we have to do something about that. Either we have to reduce the assets number or increase the liabilities and shareholders' equity number.

Oscar: You mean we solve the problem by playing with the numbers? Won't that land us in jail?

Francine: Very funny. The way we reduce the assets number is by doing something real, like purchasing less capital equipment than we had planned. The way we increase the number for liabilities and owners' equity is by raising new funds. In fact, one very good reason for engaging in this kind of planning is to help me figure out how much money I should anticipate going out and raising. Based on what we've been discussing, it looks like I should plan to raise $1,052,759 in external funding.

Mike: Where's the money going to come from?

Francine: Well, I haven't figured that out yet. Most likely, we'll turn to our venture capitalists in a new funding round. But we could also try to take out a new loan. Or we could do a combination, raising some new money by taking out a new loan and getting the remainder from our venture capitalists. For now, let's assume that we raise $786,066 from our venture capitalists and the remainder from a bank. In that case, here is how the liabilities side of our balance sheet will turn out. And if you compare the assets and liabilities sides of the balance sheet, what do you now see? (see Table 5.5).

Oscar: Okay, I see that the balance sheet now balances.

Mike: Right, and I see that it's not by playing with the numbers.

Francine: Good. Well, I think we are done with our first pass on the financial statements. We'll do another pass down the line. But at this stage, I would like for us to engage in a little capital budgeting analysis. Going forward, we need to be better disciplined about our capital expenditures. What I would like us to consider is how much value we create for our investors when we make capital expenditures.

Oscar: What's the point of doing that?

Table 5.5

Balance Sheet	2012 Liabilities
Notes Payable	$0
Long-Term Debt Due within One Year	$0
Accounts Payable	$15,000
Total Current Liabilities	$15,000
Long-Term Debt	$566,693
Other Liabilities	$0
Preferred Stock	$3,786,066
Common Stock	$0
Retained Earnings	($1,519,294)
Shareholders' Equity	$2,266,772
Total Liabilities and Shareholders' Equity	$2,848,465

Francine: Well, here are two reasons. First, we need to assess whether our capital expenditures are actually worth undertaking. If we destroy value for our investors, we are going to be toast before too long. Second, a lot of the current value of our company derives from what investors expect from us down the line, meaning our future projects. We need to start estimating what those projects might be worth.

Mike: That makes sense to me, but how do we do it?

Francine: Let's take a stab at assessing the value we estimate our 2012 capital expenditures will be creating. I'll take you all through an illustrative example to show you what I have in mind. From this point on, we will put processes in place so that the procedure becomes commonplace for us, okay?

Oscar: Well, I don't know. Let's see what you have in mind.

Francine: Take a look at this table (see Table 5.6). It displays the kind of information we need to know about the cash flows associated with our planned capital expenditure at the end of 2012. If you look at the table, you'll see that it's divided into four sections. The last section is the "bottom line." The bottom line indicates, year by year, how much of a difference doing the project will make to the overall cash flows of our company. And then

Table 5.6

1. Cash flows from investment and disposal

1 Investment	How much money are we proposing to spend on this project for new fixed assets?
2 Disposal	How much money or salvage value do we anticipate raising from selling the fixed assets associated with the project?
3 Tax on disposal	How much additional tax do we pay from disposing of the fixed assets associated with the project?
4 Subtotal	What is the subtotal of the above items?

2. Cash flows from operations

5 Sales	How much would doing this project add to the sales of our company?
6 Cost of goods sold	Excluding depreciation, how much did it cost to produce the additional items sold?

7 SG&A	Excluding depleciation, how much would doing this project add to costs associated with SG&A?
8 R&D	How much would doing the project add to the costs associated with R&D?
9 Depreciation	How much would doing the project add to the depreciation expense of the company?
10 Tax @35%	How much would doing the project add to the amount of corporate tax that the company pays?
11 Subtotal	What is the difference between sales and the subtotal of the above nondepreciation expenses?

3. Change in net working capital

12 Change A/R	How much would doing the project add to the change in accounts receiveable from the prior year?
13 Change inventory	How much would doing the project add to the change in inventory from the prior year?
14 Change A/P	How much would doing the project add to the change in accounts payable from the prior year?
15 Subtotal	What is the subtotal of the above items?

4. Net cash flows

16 Net cash flows	Total of subtotals, the difference the project makes to the overall cash flows to the company.
17 Present value	What is the present value of net cash flow in each year, from the perspective of the end of 2012?

	we do present value. The way we come up with the "bottom line" is to break up the cash flows into subcategories. Can you see that?
Mike:	Do you mean cash flows from investment and disposal?
Francine:	Right, along with cash flows from operations and cash flows from change in net working capital. Why don't we take the questions one at a time? The first one is easy: In 2012, how much money are we proposing to spend on this project for new fixed assets?
Oscar:	$200,000. But is it for a project?
Francine:	$200,000 is right. And we want to think of it in terms of a project so that we stay focused on what we are trying to accomplish. Now because that $200,000 is money that we spend as a company, money that goes out the door, we put a minus sign in front of it to mark it as a cash outflow. Okay, keeping in mind that what we're trying to do is assess the impact of the project on the company's overall cash flows, let's go through the line item questions one by one.
Oscar:	Easy enough.
Francine:	We're at line item 2. These assets have an expected lifetime of two years. After two years, do you think there will be any value in those assets if we sell them as scrap?
Oscar:	Not really. They will be pretty useless.
Francine:	Okay, then that item is $0, and so is line item 3, the associated tax, were we to get some money by selling off those assets for salvage.

And line item 4 is just a subtotal. The next item, number 5, is the first item in cash flow from operations. Mike, how much less would the company's sales be in 2013 if we didn't make that $200,000 investment at the end of 2012?

Mike: Off the top of my head, I'd guess about $1 million.

Francine: And how about the impact on sales in 2014? How much less would the company sales be in 2014 if we didn't make that $200,000 investment at the end of 2012?

Mike: Oh, that's harder. I'd guess about 15 percent more because we would be able to make more efficient use of those assets in 2014 than in 2015. So, my answer would be $1.15 million.

Francine: Thanks. Oscar, can you tell me what you would do to figure out by how much the cost of goods sold would go down if we didn't have those sales?

Oscar: I would start by multiplying sales by 35 percent because that was the figure we used to forecast costs of goods sold in the 2012 financial statements. I would probably reduce that figure to take into account future productivity improvements and so on.

Francine: And would you do the same for the other cost items as well?

Oscar: Yes. I would use the percent of sales technique as my starting point.

Francine: Good. And depreciation?

Oscar: Well, we use straight line, so depreciation would be $100,000 in 2013 and another $100,000 in 2014.

Francine: Well, we're almost finished. We can figure out the subtotal for cash flow from operations for all years. We can also apply the same technique to the next section for working capital, where we use "change in sales" instead of "level of sales" because we are estimating the "change in working capital." And that will take us to the bottom line, section 4, line 16. I've done a quick calculation, and here is how things work out (see Table 5.7). You can see that I've included line 17 to measure the present value of those estimated cash flows, where "present" means "end of 2012."

Henry: I can follow what's going on in sections 1 and 2; that's easy enough. So, for example, in section 2, line 11 shows that we expect to earn a profit of $230,000 in 2013. But I don't understand section 3 on working capital at all.

Francine: Henry, thanks so much for having the courage to say so. There are a couple of things going on here. First, the $230,000 is not profit per se. It's the extra profit we would expect the company to earn by virtue of doing the project. That $230,000 refers to the impact on the firm's overall after-tax profit.

Henry: Ah, yes. You keep stressing that it's about the impact of the project on our company's overall cash flows.

Table 5.7

Year	2012	2013	2014	2015
1. Cash flows from investment and disposal				
1 Investment	($200,000)			
2 Disposal				
3 Tax on disposal				
4 Subtotal	($200,000)	$0	$0	
2. Cash flows from operations				
5 Sales	$1,000,000	$1,150,000		
6 Cost of goods sold	($350,000)	($402,500)		
7 SG&A	($250,000)	($287,500)		
8 R&D	($100,000)	($115,000)		
9 Depreciation	($100,000)	($100,000)		
10 Tax @35%	($70,000)	($85,750)		
11 Subtotal	$0	$230,000	$259,250	
3. Change in net working capital				
12 Change A/R	($500,000)	($75,000)	$575,000	
13 Change inventory	($29,190)	($4,378)	$33,568	
14 Change A/P	$10,331	$1,550	($11,880)	
15 Subtotal	$0	($518,859)	($77,829)	$596,688
4. Net cash flows				
16 Net cash flows	($200,000)	($288,859)	$181,421	$596,688
17 Present value	($200,000)	($240,716)	$125,987	$345,306

Francine: Exactly. Now here's the thing about working
capital. Those items are actually adjustments
for the purpose of coming up with cash
flows. For example, when we say that our
expected sales will be $1 million in 2013, that

$1 million is not all cash flow because we don't expect all of our customers to pay us in 2013. If you look at line 12, you'll see that it's –$500,000. What that means is that we're expecting to increase the value of the money we're owed by $500,000 because we only collect half of the extra $1 million in sales.

Mike: I got it. We expect to recognize additional sales of $1 million in 2013 but only to bring half of that in as cash.

Francine: Correct. The other working capital items also pertain to adjustments. The money we spend on inventory that doesn't get sold won't show up in any of the items in sections 1 or 2. Cost of goods sold only pertains to items that have been sold. By definition, inventory has not been sold yet.

Oscar: What's going on with working capital in 2015? That's after the fixed assets associated with this project become worthless.

Francine: Well, look at accounts receivable, line 12, again. In 2015, we're expecting a $575,000 cash inflow associated with that item. Where do you think the $575,000 is coming from?

Mike: Well, it has to be sales. Oh, I see. It's coming from sales made in 2014, a portion of which gets collected in 2015.

Francine: Good. And remember, we're only talking about additional sales in 2014, which arise because we do the project.

Mike: I keep forgetting that. Yes, they are "additional" sales.

Oscar: Remind me again why you keep emphasizing that the sales are additional.

Francine: Because we're trying to assess whether the capital expenditures being proposed for 2012 make sense. To make this assessment, we want to identify the difference we anticipate that those expenditures will make on our company's overall cash flows. And that's what line 16 tells us on a year-by-year basis. If we do the project, the company's cash flows will be lower by $200,000 in 2012 because we made the capital purchases, and we also expect them to be lower by $288,859 in 2013. But we expect the impact to turn positive in 2014, by $181,421, and especially in 2015 in the amount of $596,688.

Oscar: I hope we would want to do this project. But by my calculations, it doesn't pay for itself until 2015, which is more than the two years that the new assets will last. Are we still okay?

Francine: We are okay to do the project. It's fine to look at payback period, but that's not the critical criterion. The critical criterion is whether doing the project increases the value of the firm. That's why we compute the present value of all those cash flows. And if we add up the present values in row 17, we get a number of $30,577. That number gives us the value impact of doing the project. In other words, doing the project leads our company to be worth $30,577 more than if we don't do the project. So we should do it.

Mike: Okay, I'm sold. More important, I understand the logic. Well, almost. One thing I don't understand is why we are forecasting that we will pay taxes in 2013 and 2014. Don't we have this tax deferred asset that is like a gift certificate from the IRS?

Francine: Whoa, Mike. A-plus. You're absolutely correct. I have to fess up and admit that I missed that. Thanks very much. You see, it's what Eve keeps telling us about working together as a team to develop good process. We all help each other.

Oscar: You know, doing this for all of our capital budgeting requests seems like an awful lot of work. Is it worth the effort? Sometimes, you just know that you need new equipment.

Eve: Oscar has a point. The thing to keep in mind, though, is that we are trying to develop our business processes so that we operate in a culture of discipline. We need to be careful that we evaluate our major decisions with a view of how much value we are creating for our company.

Oscar: I understand. But can't we use our judgment for that? After all, we are experienced.

Eve: Bias gremlins love that attitude.

Oscar: What do you mean?

Eve: Right now, we are losing money. Psychologically, we're operating in the domain of losses. We need to be aware that psychologically we're predisposed to make judgments whereby we take bigger risks as a result. Doing project cash flow projections and computing net present value will help us counter that predisposition. And because we are working as a group, we have the additional concern about polarization, meaning that we'll all get behind whoever wants to be aggressive about taking risk.

Oscar: I got the point. Okay, I accept implementing this routine on an ongoing basis.

Eve: That's wonderful, everyone. It might take some getting used to. And we have to train everyone in the company about what's involved. Moreover, there's going to be a lot of fine tuning along the way. But I'm comfortable that together we'll move forward as a well-functioning, healthy team.

Curtain falls. Much applause.

Okay, just kidding about the applause.

Anyway, I hope the dialogue gives you the general idea of what it means to combine the nuts-and-bolts part of planning with debiasing techniques. I don't want to leave you with the impression that EnviroStuff is a perfect, psychologically smart company. Perfection is an ideal. We're far from perfection. But the discussion at EnviroStuff illustrates a very solid effort.

For those readers who get very serious about this stuff, which I hope will be most of you, and decide to try their hand at the EnviroStuff simulation game, you will find yourself in dialogues just like the one I presented in this chapter. And you'll have an opportunity to try to outperform Eve, Francine, Mike, Oscar, and Henry. I'll be disappointed if you don't.

CHAPTER 6

INCENTIVES: CHOOSING CARROTS AND STICKS

In psychologically smart companies, compensation involves more than paying an honest dollar for an honest day's work. Psychologically smart companies structure compensation systems with incentives to harness the power of a financially literate workforce.

Bias gremlins thrive in organizations that downplay incentives because that is where they can successfully encourage "social loafing." Look, people respond to incentives and seek rewards. If you motivate people well, they won't engage in social loafing. If you motivate them in a psychologically smart way, they'll channel their energies to meet organizational goals.

I'm not the only one who gets on a soapbox. When the subject of incentives comes up, Jack Stack gets on a soapbox too. He knows that the majority of companies do a terrible job when it comes to structuring incentives. And he says so whenever he has the opportunity.

A few years after Stack and Burlingham published *The Great Game of Business*, SRC produced a video program called *Lessons from the Field*. The video drums home the message of how much untapped power there is when it comes to workforce incentives. Quite honestly, that message is so dominant that I initially formed the impression that incentives were almost all there is to open book management. Of course, incentives are only part of what there is to open book management. You can't forget about financial literacy, planning, and information sharing!

I want to tell you a story about incentives and Silicon Valley. I live in Silicon Valley. Most people don't realize it, but the real name of Silicon Valley is Santa Clara Valley. I work at Santa Clara University (SCU), which lies in the heart of Silicon Valley. By the way, SCU is a truly great university. I am so fortunate to be here. It is one of the great educational institutions in the country and too humble for its own good. But that's another story.

Silicon Valley is the world's center for technology innovation. Intel, Hewlett-Packard, eBay, and Google are all valley companies. During the dot-com bubble, employee stock options were a big part of valley culture. A lot of my neighbors, and some of my students, got very rich from stock options. When my students went to interview for jobs in the valley, finding out about the stock option package was near the top of their lists.

About 10 years ago, Barry Posner, the dean of my school and one of the world's leading authorities on leadership, invited Jack Stack to speak before a valley audience. I expected him to be a big hit, but it didn't turn out that way.

Jack got on his soapbox and spoke about the importance of incentives. And how do you think his Silicon Valley audience responded? Let's just say they weren't impressed. It's not that they thought he was wrong. It's that they thought he wasn't telling them anything new. They thought they knew all about stock options. They were very motivated by stock options. They were working their tails off in the hopes that their stock options would make them rich.

Well, my Silicon Valley coworkers got about 10 percent of Jack Stack's message. They missed the rest. It's not just that they missed the part about financial literacy, planning, and information sharing. They also missed a big part of how to structure incentives so that people work smart. What employee stock options accomplished was to address the issue of social loafing. But they didn't induce people to channel their energies to support organizational goals. You will understand what I mean by this a lot better when you have finished reading this chapter.

I wish I could say that most companies motivate their people in psychologically smart ways. I wish I could say that the bias gremlins don't have the upper hand. But I can't. The gremlins have the upper hand when it comes to incentives, just as they have the upper hand when it comes to financial literacy and planning.

Structuring incentives in a psychologically smart way is no easy task. It is a huge challenge. But it's a doable challenge, and in this chapter, I will share with you some best practices for structuring intelligent incentives.

Delta Airlines: Better Late Than Never

Financial illiteracy can get a company into bankruptcy. Incentives can get them out of bankruptcy. That is a key lesson we can learn from the experience of Delta Airlines.

Like its rival United Airlines, whose situation I chronicled in Chapter 4, Delta found itself reeling from the aftermath of September 11, 2001. And it followed United into bankruptcy. United's financially illiterate workforce ignored the numbers that underscored the company's accounting weakness. The same was true for Delta. Both airlines had very high cost structures. Delta carried the most expensive pilots' contract in airline history, at least for the United States. In 2004, Delta was losing money at the rate of $4 million per day!

Delta's former CEO, Gerald Grinstein, made clever use of incentives to get his company out of bankruptcy. Grinstein had been a member of Delta's board since 1987. He became CEO in 2003. He inherited a company whose financial condition was weak and whose operating performance was declining. During 2004, Delta's record of on-time arrivals was near bottom for the whole industry.

Airlines that get into the habit of having their flights arrive late don't keep their customers. Passengers don't enjoy airline flights that routinely arrive late. The company had a lot of challenges to face, and improving operating performance was one of them.

Grinstein used incentives to address the problems with Delta's operating performance. He started a bonus program for employees. The bonus program payments were based on how well Delta did relative to other airlines in the following three key categories:

1. On-time arrivals
2. Completed flights
3. Baggage handling

In 2005, Delta's record for on-time arrivals surged to near the top of the industry. During 2005 and 2006, Delta paid out almost $50 million in bonuses from this program.

Grinstein had other challenges to face besides operating performance. He did his best, managing to convince Delta's pilots to accept more that a 25 percent cut in pay. Alas, he couldn't stave off a bankruptcy filing. Delta declared bankruptcy in September 2005. However, the steps he took to improve operating performance persisted, and Delta was able to emerge from bankruptcy in 2007.

The last part of Chapter 4 discusses the importance of standards and cues. Standards and cues are the basis for action. Think about what Grinstein did at Delta. He identified three critical cues for operating performance, laid down standards, and structured rewards based on these cues and standards. That was a psychologically smart move. You manage what you measure and, I might add, reward!

Gerald Grinstein also brought emotional intelligence to Delta. He understood that people have emotional needs as well as financial needs. He understood that an "us versus them" mentality is a disincentive. Grinstein worked long and hard on building positive relationships with his workforce and on softening differences to make people from various parts of the company feel that they were in it together.

In the aftermath of September 11, 2001, airline executives across the industry rushed to cut costs. Cutting costs meant asking the workforce to accept pay cuts, smaller retirement benefits, and layoffs. However, at American Airlines, the executives quietly gave themselves increases at the same time they asked their workforce to accept decreases.

Grinstein was different. He told his executives to drive less expensive cars to work than they had been. He himself started to eat lunch in the company cafeteria. He structured executive pay at Delta so that executives would only receive pay increases after frontline workers reached the industry standard. He understood the importance of being emotionally intelligent about incentives, especially about making everyone feel that "we're all in this together."

Here is a secret. You don't have to wait for a crisis before doing what Gerald Grinstein did with Delta's incentives. In fact, if you institute psychologically smart incentives when your company is doing well, you will be in a much better position to handle crises when business conditions deteriorate! In addition, you will have a much happier, productive, fulfilled workforce if you set sensible goals and align rewards with those goals.

How Big a Challenge?

Alignment begins with the setting and articulation of goals. It is a sad fact that surveys of American workers paint a bleak picture when it comes to the articulation of organizational goals. A 2006 Harris survey of 23,000 employees found that 73 percent did not understand their organization's goals. A 2002 Franklin-Covey study of 11,000 employees found that 56 percent did not understand the most important goals of their organization. In addition, 81 percent reported not having clearly defined goals.

I'm sure you realize that compensation involves psychological rewards as well as financial rewards. After all, people are goal oriented by nature. Goals provide "meaning" in their lives.

Do you think employees who fail to understand the goals of their organizations, and how their activities relate to those goals, will find it difficult to achieve meaningful work lives? The open book management crowd answers this question with a resounding *yes*!

I am sorry to report that the survey evidence concerning meaningful work lives is not encouraging. The Franklin-Covey study reported that 91 percent of employees surveyed believe that there is only a weak relationship between their work and the major goals set by their organization. Not surprisingly, 81 percent feel at best weakly committed to their organization's main priorities.

When it comes to incentives, I like the phrase "line of sight." In a business setting, the phrase means seeing the connection between action and organizational effect. For operating performance at Delta Airlines, the illustrative example discussed earlier, line of sight means employees understanding how their personal actions affect a variable like on-time arrivals.

The combination of line of sight and commitment is incredibly important. Some people use the term *engagement* to describe this combination. Research conducted by the consulting firm Watson Wyatt finds that having employees who are engaged is central to a company's financial success.

If you ask me, the bias gremlins aren't happy when employees lead meaningful work lives. That's why they construct barriers to the structuring of intelligent incentives. Well, we can fight those gremlins with a debiasing approach that begins by looking at theory and practice. We'll begin with theory.

Theory

There is actually an economic-based theory about the structuring of intelligent incentives. The theory concerns how a principal would design an incentive contract to offer an agent who is to perform work on behalf of the principal. At the core of principal-agent contract issues are two concepts, known as *the participation constraint* and *the incentive compatibility constraint*. The participation constraint is about offering a sufficiently attractive compensation package to induce people to join a company and stay. The incentive compatibility constraint is about the principal appropriately paying the agent for performance.

Real-world contracts are very complex, in some ways too complex to be captured by theories. Nevertheless, theory does provide some guidance about sensible heuristics for constructing contracts between principals and agents.

Discussions about incentive contracts often begin with sharecropping. There are two good reasons this is the case. First, sharecropping provides a real example of an incentive contract between a principal and an agent. Second and perhaps even more importantly, sharecropping serves as a powerful metaphor for incentive contracts in general.

Sharecroppers live as tenant farmers growing crops on land owned by a principal, the landowner. In this respect, the sharecropper serves as the agent of the landowner. As compensation, sharecroppers get to keep a portion of the total crops as their "share."

Consider two alternative ways that the landowner can compensate the sharecropper. The first way is for the landowner to agree to pay the sharecropper a fixed amount of the total crop as a wage and to keep what remains from the total crop as profit. The second way is for the landowner to agree to accept a fixed amount of the crop produced as rent and for the sharecropper to keep what remains from the total crop as profit.

In the typical sharecropping arrangement, the landowner receives the fixed amount, and the sharecropper keeps any residual. Why this arrangement rather than the other way around? The answer involves incentives.

Farming is hard work. It takes effort. A contract that promises the sharecropper a fixed amount offers less of an incentive to expend effort than does a contract that lets the sharecropper keep the entire surplus once the landowner has been paid. Letting the sharecropper keep the entire surplus features pay for performance and is incentive compatible.

There is no social loafing here because the sharecropper alone captures the full benefit of going the extra mile beyond what is minimally acceptable to remain employed. In contrast, paying the sharecropper a fixed amount, regardless of the amount produced, is not incentive compatible. This is because the sharecropper would not capture the entire benefit of additional effort and so would be inclined not to go the extra mile.

There is still the issue of the magnitude of the fixed amount the landowner is to receive. Naturally, landowners want the amount to be more, and sharecroppers want it to be less. It is the participation constraint that effectively determines this amount. In a functioning labor market, landowners and sharecroppers are in search of each other. Landowners who ask for too large an amount will fail to attract sharecroppers to work their land. Sharecroppers who insist on too low an amount for the landowner will fail to be engaged.

The risk dimension associated with incentive compatibility is very important. Because crop yields are unpredictable, an incentive-compatible contract imposes a great deal of risk on the sharecropper. In a bad year, the size of the crop might not even cover the fixed amount that is due the landowner, in which case the sharecropper receives nothing.

Risk can be expensive both for the sharecropper and the landowner. The cost to the sharecropper is obvious. The cost to the landowner is less obvious. If sharecroppers cannot easily tolerate risk, then landowners will have to pay more for performance than otherwise. And this means landowners must accept lower rents.

Sometimes, there are ways around the risk issue, especially when the landowner can tolerate more risk than the sharecropper. Keep in mind that the landowner would be happy to pay the sharecropper a fixed wage if the landowner could be assured that the sharecropper would exert the appropriate effort. And how might the landowner find such assurance? One answer is monitoring.

If the landowner can directly observe how much effort the sharecropper exerts, then the compensation contract can be "pay for effort" instead of "pay for performance." In this case, direct monitoring allows for a contract in which the sharecropper either puts in the requisite effort or, if not, gets fired.

Being fired is a stick. Paying for performance is a carrot. Depending on the situation, incentives can be carrots, sticks, or some combination. Indeed, there are laws against the use of some sticks. Civilized countries do not allow their citizens to be executed for laziness. This makes paying for performance that much more important.

Suppose that monitoring is expensive, sticks are limited in scope, and sharecroppers are very averse to risk. In this case, landowners might find that they will have to accept living in an imperfect world. This might mean offering very weak or nonexistent incentives in the knowledge that crop yields are bound to be small. In the days of the Soviet Union, Soviet workers would joke about this, saying: "They pretend to pay us, and we pretend to work."

Of course, there is a middle ground between the two extremes of having the sharecropper face all the risk and none of the risk. That middle ground involves risk sharing. In a risk-sharing arrangement, the sharecropper receives a small fixed payment (base wage) and is entitled to a share of the total crop above some mutually agreed-upon threshold.

This share is more than zero but less than 100 percent. The payment above the base wage is akin to a bonus.

The sharecropping situation serves to highlight the key issues about effective compensation plans in general. Compensation plans need to be attractive enough to recruit and retain executives and employees. If there are motivational issues involving differential interests between principals and agents, compensation plans need to feature appropriate incentives that bring the interests of principals and agents into closer alignment. Incentives can be a combination of carrots and sticks. If monitoring is expensive or unfeasible because of the need for decentralized decision making, then agents need to be paid for performance. However, paying for performance might subject agents to considerable risk, and risk is expensive for both agents and principals.

In business organizations, incentives take many forms. Some are strictly financial, such as bonuses and equity sharing. Others are nonfinancial and feature psychological rewards, such as praise and gratitude. Still others feature a combination of financial and nonfinancial incentives, such as the opportunity for promotion.

Although this chapter discusses both financial and nonfinancial incentives, most of the attention is directed toward financial incentives. This is not a statement about relative importance as much as a statement about relative attention. In general, books about business pay far too little attention to issues involving financial incentives.

Practice

The gap between theory and practice is huge! Survey data indicate that in the United States, variable pay in 2006 was less than 12 percent of payroll. Nevertheless, this ratio increased from 8.8 percent in 2003 to 11.8 percent in 2007. Hewitt Associates forecasts that in 2008 the ratio will top 12 percent. Notably, merit increases have averaged only about 3.7 percent.

Still, companies take note of incentive compatibility. The data suggest that despite the flat compensation budgets reported by compensation surveys, companies typically segment the members of their workforces and pay those segments very differently from each other. Segmentation is based on employees' potential impact on value creation as well as the cost of replacement. Notably, companies pay their top segments very differently from those below the top. The real wages of those below the top have been declining, along with incentives that feature pay for performance.

In 2007, staffing and outsourcing firm Hudson reported that almost half of American workers view the differential between executive pay and nonexecutive pay as excessive. For Americans working in publicly traded companies, the corresponding figure is about two-thirds. When it comes to top executives, a little less than 40 percent of workers believe that overpayment is a problem. A little less than 40 percent also believe that top executive compensation packages feature sufficient incentives in terms of pay for performance. Although managers are more inclined than the rank and file to view top executives as being fairly paid, many managers agree with workers.

Is providing incentives only to the top segment a good thing or a bad thing? Remember what theory tells us about conditions under which bonus-type incentives do not work or are unnecessary: if individuals below the top segment are not delegated responsibility for major decisions, are effectively monitored, are easily replaced if they fail to perform, or are extremely averse to risk.

Hudson reports that when asked if they are happy with their compensation, employees who are paid for performance are more apt to respond positively than those who are not. The respective response rates are 80 percent as opposed to 60 percent. Hudson also reports evidence that companies are increasingly willing to pay for performance, which is a good thing if done well.

Human Resources' Leadership Role

Retention and attraction together make up the participation constraint. Retaining talented employees is one of the key responsibilities of any human resources department (HR). Employees leave for a variety of reasons. To be sure, money is part of it. A 2004 study by Robert Half ranked money (i.e., inadequate salary and benefits) as the fourth reason most frequently cited. However, that leaves nonmonetary reasons occupying positions one, two, and three. And almost 90 percent of employees leave for nonmonetary reasons. The third reason most frequently cited was insufficient recognition. The second was unhappiness with management. The top reason was limited opportunities for advancement.

Running a successful human resources strategy involves keeping a lot of balls in the air. This is because employees have a lot of needs, both financial and psychological. As a result, it is imperative for an HR department to understand these needs. The lesson from the Robert Half survey is to be sure to provide opportunities for employees to grow and learn, to develop their managerial skills, to recognize them for their achievements, and of course, to pay them enough.

Attracting new employees is made easier by having a strong value proposition to offer employees and being able to articulate that proposition. That proposition will quickly tell potential employees why they should want to work for one firm over another. In addition to being fairly compensated monetarily, people also want meaning in their lives. Most want their work to feature a sense of fun. The value proposition has to assure them that they will be fairly rewarded, will have a meaningful work experience, and will find enjoyment.

HR is also responsible for overseeing the incentive compatibility component of compensation. This component focuses on pay for performance. Of course, pay is not the only reward that can be linked to performance. Other possible rewards are recognition and promotion. Put somewhat differently, there are many ways to define what "pay" means.

There are also many ways to define what "performance" means. In any pay for performance system, defining performance properly is critical. Defining performance improperly can induce employees to make decisions that result in value destruction, not value creation.

HR bears the responsibility for the institution of compensation systems that aim for incentive compatibility. And it is a major responsibility, not to mention a major challenge. If HR is to meet that challenge, then it will have to be a true partner in setting the company's overall business strategy and in measuring the progress toward the achievement of those goals.

Measurement is important. There is great truth in the phrase that you manage what you measure. Many HR departments routinely make use of key performance indicators such as head count, rates of turnover, age profile of workforce, health, and safety. However, HR departments also need to focus on key performance metrics associated with the overall value creation process. These are much more complex. Examples include indicators for revenue, costs, profits, customer satisfaction, innovations in products and processes, employee satisfaction, and employee engagement.

It is one thing to define key performance indicators. It is quite another for those indicators to serve as the gauges that guide decisions made by people in the organization. Doing so means working actively with others across the organization in the development of sensible performance indicators. It means leading the effort to link performance indicators, which pertain to intermediate goals such as customer satisfaction and innovation, to higher level goals such as value creation. It means educating employees to understand and make use of key performance indicators with the view of creating value.

Incentive compatibility has both a short-run component and a long-run component. Bonus plans are the typical way of dealing with the short-run component. Equity sharing is the typical way of dealing with the long-run component. In each case, HR is charged with the task of ensuring that the bonus plans and stock ownership plans are structured to do their jobs.

Bonus Plans: Best Practice Example

A major goal of a bonus system is to create a culture of engaged employees, where engagement combines commitment and line of sight. Engagement is about providing the workforce with the means and motive to create value. Commitment is about motive. Line of sight is about means.

Bonus plans are by nature short term. Designing a good bonus plan is a huge challenge. And the task is deceptive. It is much harder to do than it looks at first blush. Theory is informative insofar as it provides general guidelines, but it has limitations. Business relationships are more complex than sharecropping arrangements. To gain insight into how to develop a good bonus system, it makes sense to consider some best practices.

Incentives are at the forefront of open book companies. If you take a look at any seminar on how to run an open book company, you will see that compensation occupies center stage. Because SRC, Jack Stack's company, is perhaps the prototypical open book example, its compensation system is well worth studying.

SRC learned about developing a good bonus system the hard way. They tried to build one and failed. There is nothing like learning from your mistakes. And learn they did. They learned how to use a bonus system like a laser pointer, identifying the path that leads to higher profits and staying off those paths that result in lower profits.

SRC's approach to line of sight is holistic in that it focuses attention on how employees' decisions affect the value of the firm. This is a tall order. We expect salespeople to see the impact of their efforts in the level and growth of sales. We expect, or at least hope, that those in operations will see the impact of their efforts on costs. We expect that people working in finance see the impact of their efforts on profits and cash flow. However, the distance from these efforts to the value of the firm is usually long, not short. And most people are nearsighted.

SRC invests heavily in educating its workforce so that workers can see the impact of their actions on the value of the firm. That investment is akin to fitting employees with corrective lenses to overcome myopia. Employees are educated to see all the way from their actions to the firm's financial statements and value.

SRC's bonus plan figures prominently in its educational process. It builds on and reinforces training programs that teach all employees the basics of financial statements. It builds on a planning process in which employees participate in developing forecasts of future financial statements. It provides a reason employees would want to understand the firm's financial position and take actions to affect that position positively.

SRC constantly reminds its workforce that as a business it needs to focus on making money and generating cash. Making money refers to earning a profit, where profit is measured according to the income statement. Generating cash refers to positive cash flow, where cash flow is measured in the statement of cash flows and reflected in how the balance sheet changes over time.

SRC aims for a bonus plan that is easily described to its workforce. It typically chooses targets that relate to the financial statements. To keep things simple, SRC bases bonuses on two goals: one from the income statement and one from the balance sheet. The income statement goal might pertain to pretax profits. The balance sheet goal might pertain to the current ratio or some other measure of liquidity.

Here is what SRC does to develop the details of its bonus plan. It begins by viewing pretax profit as a pool to be shared by the firm's shareholders and the workforce. It then identifies the following three bonus-plan components:

1. The baseline for pretax profits, as a percentage of sales, below which bonuses will be zero

2. The top target for pretax profits, as a percentage of sales, above which bonuses will be maxed out

3. The highest aggregate bonus the company is willing to pay out, expressed as a percentage of annual payroll

The first two items relate to the bonus goals for the income statement. The third item relates to the total bonus paid from both the income statement goal and the balance sheet goal.

Typical numbers for SRC are 5 percent for base, 8.6 percent for top, and 13 percent for highest aggregate bonus. This means that SRC's profit plan enables its workforce to share in any profits that lie between 5 and 8.6 percent of sales, an amount that is capped by 13 percent of annual payroll.

The balance sheet goal is typically determined with a view to ensuring that the company generates enough cash to cover the bonuses. For example, suppose SRC's revenue was $7 billion and its annual payroll was $1 billion. In this case, pretax profit would have to be at least $350 million before any bonuses would be earned. The maximum bonus SRC would pay out would be $130 million, 13 percent of $1 billion. For this to happen, pretax profits would have to be at least $602 million, given sales of $7 billion. SRC would want the $130 million bonus to come out of the incremental profit associated with the difference between its baseline 5 percent and its top target of 8.6 percent. Continuing to assume $7 billion in sales, the difference is $252 million, more than the $130 million maximum bonus. (The $252 million is the difference between $602 million and $350 million.)

Of course, the $252 million might not all be cash because net income and cash flow are not the same thing. Remember that net income has to be adjusted by depreciation and change in operating working capital to arrive at cash flow from operations. In addition, the cash might be used to finance new fixed assets. And there is also incremental net income that corresponds to 5 percent of sales. Nevertheless, to keep the discussion going, suppose that the $252 million indeed equals the incremental cash.

SRC uses its balance sheet goal to focus its workforce on how to handle the cash generated. Suppose that SRC's strategic plan called for it to use any extra cash to pay down short-term debt. How could the balance sheet goal be structured so that the workforce is provided with an incentive to make this happen?

In his book *The Great Game of Business* with Bo Burlingham, Jack Stack explains. Suppose that at the time the bonus plan is put in place, SRC's current assets are $1 billion and its current liabilities are $500 million. Therefore, the company's current ratio is 2.0 ($1 billion / $500 million). It anticipates that at the end of the year, when bonuses are paid, it will have an extra $122 million, that being what remains from the $252 million additional net income after paying the $130 million bonus. This amount is in before-tax dollars. At a tax rate of 35 percent, the amount of additional cash after tax would be $79.3 million.

There are several alternatives for using the additional $79.3 million in cash. One alternative is to hold it and build up the company's current assets (cash and marketable securities or accounts receivable or inventory). Another alternative is to use the $79.3 million to pay down short-term debt. Building up the cash balance increases the current ratio to 2.16 ($107.9 billion / $500 million). Paying down short-term debt increases the current ratio to 2.38 ($1 billion / $421 million). If SRC chooses a balance sheet goal in which the current ratio target is 2.38, then the workforce will be induced to urge that the cash be used to pay down debt rather than building up the company's current assets.

Having outlined the basic parameters of SRC's bonus plan, consider some of the finer points about both its rationale and its implementation. From the perspective of rationale, SRC chose 5 percent as its baseline pretax net profit margin because it views that amount as the lowest point of profitability that is consistent with the company's situation being secure. A 5 percent pretax net profit margin corresponds to a 3.25 percent after-tax net profit margin. That low of an after-tax margin barely allows for expenditures such as the replacement of fixed assets, management of unintended inventory, and so on without resorting to using cash or engaging in external financing. In other words, a 3.5 percent after-tax margin adds no cash to the company. Paying a bonus when the margin is so low would either use cash or require external financing.

SRC chose 13 percent of payroll as its maximum bonus pool to provide its workforce with a real stake in the outcome.

Turning to the topic of implementation, SRC divides its bonus pool into two parts. One part is associated with achieving the income statement goal. The other part is associated with achieving the balance sheet goal. It treats the two goals as equally important and therefore assigns them equal weight, meaning that the bonus pool is divided in half. Given that the maximum bonus pool is 13 percent of payroll, 6.5 percent is the maximum "share rate" associated with the income statement goal, and 6.5 percent is the maximum share rate associated with the balance sheet goal.

Thus far, we have discussed the parameters defining the maximum bonus pool. Those parameters are linked to targets of 8.6 percent pretax net profit margin for the income statement goal and a current ratio of 2.38 for the balance sheet goal. What happens if actual performance comes in below either or both of these targets? Not surprisingly, the bonus pool will be less, partly because pretax income will be less and partly because the bonus plan is structured so that share rates will be less. For example, SRC divides the improvement in the current ratio, from 2.0 to 2.38, into four equal segments. It then divides the maximum bonus pool into four equal parts, with each part associated with the demarcation points of the segments. It makes each part available as the current ratio exceeds one of those milestones.

Although SRC sets its bonus plan annually, using annual targets, it administers its plan on a quarterly basis. It does so to keep bonuses salient in people's minds so that the bonus plan maintains its motivating function. SRC is absolutely explicit in saying that the bonus plan is the center of attention in its culture.

In practical terms, SRC divides the maximum annual bonus into four portions, one per quarter. These portions are not equal in size. Instead, the smallest portion is available to be paid in the first quarter, and the portions subsequently grow from one quarter to the next.

SRC determines the size of quarterly bonuses by applying the bonus-plan criteria to its quarterly financial statements. Notably, it links quarters within the same fiscal year by allowing for bonus pool rollover. If the workforce fails to earn the maximum bonus available in any quarter except the last, the unearned portion rolls over into the maximum pool available to be paid in the following quarter. Once paid, bonuses are not retracted, even if a year begins well but ends up problematically with missed annual targets.

Stock Ownership

Although a bonus plan focuses on the short-term aspects of incentive compatibility, employee stock ownership is intended to focus on the long-term aspects. Employee stock ownership is something of a double-edged sword. Theory tells us that in the absence of perfect monitoring, incentive compatibility typically requires the agent in a principal-agent relationship to bear more risk than is ideal. This feature can hold in spades when it comes to employee stock ownership.

In an ideal world, employees hold diversified portfolios and not just stock portfolios. Employees' portfolios consist of their financial assets, their real estate, their future earning power (also known as their human capital), and their insurance coverage. Diversification is about not putting too many eggs in one basket to hedge different types of risk. Holding a lot of company stock typically leads to insufficient diversification because a person's human capital egg and equity egg are in the same basket. If that basket falls to the ground, individuals can lose their livelihood for an extended period and lose financial wealth.

Although rational employees would want to exchange the stock of companies for which they work with the stock of companies for which they do not, doing so would interfere with long-run incentive compatibility. The key issue here is that the value of a firm's stock reflects its future cash flows, not just its immediate cash flows. It is possible for employees to make decisions that play out well in the short run but are disastrous in the long run. Providing employees with company stock is intended to counter this possibility.

For most employees, line of sight to bonus is much clearer than line of sight to the value of the company's stock. Just think about how difficult is the capital budgeting procedure described in Chapters 2 and 5. In theory, computing the net present value (NPV) of a project tells managers what the impact of project adoption would be on the company's market cap. Yet very few companies do capital budgeting with anything like the degree of precision and accuracy that are required to accomplish this task. A similar remark applies to economic value added. The line of sight from most employees' decisions to the present value of the future expected economic value stream is enveloped in thick fog!

Most companies fall back on heuristics to make the connection from decisions to the value of the company's stock.

For example, at SRC the P/E heuristic is used. The argument goes that the value of the company's stock is the product of the stock's P/E and its earnings. Of course, this is a tautology in that the E in P/E is earnings, and so multiplying P/E by E is nothing more than P, after cancelling out the Es. Nevertheless, the point is that P/E serves to multiply earnings. As a result, SRC executives can exhort employees that anything they can do to increase future earnings will magnify the value of their stock holdings because of the impact on P/E. Therefore, taking an action today that increases current earnings but significantly reduces future earnings might increase the value of the stock today but will cause the future value of the stock to tank.

In theory, magnification makes equity much more powerful than annual bonuses. In practice, for companies whose stock is publicly traded, there is so much volatility caused by factors outside the control of the company that attention will shift to factors that are within the company's control. And this means that most of the attention will be on the targets associated with the bonus plan.

A good resource for information on stock ownership plans is the National Center for Employee Ownership.[1] One of the most popular stock ownership plans is the ESOP. ESOP is an acronym for employee stock ownership plan. Here is how an ESOP works.

ESOPs are multifunctional. They are most commonly used for the following reasons:

1. To provide an exit mechanism for owners of closely held companies to sell their shares

---

[1]See its Web site at http://www.nceo.org/library/esops.html.

2. To provide incentives that motivate and reward employees

3. To make use of tax advantages in connection with borrowing money for acquiring new fixed assets

Typically, ESOPs are structured so that the company grants employees company stock rather than enabling them to buy that stock. The granting of stock is accomplished through a trust fund. The company can either contribute newly issued shares of its own stock, or it can contribute cash that is used to buy existing shares. If the company contributes cash, the cash might come from the company's cash and marketable securities. Or the cash might be borrowed. If borrowed, the company would typically make a series of cash contributions over time that would enable it to repay the loan at a future time.

Typically, all full-time employees over the age of 21 generally participate in the plan. The ESOP trust is structured so that employees maintain individual accounts.

The basis for allocations of stock across employees is typically relative pay. However, some ESOP allocation rules are more egalitarian.

To encourage a long-term perspective, employees do not automatically take ownership of their shares. Instead, they acquire an increasing right to the shares in a process known as *vesting*. ESOP rules call for employees to be 100 percent vested within five to seven years.

When employees leave the company, they receive their stock, which the company must buy back from them at its fair market value (unless there is a public market for the shares). Private companies must have an annual outside valuation to determine the price of their shares.

In public companies, employees must be able to vote on all issues. In private companies, employees must be able to vote their allocated shares on major issues, such as plant closings or relocation. However, the company can choose whether to pass through voting rights (such as for the board of directors) on other issues.

The Fascinating Example of Whole Foods

Whole Foods is one of the leading retail firms selling organic foods. Whole Foods prides itself on being an environmentally friendly company. It is also an open book company. Open book companies are serious about incentives. In fact, providing proper incentives to employees is what open book companies most emphasize.

On its Web site, Whole Foods states that its purpose is "selling the highest quality natural and organic products available." Do you think its employees understand that this is one of the organization's top goals? I wondered about this question.

As it happens, I am a Whole Foods customer. Shopping at Whole Foods provides me with an opportunity to do a little informal research as well as buy groceries. So, when I visit a Whole Foods store, I typically engage Whole Foods' employees in short conversations about their company. One question I ask is whether they know what the company's main goals are. More or less, most employees do know.

Whole Foods describes itself as structuring an empowering work environment that supports employee excellence and happiness. It divides its workforce into self-directed teams. Every employee belongs to a team and is called a team member. The company speaks about "motivated" team members whose efforts it appreciates and whose results it rewards.

Whole Foods' CEO is John Mackey. Mackey is a bit odd, and some might say goofy. But he does understand his business. In a December 4, 2006, interview with *The Wall Street Journal*, he explained that in the retail food business, the competitive environment is local. For this reason, Mackey has developed what he calls an empowered, decentralized culture for Whole Foods. This means that the teams in each Whole Foods store are the ones who assess the needs of their customers, evaluate their unique competitive environment, and decide on their store's product mix. In other words, Whole Foods' business culture features line of sight!

The focus of Whole Foods' incentive system is on its team leaders. In 2007, the company had more than 39,000 employees, and about 500 were team leaders. Their rewards are tied to the firm's financial performance. Whole Foods measures its performance in terms of economic value added, a concept introduced in Chapter 2. It rewards team leaders for improvement in economic value added, with the associated incentive plan participants consisting of the senior executive leadership, the regional leadership, and the store team leaders. Notably, financial rewards for each group are based on measures of economic value added that are specific to the decision environment faced by each. In other words, rewards are tied to line of sight decisions.

For psychological reasons, large pay differentials can create disincentives because of perceptions about unfair treatment. This is an important reason that Whole Foods caps the ratio of executive pay to the pay of the average full-time worker. In 2007, that ratio stood at 19. In 2006, that amounted to $607,800 as a dollar figure. Whole Foods has always maintained a cap. In years past, the cap was lower. It began at 8 but drifted up over time as the company came up against the participation constraint and had to pay more to recruit and retain talented executives. Overall, the workforce at Whole Foods seems content. For 10 years in a row, the company has been in *Fortune* magazine's edition of the

"100 Best Companies to Work For." In 2007, it ranked number five.

Earlier, I mentioned that John Mackey is a bit odd. Actually, he has more than a few gremlins of his own. Over an eight-year period, Mackey participated anonymously on a Yahoo! finance message board dedicated to Whole Foods. He did so using the screen name "rahodeb," an anagram based on the name of his wife, Deborah.

As rahodeb, Mackey's comments ranged from Whole Foods' earnings to the quality of its competitor Wild Oats to the quality of his own haircut. On the message board, rahodeb played up Whole Foods' earnings, played down Wild Oats, and responded to a critical remark about Mackey's haircut by saying that he looked cute.

The Federal Trade Commission (FTC) became involved when Whole Foods sought to acquire Wild Oats and submitted a package of materials that disclosed the postings. The FTC was not amused. Although he might not have broken any laws, Mackey came under intense criticism for his lack of judgment in participating in the message board. Although the acquisition eventually went through in August 2007, Whole Foods paid millions in court costs to deal with the issues that troubled the FTC.

In July 2007, *The St. Petersburg Times* ran a story that touched on Mackey's psychological biases. The bias they focused in on was hubris, a form of overconfidence. The article pointed out the irony of rahodeb's final posting, which appeared in August 2006. The posting was titled "Congratulations to hubris and goodbye." The title refers to Mackey having lost a bet with chat room poster hubris12000 in connection with Whole Foods' earnings and stock performance.

Although Whole Foods deserves a lot of credit for the way it has structured incentives in the past, it is worthwhile looking at history for some psychological lessons in connection with the incentives it will use in the future, especially when those incentives involve company stock.

During the 1990s, Whole Foods stock earned about the same return as the S&P 500. However, between 2001 and 2004, Whole Foods stock returned 214 percent, while the S&P returned about −3 percent. On January 14, 2005, John Mackey was very upbeat about the stock. He predicted that in 13 years, the stock price would rise from its price at the time, $46.85, to more than $800 before splits. This represents an 18 percent cumulative average growth rate!

From a psychological perspective, this kind of prediction from a CEO is strongly suggestive of unrealistic optimism and overconfidence. Long-term predictions are notoriously difficult to make, and 18 percent a year is much higher than the return on the average stock. Nevertheless, the period that followed Mackey's prediction did lend support to his optimism. In the three months after he made his prediction, Whole Foods stock earned a return of 33 percent (annualized). Interestingly, this led Mackey to suggest on April 15, 2007, that Whole Foods stock was undervalued. This comment is also suggestive of unrealistic optimism and overconfidence.

The next two years represented an interesting period in the life of Whole Foods stock (see Figure 6.1). Certainly, the remainder of 2005 was a banner year. For the year as a whole, the stock returned 63.6 percent! Alas, that represented the peak for Whole Foods' market cap. For the next two years, the stock trended down.

On November 3, 2006, Whole Foods' stock price declined by 23 percent. The market was responding to a forecasted decline in the growth rate of its same-store sales from about 15 percent in 2004 to about 7 percent in 2007. In an interview with *The Wall Street Journal* on December 4, 2006, Mackey indicated that he did not know why the

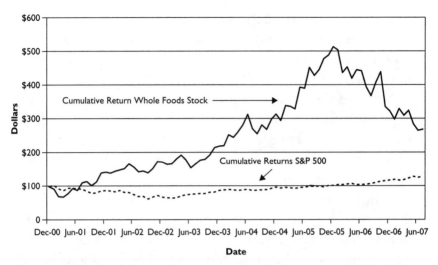

Figure 6.1 Cumulative Returns, Whole Foods and S&P 500, January 2001–June 2007

growth rate was down by as much as it was. At the same time, he acknowledged that Whole Foods was facing stiffer competition.

Finance theory tells us that you cannot expect to earn 18 percent a year over a 10-year period without being very risky or very lucky. By its nature, Whole Foods' business is not extraordinarily risky, as reflected by the fact that it uses a cost of capital of 9 percent. Finance theory tells us to be careful about expecting highly positive net present value (NPV) from projects. Positive NPV projects are expected to earn a higher return than the return associated with the next best opportunity of comparable risk. Finance theory tells us that when a company consistently earns rates of return in excess of the opportunity cost of capital, it will attract competitors. Competition from others in the form of lower prices or better quality will serve to lower future rates of return.

Whole Foods is facing competition in the market for organic foods. Notably, Wal-Mart, Safeway, and British food chain Tesco have been shifting resources to compete in this segment of the U.S. market.

NPV can be computed as the present value of the expected future economic value added stream. Remember from Chapter 2 that economic value added is the amount by which net income exceeds the level a company requires to earn its cost of capital.

Whole Foods reports that its economic value added in 2006 was $64.4 million, computed as the difference between its net operating profit after tax (NOPAT) of $215.3 million and its charge to capital of $150.9 million. It also reports that its economic value added grew by $38.6 million from 2005. This is well and good. But in a competitive industry, nobody should expect economic value added to stay positive and keep growing over time. What makes this point germane to the structure of bonuses is that Whole Foods bases its bonuses on the growth rate in economic value added.

Economic value added is a deceptive concept. It sounds plausible. However, most people have difficulty remembering its exact definition. They might remember that it is based on the concept that investors require a return on their capital. In practice, a bonus plan based on economic value added is essentially a plan based on a goal for net income. This is because economic value added is net operating profit after tax minus the charge to capital. There are a lot of mistakes that can be made in developing bonus plans. Making the plan too complex for employees to understand is one of them.

Economic value added is subtle. To help you understand one of its subtleties, let me ask you a question. Suppose that last year, a company's economic value added was $1 million. Does that mean that employees should be entitled to a large share of that $1 million because the investors have already been paid their cost of capital for the year?

The answer to this question is: not necessarily. What you need to remember from Chapter 2 is that the fundamental value of a company's stock is the sum of its book value (shareholders' equity) and the present value of its *expected* future economic value-added stream.

Think about a company whose fundamental value is the same as shareholders' equity. The present value of the company's future economic value-added stream will be zero. But economic value added will typically not be zero every year. In some years, it will be positive, and in other years, it will be negative. It is only zero on average. If a company structures its bonus plan to pay the bonus out of economic value added only when the latter is positive, then it effectively appropriates shareholders' money. This is because shareholders bear the full burden for negative economic value added but share only partially in positive economic value added.

One More Example: PSS

Physicians Sales and Service was the first national company to provide medical supplies to physicians' offices, nursing homes, and hospitals. The company was founded in 1983 by Patrick Kelly, Bill Riddell, and Clyde Young. At that time, all three had sales experience in the industry.

The three split their equity stakes unevenly. Kelly's share was 31 percent, while Riddell's and Young's shares were 23 percent each. The remaining equity stake, also 23 percent, went to an outside investor. Kelly's share was disproportionately more because he took a more active role in decision making. Ultimately, Kelly became CEO and chairman of the board until his retirement in October 2000. His replacement as board chair was Clark Johnson. David Smith was elected president and later assumed the roles of CEO and board chair.

PSS is an open book company. Kelly was the driving force behind the development of its culture. Right from the outset, Kelly focused on incentive issues. Even before the company was generating enough cash flow to pay bonuses, Kelly was distributing stock to employees.

Once its cash flow became sufficiently positive, PSS did develop a bonus plan. The company is divided into branches, and each branch has its own bonus pool. Unlike the bonus plan at SRC, where the size of an employee's bonus is linked to his or her wage or salary, PSS's bonus plan is completely egalitarian. All bonuses at a branch feature the same dollar value.

PSS describes its bonus plan in baseball terms. There are four levels dubbed single, double, triple, and home run.

To hit a single, a branch's net profit margin must be at least 5 percent. Dollar profits greater than 5 percent serve as the base for the bonus pool, and 5 percent of the base is "deposited" into the bonus pool.

To hit a double, a branch must first hit a single and also achieve the minimal acceptable sales forecast developed in the company's business plan. If it does so, a second 5 percent of the base is deposited into the bonus pool.

To hit a triple, a branch must first hit a double and also turn its assets quickly enough. Remember that asset turnover is measured by the ratio of assets to sales and represents the number of times the company must turn its asset wheel to generate sales. If the asset wheel turns too slowly, then the company's cash is not being used efficiently. PSS's target for asset turnover is one. If a branch meets the asset turnover threshold, then another 5 percent of the base is deposited into the bonus pool.

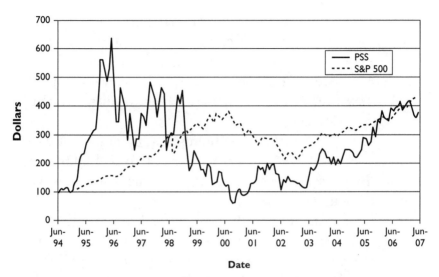

Figure 6.2 Cumulative Returns, PSS and S&P 500, June 1994–June 2007

To hit a home run, a branch must hit a triple, and net sales must exceed the minimal acceptable forecast by at least 2 percent. In that case, another 5 percent of the base is deposited into the bonus pool.

In 2007, PSS was a publicly traded company with $1.742 billion in sales. The company grew steadily under Kelly's leadership, but its stockholders experienced a rocky period after he stepped down. Circumstances eventually improved, as Figure 6.2 demonstrates.

Bonuses and Emotions

In closing this chapter, I want to mention a few additional issues about the psychological questions associated with bonuses.

If you are running a bonus plan, it's important to structure it so that people don't count on receiving the bonus. If people count on a bonus and don't get it, the pain of loss is high. Moreover, people are inclined to be aggressive about risk when they feel that they are likely to miss a goal to which they strongly aspire.

When people make their bonuses, they don't just earn more money. They also earn the right to feel additional pride. By the same token, there will be times when they will miss a bonus target and come up empty-handed. If they missed receiving a bonus by only a small amount, they are likely to experience the emotion of regret. Regret stems from the pain of imagining doing something a bit differently and having the outcome turn out fine. Regret can be a demotivator, and a good leader knows how to say things to bring down the level of regret.

CHAPTER 7

INFORMATION SHARING: EYES ON THE PRIZE

People who work for psychologically smart companies share information that belongs on the front burner. That way, they keep their eyes on the prize.

I have the feeling that the information-hoarding gremlins are the biggest obstacles a company has to overcome in becoming psychologically smart. Bo Burlingham, the executive editor at *Inc.* magazine, says that middle managers are prone to torpedo a company's attempt to institute an open book culture. Can you guess why?

For middle managers, information is power. Middle managers serve as information channels between upper management and line workers. And for this reason, middle managers worry that excessive information sharing will make their functions redundant. Moreover, financial managers are reluctant to share financial information, especially in companies whose stocks are publicly traded.

Group dynamics give the information-hoarding gremlins extra strength. Do you remember our discussion about groupthink in Chapter 5? Groupthink tends to occur because group members become overly prone to supporting other group members' positions instead of having the courage to play devil's advocate. In technical terms, groups are vulnerable to collective confirmation bias. The same dynamic operates when it comes to information hoarding. Specifically, managers appear to offer information that confirms or supports a proposal by an executive leader, but they withhold information that would fail to confirm or support that proposal.

Addressing the challenges of effective information sharing requires process. Effective information sharing transpires when managers put effective information-sharing processes in place.

This chapter presents a few examples to lead readers through the principles that underlie the development of effective processes for sharing information. An important part of these principles is the use of a behavioral checklist.

Psychology, Relationships, and Sharing Information

Most of the material I write about in this chapter focuses on how to structure processes to get people to share the right information and make that information highly salient so that it gets placed on the front burner. But in this section, I want to talk about the emotional climate in which this sharing takes place.

I imagine that the psychology you are used to reading about is a bit different from the kind of psychology associated with the bias gremlins. Most people think about psychology as pertaining to the emotional needs that motivate people. Please don't think that my emphasis on psychological biases means that I view emotional needs as unimportant. Emotional needs are extremely important, especially in organizations.

You cannot address the problems caused by groupthink and information hoarding without appreciating the emotions that cause them. These emotions involve the nature of our relationships with others. Most of us want to be liked. We like others to hold us in high esteem, to respect us. We seek to advance in social position. We like others to agree with us. So, when others disagree with us, we become concerned that they might not like us, might not hold us in high esteem, and might take actions that lead us to decline in terms of social position.

Okay, do you see the point? Suppose I belong to a group and my leader makes a proposal that I don't favor. Is my first inclination to share information in my possession that would argue against my leader's position? Or instead, do I inherently worry that doing so will make me appear disloyal, which in turn will have negative ramifications for me? And I'm not even suggesting that such thoughts are conscious. However, I am suggesting that emotions pertaining to group acceptance, loyalty, and social bonding lie at the heart of information hoarding and groupthink.

Group leaders also worry about sharing negative information. They fear being viewed as ineffective. And they fear that bad news will demoralize the workforce.

In January 2006, *BusinessWeek* published an article about *Inc.* magazine.[1] The article documents a memo that *Inc.*'s CEO John Koten had written to his staff in connection with

---

[1] See Jon Fine, "Hard Times at *Inc.* and Fast Company," *BusinessWeek*, January 11, 2006.

the company's $10 million loss in 2005. The article describes the memo as "stunningly frank."

Bo Burlingham is *Inc.* magazine's executive editor. He says that *BusinessWeek*'s reaction shows just how widespread information hoarding is in the business world. John Koten, too, understands the resistance to communicating bad news. The article quotes him as saying that communicating bad news is one of the drawbacks of open book management. Koten might have made this point in an attempt to be humorous. But the issue is very serious.

Despite having championed open book management as a publication, as a company *Inc.* was run along closed book lines. In 2006, it began a process to transform itself into an open book company. A year later, Burlingham reported being very disappointed in the pace of the transformation.

Dealing with information hoarding and groupthink in organizations takes informed leadership. Such leadership requires more than a clear sense of how people relate to each other at an emotional level. It requires knowing how to manage the way people relate to each other.

Daniel Kahneman and Amos Tversky are the psychologists who developed many of the insights that underlie behavioral finance. Sadly, Tversky died in 1996. When, in 2002, Kahneman was awarded the Nobel Prize for Economics, the Nobel committee singled out his work with Tversky about the importance people attach to gains and losses.

Leaders need to be especially attentive to the gains, losses, and emotional subtext of the way people communicate with each other in their organizations. Every interaction between people holds the potential for perceived gains and losses, especially when it comes to the issue of respect.

Leaders understand that communication styles are important because when people communicate ideas, they often send emotional messages at the same time. That is, why and how people express themselves can be as important as what they say. Criticizing somebody's idea can have the unintended side effect of somebody experiencing loss in terms of self-respect. On the flip side, there is a counterworry: If I disagree with her tonight, will she still respect me in the morning?

Human communication is deep stuff. I mentioned John Gottman's work in Chapter 4. Gottman's main research focus has been on how couples relate to each other. However, his insights apply more broadly. I particularly like his book *The Relationship Cure*, which he begins by discussing a workplace issue.[2]

Gottman tells us how important it is to understand the emotional subtext in our communications with each other. He tells us to be aware that people routinely make overtures to connect to each other at an emotional level and wait to see how others respond to those overtures.

Gottman's book is basically a five-step guide to developing better relationships. He asserts that people can build strong relationships with each other through a series of overtures and associated positive responses that over time build strong bonds. He suggests that those bonds are like money in the bank so that when people find themselves in conflict, they can draw on that bank account to keep the relationship positive.

Here is the connection between Gottman's insights and the information sharing–groupthink dynamic. If I am to be the messenger of bad news, my big fear is that those who receive the bad news will react by killing the messenger. Of course, I am speaking figuratively. What I worry about is the damage to my relationship with my group, its leader, and

[2]See John Gottman and Joan DeClaire, *The Relationship Cure: A 5 Step Guide to Strengthening Your Marriage, Family, and Friendships* (New York: Three Rivers Press, 2002).

my fellow group members. Gottman's five-step guide provides direction on how to build up emotional money in the bank so that people feel more comfortable sharing negative information.

Ford: Information Hoarder

Companies that do not have a culture of sharing information can get into deep trouble.

In about a decade, Ford's performance went from excellent in the mid-1990s to dismal. Its share of the U.S. market fell from 25 to 16 percent, as it posted a record loss of $12.7 billion for 2006. To try to restore the firm to profitability, Ford recruited Alan Mulally as its new CEO.

In September 2006, Mulally took charge of the ailing Ford Motor Company. He had previous experience with corporate repair, having put a successful turnaround plan in place at Boeing. Mulally brought with him some of the valuable techniques he had used successfully at Boeing. Among these was a regular Thursday managers' meeting designed to share information and focus on business plans.

Mulally found out the hard way that his company took more of a closed book approach to management than an open book approach. With the intent of restoring Ford to profitability by 2009, Mulally brought the heads of Ford's business units together for a Thursday session focused on financial strategy. He asked each business head to share his or her financial forecast with the group.

After the presentations, Mulally pointed out that in the aggregate, the financial plans for the individual business units did not square with the overall corporate financial plan. When he quizzed his executives about the inconsistent numbers, one manager explained that the custom at Ford was not to share everything but instead to hold some things back. Usually, what got held back was bad news.

It was at this point that Mulally began to understand the depth of the challenge he faced in changing Ford's corporate culture. He began to call for information sharing and was emphatic about not penalizing managers for delivering bad news. Instead, he applauded them for their honesty and began to focus them on taking actions to improve the results.

By July 2007, Ford's numbers began to improve. It reported a second quarter profit of $750 million at a time when analysts were expecting deep losses. When asked by the *Detroit News* what accounted for the good news for that quarter, Mulally responded that it was greater involvement throughout the organization. At the same time, he sounded a cautious note, pointing out that although the company may have turned a corner, returning to health was a long-term project that might take until 2009.

In an interview with *The Wall Street Journal* in July 2007, Mulally emphasized the degree to which he encouraged Ford's stakeholders, including its customers, to share their views and knowledge with him; as he listened to them, he took careful notes, which he kept in marked binders. In saying this, he also commented that he interprets all information through the filter of profitability growth and corporate value.

The weekly Thursday meetings serve as the heart of Ford's information-sharing process. The number of participants is 16, comprising the senior executives who are responsible for their areas of business. The main agenda item is always to review the business plan. That review serves as the vehicle for eliciting and discussing key information within the company.

The business plan that Mulally developed to bring Ford back from the brink is specific. Every participant at the

Thursday meeting shares information about how the businesses for which they are responsible are performing relative to the plan.

Mulally uses a color-coding system to denote the condition of each business. Not surprisingly, red means problematic and green means successful.

Leaders need to build up an emotional climate in which people feel comfortable sharing negative information. This is the key point of John Gottman's analogy about "money in the bank." A really great leader can sometimes find a way to add money to an account when someone delivers negative information. In this respect, Mulally provides much praise when executives report that their businesses are moving from red to yellow or yellow to green.

Here is an anecdote about the launch of Ford's new model, Edge. Executive Vice President Mark Fields had color coded that item red because he had identified problems with the car and wanted to delay the launch to address the problems. When Fields described his intention, the room fell silent. However, Mulally applauded him for bringing the problem to everyone's attention in a very visible way. And the story had a happy ending because Ford did address the problems in question and achieved a successful launch.

SRC: The Fine Art of Huddling

SRC has more than 20 years of experience putting into practice the information-sharing processes that Alan Mulally introduced at Ford. How does it work?

Lying at the heart of information sharing at SRC is a weekly meeting called the "huddle." The huddle takes place at 9 a.m. on Wednesdays. Jack Stack is very clear about the main goal of the huddle. It is to keep the workforce focused on why what they do matters by drawing people together around common goals and developing the company's human capital through training and education.

The focal point of the huddle is SRC's financial plan. During the huddle, people provide their best forecasts of how close the company will perform relative to the plan during the current month. Almost everyone present at the meeting is responsible for reporting on particular line items whose values they can influence.

Reports are more than numbers. Reports are about the business conditions that underlie the forecasts. In particular, reports are about making problems visible and bringing them to the surface. In this way, the workforce becomes aware of threats to successfully achieving the plan.

As people report their forecasts, the CFO inputs the numbers into a financial statement spreadsheet. At the conclusion of the reporting sequence, the CFO then updates the pro forma financials.

The updated pro formas serve several purposes. In terms of self-interest, the pro formas provide the best information about the likely magnitude of future bonuses. Remember, eyes on the prize! In the culture at SRC, bonus payouts are very salient. The idea is to use the bonus as a carrot to get people in the company focused on the financials, and that means the future financials that they can still affect, not the past financials that they cannot. In this respect, the pro formas also provide a broad view of the status of the company— where it is doing well and where it is doing poorly.

Earlier in this chapter, I described John Gottman's five-step approach to building strong relationships. His fifth step is finding shared meaning with others. The powers that be at SRC understand this point very well! That is why they use a single bonus system for each business, so that everyone's bonus in the business is determined by a common formula. And what the huddle does is induce the sharing of information most germane to making those bonuses as big as possible.

The huddle also introduces psychological incentives. Nobody likes to report bad news. Therefore, people will be motivated to take actions that will lead them to report good news in the future. More importantly, the sequence of weekly huddles provides evidence on how much control managers exert over their areas of responsibility. Do they provide information over time that is consistent both with past information they have provided and with other information being shared? Jack Stack says that he seriously thinks about firing a manager whose forecasts are erratic and who has difficulty explaining the business conditions underlying those forecasts.

Jack Stack is big on metaphors. Football is obviously the metaphor for the *Great Game* in the title of his book. In his view, once the huddle is over, everyone can see how the game is unfolding and what individual employees need to do to move the ball closer to the goal line.

Of course, the entire workforce does not attend the huddle. Most people learn about the information that was shared from someone who attended, either directly or indirectly. At SRC, the posthuddle sessions are called "chalk talk." Chalk talk sessions are group meetings designed to produce operational plans to address threats or to exploit opportunities.

Do you know the phrase "out of sight, out of mind"? It means that people attach greater importance to information that is readily available than to information that is less available. Psychologists call this phenomenon *availability bias*.

Jack Stack understands availability bias intuitively. Early on, he was using electronic information boards at SRC to update critical numbers and make those numbers salient for the workforce. It was that practice as much as any other that captured the imagination of *Inc.* magazine's staff back in the 1980s. You might recall the story I told in Chapter 2.

Salience is a key issue. It's not enough just to share critical information. You have to make sure the information is salient. You need to make sure it's on the front burner and glowing in neon lights! Otherwise, the bias gremlins will make salient something that is less relevant.

At Delta Airlines, Gerald Grinstein also understood salience. When he instituted his new employee bonus system in 2005, he didn't just communicate the bonus formula. He took a leaf out of Jack Stack's playbook and had large digital boards placed in work areas to track service improvements.

Commercial Casework: A Case in Best Practices

Jack Stack is definitely an inspiring guy. One of the many people he inspired was Bill Palmer, the CEO of Commercial Casework. Palmer read *The Great Game of Business* and was so impressed that he instituted open book principles at his own company. At the same time, putting those principles into practice was neither easy nor 100 percent successful. In this respect, Commercial Casework offers some extremely valuable lessons.

Commercial Casework is a small firm in Fremont, California, that manufactures high-end custom furniture for businesses and homes. The company was founded in 1976 by four brothers from the Palmer family. In 2007, Bill Palmer was CEO and the only brother still working at the firm.

Commercial Casework's early customers were jewelry stores. During the late 1970s, as California's banking industry grew rapidly, it shifted its focus to the manufacture of custom teller counters. In the 1980s, the technology industry in

Silicon Valley was giving rise to many new businesses in need of custom woodwork for their corporate headquarters. Commercial Casework leveraged its experience in producing teller counters to producing complex custom office interior woodwork. Among its customers were IBM, Apple Computer, and Oracle.

Bill Palmer read *The Great Game of Business* in 1993, a year after it was published. Enthusiastic about what he read, he purchased copies for the entire management team at Commercial Casework. The team loved the book.

Palmer then attended some of the seminars that SRC offers and became even more enthusiastic. When he got back home, he expected everyone to be as enthusiastic as he was. He expected to institute the great game at Commercial Casework with 100 percent buy-in on the part of the workforce.

As it happens, not everyone was as enthused by *The Great Game* as was Palmer, and to this day, some of his workforce has not bought into the concept. Yet despite that, for over a decade, Commercial Casework has managed to operate according to key open book principles.

Here we have an important point. Instituting *The Great Game* does not require 100 percent buy-in. Instead, it requires an informed, skilled leadership team and a critical mass below those who have bought in.

At Commercial Casework, the counterpart to SRC's huddle takes place on Tuesday afternoons at what is called the "managers' meeting." The managers' meeting is held in a conference room that Commercial Casework calls its game room. Those present for the managers' meeting are:

- Chief executive officer
- General manager
- Estimating manager

- Purchasing manager
- Production manager
- Manager in charge of installation and engineering
- Corporate controller

The people attending the managers' meeting are effectively the department heads. Each department is responsible for a particular aspect of the business. The estimating manager is responsible for putting together successful bids to win business. The purchasing manager is responsible for purchasing raw materials used to manufacture custom furniture. The production manager is responsible for manufacturing operations, meaning the actual construction of the furniture. The installation manager is responsible for the process of installing the furniture at job sites. The CEO, general manager, and controller are responsible for activities that support the main functions of the business.

The key questions for this chapter are: What do the managers talk about at their managers' meeting? How is their discussion structured?

The answer to the first question is simple. The managers talk about how well their annual plan is being implemented. The annual plan is the game plan. This is the plan that is the focus of discussion in Chapter 5. That plan and its associated objectives are highly salient. The game plan is on the front burner, not the back burner, so that all eyes are on the prize. If distractions should move the game plan to a back burner, the plan will return to the front burner the following Tuesday.

Take a look at Table 7.1, which displays a portion of a spreadsheet for Commercial Casework's 2007 game plan. It provides the beginning detail for what will prove to be a pro forma income statement.

Table 7.1 The Plan for Bids, Awards, Backlog, and Revenue

Commercial Casework Inc 2007 Game Plan

	JAN	FEB	MAR	APR	MAY	JUN	JUL	AUG	SEP	OCT	NOV	DEC	EST	PLAN	2006
BIDS															
TOTAL BIDS	4,103	6,394	4,651	3,975	4,717	6,606	8,731	5,663	4,430	5,540	4,430	4,430	63,670	57,600	**53,129**
HIT RATE	24.03	7.63	22.38	14.84	25.84	17.24	12.77	21.19	29.35	23.47	29.35	27.09			
CUM HIT RATE	24.03	14.04	16.60	16.24	18.14	17.94	16.79	17.35	18.43	18.93	19.71	20.23	20.23	25.00	**24.00**
AWARDS															
PLAN	900	1,000	1,200	1,200	1,200	1,200	1,200	1,200	1,300	1,400	1,400	1,200	12,878	14,400	
CURRENT EST	986	488	1,041	590	1,219	1,139	1,115	1,200	1,300	1,300	1,300	1,200	12,878	14,400	**12,749**
MTD								757							
ACCUM BACKLOG	3,385	2,924	2,806	2,392	2,646	3,037	3,217	3,117	3,317	3,317	3,517	3,617	3,617	3,889	**3,489**
CONTRACT REVENUE															
PLAN	1,100	1,200	1,200	1,200	1,200	1,100	1,100	1,300	1,100	1,300	1,100	1,100		14,000	
CURRENT EST	1,089	980	1,144	1,004	965	717	935	1,300	1,100	1,300	1,100	1,100	12,735	14,000	**13,390**

Commercial Casework's game plan for 2007 was developed in November and December of 2006. As you can see in Table 7.1, the plan is structured along monthly lines. The first category of line items is Bids. When the plan was developed, those putting the plan together predicted that in 2007, Commercial Casework would bid on 57,600 jobs and would be awarded 14,400 of those jobs. You can see these numbers by examining the second column from the right. You can also see that the column at the far right shows that Commercial Casework bid on 53,129 jobs in 2006 and was awarded 12,749 of those, a "hit rate" or yield of 24 percent.

The spreadsheet in Table 7.1 reflects the situation during the last week of August 2007. All the numbers to the right of the August column are forecasts. All the numbers to the left of the August column reflect what has already occurred. For example, Commercial Casework's plan calls for it to bid on 4,430 jobs in September 2007 and to be awarded 1,300 of these. During June, Commercial Casework actually bid on 6,606 jobs and was awarded 1,139 of these, less than the 1,200 it had forecast as part of its plan.

The line item Accum Backlog for accumulated backlog represents the jobs that have been awarded and have either not yet been started or have started and are ongoing. This item is the key leading indicator of future revenue. The August number for this line item is 3,117, which represents about 2.6 times the new job awards that were planned for August. Notice that the accumulated backlog rose during the first half of the year, suggesting that Commercial Casework was developing new work at a faster rate than it was completing jobs for which it had been awarded contracts.

The section Contract Revenue means just what it says but in thousands of dollars. The line item Plan in this section is the annual forecast that was made during the previous

November–December. The line item Current Est is, of course, the current revenue estimate for the month.

In any event, let us be sure to keep ourselves focused. Again, what do Commercial Casework's managers talk about during their Tuesday managers' meeting? They talk about their updated forecasts for the current month of the key items in the game plan spreadsheet. Because managers only update their forecasts for the current month, estimates for months after August coincide with the game plan.

Every line item is the responsibility of some manager. When August was the current month, the estimating manager took responsibility for updating the August estimate for Total Bids and the Current Est for August awards. When the estimate is close to the game plan, the discussion is routine. When the estimate is very different not just from the game plan but from the prior updates, the managers talk about how business conditions are changing and what effect this might have on their company down the line.

As you can see, the estimate for annual revenue lies below the game plan forecast, with $14,000 forecast in the game plan and $12,735 being the most recent estimate. In this respect, notice that actual revenue has been below the game plan for every preceding month. This pattern is symptomatic of unrealistic optimism and might merit some behavioral attention. You can be sure that this is an issue to which we will return. But first, let us keep going with the game plan spreadsheet.

Table 7.2 is the part of the spreadsheet that relates to the costs of production. This table refers to the extent to which the direct costs associated with jobs currently being worked on are estimated to be completed over budget or under budget. For example, in January, Material costs were $8,000 under budget, and Project Management costs were $1,000 over budget. For the month, total direct costs turned out to

Table 7.2 Costs of Production Relative to Budget

Commercial Casework Inc 2007 Game Plan

	JAN	FEB	MAR	APR	MAY	JUN	JUL	AUG	SEP	OCT	NOV	DEC	EST	PLAN 2006
JOB COST OVER/UNDER														
MATERIAL	(8)	(2)	(10)	(8)	(6)	(16)	13	(11)	(22)	0	0	0	(70)	(45)
PROJECT MANAGEMENT	1	(3)	(8)	(4)	(16)	(9)	(7)	(5)	(37)	(10)	(2)	0	(100)	(154)
SHOP DRAWINGS	1	(1)	1	(1)	1	(2)	(2)	(3)	(19)	(4)	(3)	0	(32)	(24)
LAYOUT	1	0	2	(7)	(9)	(7)	(7)	(6)	(37)	(8)	(4)	0	(82)	(76)
MACHINE	0	2	(2)	(10)	(5)	1	0	1	2	(4)	0	0	(15)	4
CUST ASSEMBLY	0	(2)	0	44	(11)	(10)	(9)	(1)	(31)	(22)	(5)	0	(47)	(84)
STD ASSEMBLY	(1)	(3)	(6)	(6)	(10)	(13)	(5)	(5)	(24)	0	(2)	0	(75)	8
FINISHING	4	2	5	6	5	10	5	2	(4)	1	0	0	36	76
DELIVERY	3	4	13	9	18	12	4	2	3	3	0	0	71	173
INSTALLATION	(3)	0	8	(19)	(26)	(5)	2	30	(27)	5	0	0	(36)	209
MISC COSTS	2	(2)	2	(1)	11	0	1	2	0	0	0	0	15	18
TOTAL OVER/UNDER	0	(5)	5	3	(48)	(39)	(5)	6	(196)	(39)	(16)	0	(334)	105
AS A % OF SALES	0.00%	-0.51%	0.44%	0.30%	-4.97%	-5.44%	-0.53%	0.46%	-17.82%	-3.00%	-1.45%	0.00%	-2.62%	0.78%

be at budget. In February, total direct costs came in under budget by $5,000, which was 0.51 percent of February sales. In March, total direct costs were over budget by $5,000. For the year, total costs are estimated to come in at $171,000 under budget.

Excessive optimism leads people to produce budgeted costs that are too low, thereby leading to jobs tending to come in over budget. At Commercial Casework, managers are encouraged to set conservative cost estimates when developing their budget numbers. It is possible to overcorrect for unrealistic optimism. If jobs routinely come in under budget, then it is likely that overcorrection is occurring.

Again, what do managers talk about in the managers' meeting? They talk about updating estimates. As with sales, when the over/under numbers are close to zero, meaning that estimates are close to the game plan, the discussion is relatively short. When the over/under numbers are not close to zero, it is time for a more detailed discussion.

For example, Bill Palmer describes a past occasion when the cost overrun appeared to jump suddenly to 10 percent and not decline. This observation led to a conversation about identifying the source, with the spreadsheet pointing to the line item Cust Assembly. This line item refers to custom assembly, and it was over by 30 percent. As it happens, a newly hired person doing estimation failed to implement a cross-checking procedure that was part of Commercial Casework's standard operating procedures.

The procedure called for the estimator to get his estimates validated by the production team, but he had not done so. Had he followed procedure, he would have received feedback to the effect that his estimates were off. The new hire explained that he had skipped the validation step because he was feeling overworked. Notably, the new hire's manager had failed to check to see whether the procedure was being followed. It should come as no surprise that once the problem was identified, it was quickly corrected.

The general point of the example is that the processes used to structure discussion in the meeting induced managers to uncover, discuss, and solve an important problem through the sharing of information.

After the game plan spreadsheet gets updated during the Tuesday managers' meeting, it is reprinted on a large sheet and posted in the game room for the entire workforce to see. In other words, the game plan is information that is freely and fully shared.

At Commercial Casework, the game room is a central location for the sharing of all kinds of critical information. Some of the most important information involves the detail that underlies the Job Costs Over/Under figures in the game plan spreadsheet. The manner in which this information gets shared is through a worksheet, a portion of which is displayed in Table 7.3.

Table 7.3 Specific Project Detail: Drilling Down

September Projects
Projected Over/Under Results

JOB#	CUSTOMER	PROJECT	EST	MTL	M/O	P/M	P/M	F/D
				ROBERT	LARRY			
9642	DPR	BARNEY'S NY	ED	$500	($300)	AZ	($2,400)	($500)
9652	BCCI	SANTA CLARA HSG AUTH	PAUL	($3,000)	($500)	CC	($6,200)	$1,400
9770	CCI	290 KINGS ST	PMP	$0	($200)	PG	($500)	($150)
9781	HILLHOUSE	CAL STATE 9 CREDIT UNION	EAG	$1,000	($600)	PG	($2,300)	($1,500)
9798	CANNON	W HOTEL FIREPLACE	EAG	$0	$0	PG	($500)	($450)
9828	TBI	ST JOSEPHS CHURCH	EAG	$0	$0	RC	($700)	$0

This worksheet occupies a large area along one of the walls of the game room. During the week, members of the operations team working on the various projects update their own estimates for the extent to which the jobs on which they are currently working will come in over or under budget. These entries form the basis for the estimates that are presented during the Tuesday managers' meeting. Notice that the suppliers of the information identify themselves.

People who share information do so with accountability, not anonymity. Moreover, the game room display is highly salient. Remember, it's critical to fight the availability bias gremlins.

Do you know why it is so important to share information frequently? The answer is that if problems or opportunities are identified early enough, then managers can take actions to address the situation. For Commercial Casework, that can mean reoptimizing production schedules or redesigning layouts to reduce installations costs. The saying that information is power might be a cliché, but it is a true cliché nonetheless.

Table 7.3 is a small extract from a large worksheet. In the cliché about not seeing the forest for the trees, Table 7.3 represents the trees. The game plan represents the forest seen through the filter of an income statement.

Lying below the Job Cost Over/Under section of the game plan is summary information about costs. Table 7.4 presents this portion of the game plan.

The section Direct Margin refers to dollar profit margins associated with direct costs. To illustrate, for January, the game plan forecast for Direct Margin was $363,000. This forecast was developed using the percent of sales technique described in Chapter 6, with the percent of sales taken to be 33 percent. As a percent of sales, the actual margin for January came in at 29.78 percent.

Table 7.4 Financial Plan: Computation of Gross Margin

Commercial Casework Inc. 2007 Game Plan

	JAN	FEB	MAR	APR	MAY	JUN	JUL	AUG	SEP	OCT	NOV	DEC	EST	PLAN	2006
DIRECT MARGIN															
PLAN	363	396	396	396	396	363	363	429	363	429	363	363		4,620	
CURRENT EST	324	321	370	311	299	233	286	365	315	377	337	343	3,882		
% CURRENT EST	29.78	32.74	32.34	31.01	30.95	32.49	30.64	28.08	28.64	29.00	30.64	31.48	30.48	33.00	31.39
FACTORY OVERHEAD															
PLAN	126	120	121	121	126	117	125	134	124	132	125	126		1,498	
CURRENT EST	117	116	119	115	120	105	105	134	124	132	126	126	1,439		1,394
% CURRENT EST													11.30	10.70	10.41
GROSS MARGIN															
PLAN	237	276	275	275	270	246	238	295	239	297	238	237		3,122	
CURRENT EST	207	205	251	197	178	128	182	231	191	245	212	217	2,443		2,809
% MARGIN PLAN	21.57	23.02	22.91	22.89	22.61	22.66	21.00	22.66	21.72	22.81	21.60	21.57		22.30	
% MARGIN CURRENT EST	19.05	20.87	21.95	19.58	18.48	17.82	19.45	17.77	17.35	18.81	19.23	19.75	19.19		20.98
% MARGIN CUM PLAN	21.57	22.33	22.53	22.62	22.60	22.56	22.43	22.46	22.39	22.43	22.36	22.30			
% MARGIN CUM EST	19.05	19.91	20.64	20.39	20.03	19.76	19.72	19.41	19.16	19.12	19.13	19.19			

The section Factory Overhead pertains to indirect costs, which are allocated rather than traced. Taken together, direct costs and indirect costs of manufacturing comprise gross costs, which is the basis for computing Gross Margin. To illustrate, for January, Gross Margin was forecast to be $237,000 in the plan and came in at $207,000. As a percent of sales, Gross Margin was forecast to be 21.57 percent in the plan and came in at 19.05 percent.

There is more information to be shared. The next block of the game plan involves Bonuses, General and Administrative Expenses, and an item labeled Variable Comp, which stands for variable compensation, as Table 7.5 illustrates.

The information displayed in Table 7.5 is necessary for computing Net Income, the bottom line of the income statement. And Net Income is a key aspect of the prize on which managers' eyes are supposed to focus. At the same time, the workforce will be inclined to focus on prizes in which they share. And the Game Plan Bonus and Variable Compensation represent prizes of direct interest to the workforce.

The workforce at Commercial Casework is unionized; and much of the compensation is already fixed. However, Commercial Casework has established an additional bonus to be paid out to workers if particular thresholds are met. What the game plan displays is the size of the bonus pool, the total amount of bonus money to be paid to the workers.

The size of the bonus pool is tied to company performance against the game plan. For example, in 2006, Commercial Casework contributed $60,000 to the bonus pool if the company was able to meet its game plan. The company contributed 1 percent of sales over $12 million and 50 percent of gross margin over 21.25 percent to the bonus pool. In 2006, Commercial Casework paid out $128,000 in bonuses.

The company's 2007 game plan featured a forecasted bonus payout of $126,000. As of August 2007, the company's

Table 7.5 Planned Bonus Payments and Variable Compensation for Executives

Commercial Casework Inc 2007 Game Plan

	JAN	FEB	MAR	APR	MAY	JUN	JUL	AUG	SEP	OCT	NOV	DEC	EST	PLAN	2008
GAME PLAN BONUS															
PLAN	6	15	14	14	12	10	6	14	7	15	6	6			
CURRENT EST	(8)	2	8	(5)	(10)	0	(5)	3	3	3	3	3	(0)	126	128
GENERAL & ADMIN EXP															
PLAN	166	140	140	149	163	139	159	165	141	194	151	155			
CURRENT EST	159	155	140	146	158	130	138	168	141	194	151	155	1,833	1,862	1,773
% CURRENT EST													14.39	13.30	13.24
OTHER EXPENSE															
PLAN	3	4	4	4	4	3	3	4	3	4	3	3			
CURRENT EST	1	1	1	2	1	2	1	4	3	4	3	3	27	42	38
% CURRENT EST													0.21	0.30	0.28
VARIABLE COMP															
PLAN	21	39	39	36	30	31	23	37	29	28	26	24			
CURRENT EST	18	16	34	18	10	(1)	16	19	15	15	18	18	194	364	325
CUM V/C SHARE VALUE															
PLAN	8.34	23.98	39.50	53.92	66.06	78.43	87.70	102.58	114.36	125.55	135.91	146.80		145.60	120.59
CURRENT EST	7.39	13.65	27.27	34.28	38.20	37.68	44.08	51.52	57.35	63.17	70.42	77.79	77.79		

best estimate was that it would not be paying out any bonuses for 2007. To see why this is the case, look at the most recent estimated annual revenues for 2007 against the game plan. The most recent estimate is for Sales to come in at $12.375 million, less than the $14 million in the game plan. Likewise, estimated Gross Margin at 19.19 percent is less than the 22.3 percent forecast in the game plan.

By August 2007, it was no secret that Commercial Casework was not performing well against its game plan. This information was shared with the workforce in a way that appealed to workers' self-interest—through the bonus plan. Those interested in how close they might be to earning a bonus would be aware that direct margin was about 3 percent less than called for in the game plan. They would also be aware that the most recent estimate for factory overhead was that it would end the year a bit higher than the number in the game plan. The direct margin is a number over which they have some influence, but they have no influence over factory overhead.

For Commercial Casework's executives, it is Variable Compensation rather than the Bonus Plan that reflects pay for performance. Notice that in Table 7.5, the amount for Variable Compensation in the game plan is about three times as high as the amount for the Bonus. Whereas the Bonus per capita is actually quite small, this is not the case for Variable Compensation, which comprises between 20 and 40 percent of overall compensation for executives. Variable Compensation is based on pretax income, meaning earnings before tax.

Variable Compensation features both a cash component and an equity component. The game plan shares information about the current value of the equity component on a per share basis.

The final line items making up the game plan display Net Income, both before and after tax. Table 7.6 provides the

Table 7.6 Net Income and Net Profit Margin

Commercial Casework Inc 2007 Game Plan

	JAN	FEB	MAR	APR	MAY	JUN	JUL	AUG	SEP	OCT	NOV	DEC	EST	PLAN	2006
TAXABLE INCOME															
PLAN	42	78	78	72	61	62	46	74	59	56	52	48			
CURRENT EST	37	31	68	35	20	(3)	32	37	29	29	36	37	389	728	**546**
% CURRENT EST													3.05	5.20	**4.08**
PROVISION FOR TAX															
PLAN	17	31	31	29	24	25	19	30	24	22	21	19			
CURRENT EST	15	13	27	14	8	(1)	13	15	12	12	15	15	156	291	**213**
NET INCOME															
PLAN	25	47	47	43	36	37	28	45	35	34	31	29			
CURRENT EST	22	19	41	21	12	(2)	19	22	17	17	22	22	233	437	**333**

	CURRENT	
	EST	PLAN
CONTRACT REVENUE CURRENT EST ($000)	$12,735	$14,000
NET INCOME CURRENT EST ($000)	$233	$437
NET PROFIT MARGIN (PERCENT)	1.83	3.12

bottom line detail for the income statement. In terms of net profit margin, the current estimate of 1.83 percent trails the game plan number of 3.12 percent.

Sharing information systematically, effectively, and widely within the organization is not a panacea for preventing all problems. The anecdote about the new estimating manager is a case in point.

Bill Palmer describes other examples of problems he has encountered, which the information-sharing culture has helped him address. One of my favorites involves a manager whose office displayed an organized set of white binders, each labeled on the outside with a job number and customer name. Let's call the manager Mr. Binder.

No other project manager at Commercial Casework appeared to be more on top of his jobs than Mr. Binder. Being in control is important. Jobs vary by stage of completion, and the different Commercial Casework teams become involved in a project at different stages. For example, the production team is involved at the beginning and middle of a project, when the furniture is being manufactured, whereas the installation team is mostly involved in the late stages of a project. It is the project managers who are responsible for coordinating the different project phases.

Palmer's management style is to walk around his work world a lot to keep his finger on the pulse of the company. One day, Palmer decided spontaneously to visit a particular job site for which Mr. Binder was the project manager. Based on Mr. Binder's communications, production on this job at Commercial Casework had not yet begun. When Palmer mentioned to Mr. Binder that he was headed out to the job site, Mr. Binder gulped. This was not a good sign.

When Palmer arrived at the job site, he naturally expected to find a project in its early stages, several weeks away from being ready for a Commercial Casework crew to begin installation. What he found instead was a project that was on the verge of being ready for a Commercial Casework crew to begin installation. He quickly grasped that Mr. Binder had misled the customer into believing that the furniture installation would begin shortly.

Palmer realized he had a crisis on his hands. Why a crisis? Commercial Casework had not yet begun production on this job. Yet, its customer was expecting Commercial Casework to begin installing furniture very shortly. Commercial Casework's failure to do so would cause his customer to fall behind schedule, incur large delay costs, and be very unhappy. Commercial Casework's high reputation for quality and efficiency was at risk.

Palmer made a quick phone call to his management team back in Fremont, explaining the nature of the crisis. He then quickly drove back to the company. When he arrived, he discovered that his production team had already put a plan in place to address the issue. They had assessed the material requirements for the job, assessed resource availability, reprioritized other jobs to free up equipment and workers, and secured commitments from the workforce about working overtime.

The members of Commercial Casework's management team were able to respond to the crisis quickly by sharing important information with each other. Doing so had become second nature. It was part of their culture.

As for Mr. Binder, well, he did not last out the day as an employee. After he left and the company began to clean out his office, they found that every single one of his binders was empty. Talk about the illusions!

Bill Palmer understands psychological issues such as unrealistic optimism and overconfidence at an intuitive level. He understands the importance of training his work-force to understand financial statements. In this regard, one of the criteria for being eligible to receive a bonus at Commercial Casework is reading *The Great Game of Business* as well as an SRC publication on understanding financial statements. Doing so provides employees with an incentive to understand the basic principles of open book management.

I have one additional point to make about open book companies in general. Because of their focus on common goals and service to others, open book companies tend to be community oriented. People who work for open book companies participate in projects that help those who are less fortunate. In *The Great Game of Business* Jack Stack talks about this feature of his company. I could see the same spirit at work in my visits to Commercial Casework.

UBS: A Debiasing Toe in the Water

Open book management does not necessarily include for-mal processes for mitigating psychological obstacles. In fact, debiasing games do not come naturally. They need to be purposefully structured and implemented. In this section, I describe the nascent efforts of one company to introduce some efforts at debiasing.

UBS is a major financial services firm that deals with behavioral finance issues every day. Its experience offers important lessons for all companies.

There are times when financial markets become irra-tionally exuberant and times when they become irrationally pessimistic. On any given day, a stock can be overpriced, or it can be underpriced. Investors who buy stocks when they are underpriced and sell them when they are overpriced are said to earn positive alpha. UBS is in the business of seeking positive alpha.

Proponents of behavioral finance assert that earning positive alpha is possible. But they don't say that it's easy. If anything, they assert that it's harder than it looks. Yes, that's right. If somehow you had the impression that one of the key messages of behavioral finance is that it's easy to beat the market, you've been misinformed. One of the biggest misconceptions about behavioral finance is that it tells us that if we learn a little bit about psychology, then we'll be able to go out and beat the market.

Here is a key message about behavioral finance that many people miss. The psychology that leads some investors to cause mispricing in the market can also prevent other investors from taking advantage of the profit opportunities so created. Some at UBS understand this message. Other companies can learn from their insights.

On October 11, 2006, UBS published a newsletter with the title "Alpha + Anti-consensus: What's the Street Missing?" The cover of the newsletter featured a picture of a highway traffic jam, with a lone car taking an exit ramp. The picture was a metaphor. The traffic jam represented the crowd, the consensus. The lone car on the exit ramp represented UBS.

Being anticonsensus means going against the crowd. Almost by definition, finding positive alpha requires going against the crowd. An investor who earns positive alpha does so by getting market mispricing right when so many other investors are getting it wrong.

The UBS newsletter discusses a group of stocks where the views of UBS analysts are distinctly different from their counterparts at other financial firms. In itself, this is hardly unusual. What is unusual is that the newsletter describes techniques for debiasing. These techniques are based on three specific questions that the UBS analysts described in the newsletter asking themselves about their views. The questions are:

1. What is the Street missing?
2. What could be a trigger for consensus to come in line with UBS?
3. Where could we be wrong?

The UBS newsletter discusses anticonsensus with respect to several stocks. One of these is BG Group, an energy firm headquartered in the United Kingdom. BG Group describes itself as a leading player in the energy market, whose focus is supplying natural gas on world markets. The company has operations in more than 25 countries and across five continents.

BG Group operates in four key business sectors: Exploration and Production, Liquefied Natural Gas, Transmission and Distribution, and Power. In this respect, BG Group operates along the entire supply chain for natural gas, which provides the flexibility to make adjustments to capture value along the chain when opportunities present themselves.

Figure 7.1 provides a sense of how the stock of BG Group has fared relative to that of Exxon Mobil and the S&P 500 over about a decade. Although the stock did relatively poorly during the recession of 2001 that followed the bursting of the dot-com bubble, it performed much better after the recession. Of course, there were some dips. In particular, BG Group's stock experienced a dip in August and September of 2006.

On October 11, 2006, UBS upgraded its recommendation for BG Group's stock from neutral to buy. This upgrade set UBS apart from the consensus. In other words, it was an anticonsensus move.

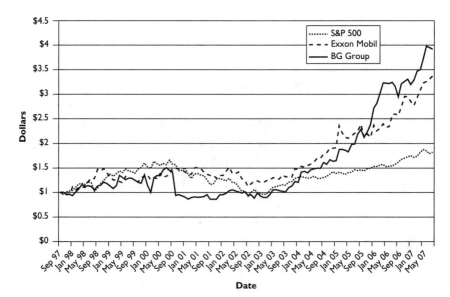

Figure 7.1 Cumulative Returns—BG Group, Exxon Mobil, and S&P 500, October 1997–August 2007

Consider now the first of the three questions: What is the Street missing? UBS analysts asserted their view that the consensus valuations did not reflect the potential upside from BG Group's exploration activities. They noted that during the previous 18 months, they believed that BG Group had added 640 million barrels of oil in new reserves. The UBS analysts judged that the fundamental value of the company had risen by about 8 percent as a result. At the time, BG Group's share price was about $62. In a nutshell, UBS analysts believed that the Street underestimated the value of BG Group's exploration projects.

UBS's second question asks: What could be a trigger for consensus to come in line with UBS? UBS analysts respond by saying that they believe the trigger will be the drilling of new wells, particularly in Norway, Brazil, and Madagascar. They point out that drilling activities rose by 40 percent in 2006; and they expected even more activity in 2007.

UBS's third question asks: Where could we be wrong? The analysts' answer is remarkably short. They simply say that exploration is risky and that their estimates of how much oil BG Group will really discover could be off.

UBS analysts express a great deal of conviction in their anticonsensus view of BG Group. They clearly assert their opinion that the company's stock is undervalued, pointing out that in the past they had judged the stock as being over-valued by 22 percent. Their recommendation change is accompanied by a forecast that the stock will increase by 22 percent in the subsequent 12 to 18 months. As it happens, the stock price rose by 32 percent over the subsequent 10 months, at a time when the S&P 500 rose by 12 percent and Exxon Mobil's stock rose by 30 percent. The company did indeed announce that it would be increasing its drilling activity in both Norway and Brazil. BG made its announcement about Norway in February 2007 and its announcement about Brazil in April 2007.

In November 2006, UBS published a second paper titled "Valuation and Accounting Footnotes," which provided a behavioral perspective on the anticonsensus paper that had appeared a month earlier. This second paper was written by a different group of analysts. One of the authors, Dennis Jullens in UBS's Amsterdam office, wrote to me after reading the October UBS report, posing the following question: Has UBS gone behavioral?

Jullens thinks so. He thinks that explicitly asking where analysts differ from the market, and writing down their responses, will help analysts limit some of the errors that are common to investors and analysts. His checklist of errors and biases that the process mitigates includes:

1. *Self-attribution bias:* People have a tendency to attribute favorable outcomes to their own skill and

unfavorable outcomes to bad luck or the mistakes of others. The three-question process provides a check for the future, to see where attribution is appropriately assigned.

2. *Confirmation bias:* People have a tendency to overweigh evidence which confirms their views but underweigh evidence which does not. By explicitly asking, "Where could we be wrong?" analysts limit the tendency to seek only confirming evidence, as it requires them to identify disconfirming evidence as part of the exercise.

3. *Hindsight bias:* People have a tendency to view events in hindsight as if they were highly predictable, whereas in foresight those events appear far less predictable. Writing up "What is the Street missing?" means that analysts have put a mechanism in place to prevent hindsight bias. This is because the reasons underlying their anticonsensus views get recorded for posterity. Hence, it will be possible in six to nine months time to revisit those reasons and see where either they got it wrong or the Street got it wrong.

4. *Overconfidence:* People tend to think they know more than they do or are smarter than they actually are. In asking where they might be wrong, analysts implicitly ask whether they might be overconfident. However, this question also raises the issue of other potential behavioral biases. Three examples that are especially pertinent are "hot hand bias," "gambler's fallacy bias," and "recency bias." *Hot hand bias* is the mistaken tendency to predict that recent trends will continue into the future. *Gambler's fallacy bias* is the mistaken tendency to predict that recent trends will reverse in the future. *Recency bias* is the mistaken tendency to overweigh recent events relative to more distant events.

The November publication concludes by suggesting that limiting the impact of these biases should improve the feedback mechanism and learning experience. In this regard, the publication stresses the importance of a written record as opposed simply to answering questions in one's own head.

You, Us, and Subprime Bias

"You and us" is UBS's global brand campaign slogan. In 2007, that slogan might have included "and behavioral bias." Despite putting a toe in the water, not everyone at UBS uses behavioral checklists. In the last half of 2007 UBS wrote down more than $18 billion in losses stemming from bad bets it made in the mortgage market. In this regard, UBS had plenty of company. Many other financial service firms, such as Citigroup and Merrill Lynch, experienced similar losses.

One of the biggest stories in behavioral finance in 2007 and 2008 involved the collapse of a real estate bubble that had begun several years earlier. The bursting of the bubble began in the subprime mortgage market, where the risk of default is relatively high.

Here is a quick sketch of how UBS and other financial services firms got so badly burned. Suppose you were lending money to someone who wanted to buy a house, but had shaky credit. That shaky credit presents a risk, a risk that the borrower might not be able to make his or her monthly payments to you. Now it's only a risk if you hold the borrower's note for any length of time. You can shed the risk if you quickly sell the note to someone else. In fact that is what most originators of mortgage loans do, namely sell the mortgage to someone else.

Typically the buyer of that mortgage loan will combine it into a pool with many other similar mortgage loans. Because of diversification, the mortgage pool is less risky than just holding a single individual mortgage. After all, a person with a mortgage might lose their job and be unable to make their monthly mortgage payments. However, it is much less likely that all those holding mortgages in the pool will experience this fate. Therefore, a security whose cash flows are the monthly payments from a pool of mortgages is less risky than its individual constituents. This type of pooled security is called a *mortgage-backed security* (MBS).

Pooling reduces some risk, but not all. The quality of an MBS backed by a subprime mortgage pool is below investment grade. Suppose that a financial services firm wanted to sell such an MBS to a pension plan whose investment policy is quite conservative. How might the financial services firm make the subprime MBS look appealing to the pension fund managers? One way is to offer insurance along with the MBS, where the insurance would cover the lost income stemming from default.

In practice, this default insurance took the form of a derivative product known as a collateralized debt obligation (or CDO). A CDO essentially provides partial insurance against default. For example, one type of CDO might cover the first 5 percent of losses, but no more. Another type of CDO might be like an insurance policy with a 5 percent deductible that covers losses up to 39 percent. Yet another type of CDO might be like an insurance policy with a 39 percent deductible that covers all losses. These types of CDOs have names such as senior, mezzanine, and subordinated.

When a financial services firm sells a subprime MBS packaged together with insurance, there needs to be investors willing to provide the insurance. Some of these investors were hedge funds operated by UBS. The hedge funds were willing to provide insurance in exchange for the associated premiums.

Insurance companies make money when the premiums they collect are larger than the claims they have to pay. UBS made money while default rates were low. They lost money when the real estate bubble ended and default rates began to soar. Rising defaults made the value of the securities they held, namely the obligation to cover losses from defaults, decline in value. UBS's writeoffs reflected their assessment of the amount by which their CDO positions had declined.

Robert Shiller documents the real estate bubble in his book *Irrational Exuberance*. After the collapse of the Nasdaq bubble in 2000, and the subsequent recession, the Federal Reserve maintained low interest rates. The low interest rates encouraged people to buy homes at very favorable mortgage interest rates. Some of the deals mortgage brokers offered homebuyers featured "teaser rates," meaning very low initial mortgage rates that would increase sharply over time. Many homebuyers took out such mortgages, planning to refinance these mortgages before the higher rates kicked in. However, when real estate prices began to decline in 2007, many homebuyers discovered that they were unable to qualify for new loans. Many found that they could not make mortgage payments at the higher rates. Adding insult to injury, the prices of many homes fell below the amounts many homeowners had originally paid. As a result, these homeowners were either forced to default on their mortgages or chose to default.

Would a checklist have helped UBS's hedge funds avoid their disastrous CDO investments? I would like to think that a behavioral checklist would have helped. My sense is that UBS managers' decisions reflected a combination of hot hand bias, confirmation bias, and overconfidence. Hot hand bias applies to managers who simply extrapolated past housing price increases. Confirmation bias applies to managers who discounted the possibility that housing was overpriced, just as stocks had been overpriced in 1999 and 2000. Remember, Robert Shiller made a strong case that the housing market was in the midst of a bubble. Overconfidence applies to managers who underestimated the risk that the values of their CDO positions would drop sharply.

In concluding this section, I want to offer a word of caution about exploiting mispricing, especially bubble mispricing. Proponents of behavioral finance point out that mispricing often gets bigger before it gets smaller. Therefore, investors who bet that a bubble is about to pop might find that they lose money when the bubble expands rather than contracts. Betting successfully on mispricing takes both luck and skill.

Some investors took the other side of the CDO trades that hit UBS, Citigroup, and Merrill Lynch so hard. Those investors profited handsomely. On January 16, 2008, *The Wall Street Journal* described the successful trading strategies of Goldman Sachs and hedge fund Paulson & Co. In particular, the article noted that Paulson's bets initially lost money as the housing bubble got bigger. But Paulson was lucky: he was able to wait for the bubble to burst.

What Have We Shared?

You've just finished reading about some best practices for information sharing at SRC, Commercial Casework, and some not-so-best practices at Ford. Sharing information in a psychologically smart way is quite a challenge. The tips from UBS provide some guidance about the use of behavioral checklists for debiasing.

In closing this chapter, I want to reiterate the emotional dimension of information sharing. You cannot underestimate the emotional element that underlies the exchange of information. When people share information, they often perceive themselves as rising or falling in social hierarchies. They worry about whom they are pleasing or displeasing. They worry about their self-images as well as the images others have of them.

You need to pay attention to the emotional dimension. When I wrote up the planning dialogue in Chapter 5, I tried to capture the flavor of the emotional subtext. If you go back and reread that dialogue, see if you can spot the emotional exchanges and how the tone of conversation either strengthens the relationships or weakens the relationships.

We have reached a point where you have encountered the basic building blocks of a psychologically smart company. What comes next is a discussion about how to put the whole thing together.

CHAPTER 8

THE WHOLE BALL OF WAX: HOW PSYCHOLOGICALLY SMART COMPANIES DO IT

The people who work in psychologically smart companies are financially literate. They engage in planning that builds in clear financial standards. They are motivated to create as much value as possible for their companies. And they freely share important information with each other.

The people who work in psychologically smart companies understand the bias gremlins. They understand unrealistic optimism and overconfidence. They understand availability bias. They understand the planning fallacy. They understand the escalation of commitment. They understand emotional intelligence[1] and its cousins, spiritual intelligence and moral intelligence.

---

[1]See Daniel Goleman, Richard Boyatzis, and Annie McKee, *Primal Leadership: Realizing the Power of Emotional Intelligence* (Boston: Harvard Business School Press, 2002).

The people who run psychologically smart companies have techniques to fight the bias gremlins. They set up training programs for financial literacy. They structure planning processes with built-in bias checks. They structure incentives that are transparent and tie directly to value. They structure information-sharing processes that encourage the open and free exchange of critical information.

By the whole ball of wax in the chapter title, I mean the integration of accounting, planning, incentives, and information sharing into a powerful, coordinated business culture.

The whole ball of wax does not happen by itself. Even if you were to bring together its separate components, the whole ball of wax will not magically assemble itself. It is kind of like baking a cake. You certainly start with the ingredients, but there's a whole lot more to baking the cake than mixing the ingredients together.

To become psychologically smart, companies need true leadership. Behavioral intelligence does not come from the ground up. It comes from the top down.

Leaders of psychologically smart companies understand the knowledge that comes from having a workforce that knows how to measure the financial health of their organizations. Therefore, they invest in their employees' financial literacy.

The leaders of psychologically smart companies understand the direction that comes when members of a financially literate workforce take ownership of a business plan. Therefore, they develop clear plans that feature extensive involvement and buy-in from a workforce that both understands and contributes to the financial standards embodied within the plan.

The leaders of psychologically smart companies understand the effort that comes when rewards are based on company performance relative to the plan. Therefore, they use bonuses and equity sharing to align the financial interests of employees with those of the company's investors.

The leaders of psychologically smart companies understand the efficiency that comes from effective communication among the members of the workforce. Therefore, they structure regular meetings in which pertinent information about performance relative to the plan goes on the front burner to be shared, not on the back burner to be ignored.

These are the ingredients. Here is how they combine to form a whole ball of wax. A financially literate workforce participates in the creation of a realistic plan, commits to that plan, learns how their actions will affect the degree to which the company achieves the plan, are provided with incentives that induce them to want the company to do as well as possible relative to the plan, and are given the information they need to adapt their actions in the course of implementing the plan. A company that puts all of this in place fires on all four cylinders: accounting, planning, incentives, and information sharing.

There is also the emotional glue that binds. The leaders of psychologically smart companies understand that psychological forces can be both beneficial and destructive. Therefore, they are explicit about encouraging emotionally intelligent behavior. The leaders of psychologically smart companies understand that the best incentives package financial rewards together with nonfinancial rewards. Therefore, they combine money, stock, praise, and recognition.

The leaders of psychologically smart companies understand that they need to foster the right kind of emotional environment. This means cultivating within people the need to feel like winners. It also means providing people with support when they end up not feeling like winners. Remember that people who perceive themselves to be in the domain of losses are prone to take bad risks, hoping to beat the odds.

I will tell you that building a successful culture takes effort. It takes focus. It takes practice. If it were easy to do and came naturally to most, many companies would already be doing it. But they are decidedly not doing it.

Most people find accounting and finance dull and dry. Psychologically, they lack the self-control to develop that knowledge and apply it. Therefore, the workforces of most companies are financially illiterate. Psychological biases such as unrealistic optimism and overconfidence underpin the planning fallacy, which explains why most companies plan poorly. These same biases operate to inhibit sensible reward mechanisms. Finally, psychological factors are also at work to inhibit the effective sharing of information, which is why managers of most companies tend to hoard valuable information.

Psychologically smart companies make the effort and then succeed. How do they do it? In their book *A Stake in the Outcome*, Jack Stack and Bo Burlingham offer a set of principles. Know the rules of the game, obtain information on how the business is performing, take the best action within the rules of the game, and experience the rewards of success. Is it that simple?

Southwest Airlines: How They Do It

Southwest Airlines does it. They run a psychologically smart company, at least most of the time. They train their employees to be financially literate. They plan. They use a mix of financial and nonfinancial incentives. And they absolutely excel at sharing information. They've got the whole ball of wax!

What is really important is not just the fact that Southwest has structured processes for accounting, planning, incentives, and information sharing. What is really important is that they have figured out how to make these four processes work together! They are like a car firing on all four cylinders.

Southwest has succeeded against the backdrop of an airline industry in deep trouble, which makes its success especially impressive. Just to remind you, in Chapter 4, I pointed out how financial illiteracy got United Airlines into bankruptcy. In Chapter 7, I pointed out how improved incentives and information sharing helped Delta Airlines get out of bankruptcy. In contrast, Southwest Airlines has thrived! According to some analysts, Southwest carries more passengers within the United States than any other airline.[2]

Let's take stock of Southwest's financial performance. Southwest is a publicly traded company, so we can track the return to investing in its stock. Suppose that at the end of 1989, you invested $1 in the stock of Southwest Airlines. How well would you have done, both absolutely and relative to investments in other airlines like United or Delta, or for that matter relative to an S&P 500 index fund?

Take a look at Figure 8.1. Had you invested in Southwest Airlines, your $1 would have grown to $14.79! In contrast, a $1 investment in American Airlines would have been

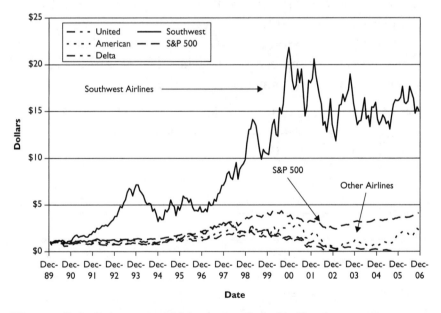

Figure 8.1 Subsequent Value of a One-Dollar Investment on December 30, 1989, in Southwest Airlines and Other Airlines Compared to the S&P 500

[2]See Micheline Maynard, "Another Route for Sick U.S. Airlines? Delta and Northwest May Need to Go beyond Traditional Tactics," *The New York Times*, September 29, 2005; see also Drew Griffen and Scott Bronstein, "Records: Southwest Flew 'Unsafe' Planes," *CNN*, March 6, 2008.

worth $2.92 at the end of 2006. Over the same period, a $1 investment in the S&P 500 would have been grown to $4.14. As for investing in United or Delta, well, you can see the bad news for yourself.

Southwest Airlines is a special company. You only have to look at the time path of its earnings since 1971, which I display in Figure 8.2, to see that this is so. In 2006, Southwest ranked number one among all U.S. airlines in financial performance, number one in operating performance, and number two in the quality of its customer service. Southwest claims to be the only U.S. airline that actually increased its profits in the immediate wake of September 11. It was even profitable during the recession of 2001–2002, although you can see from the figure that earnings in 2002 did fall dramatically after 2001.

What has made Southwest Airlines so special? The answer is simple: Its culture features the whole ball of wax. It's a psychologically smart company.

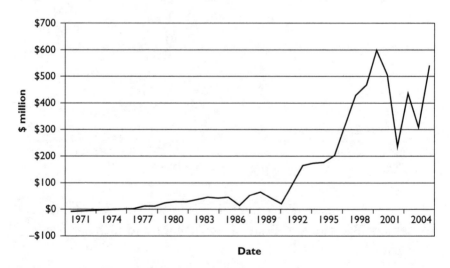

Figure 8.2 Earnings, Southwest Airlines, 1971–2005

Rollin King and Herb Kelleher are Southwest's cofounders. They first sketched out the strategic idea for Southwest Airlines in 1967 on a cocktail napkin. Rollin King did the sketching, and Herb Kelleher did the responding, telling him, "Rollin, you're crazy." After a pause, Kelleher continued: "Let's do it!"

Kelleher, Southwest's longtime, legendary board chair had a mantra that he repeated often: "In good times, manage as though bad times are just around the corner because they're sure to come."[3]

Think about this mantra. Does anything come to mind? Any concepts described in Chapter 1? Any psychological biases attributed to other executives? Yes, indeed: unrealistic optimism and overconfidence. Kelleher's mantra serves as a constant reminder to beware of becoming too optimistic and too confident.

What does Southwest do when it comes to financial literacy, planning, incentives, and information sharing? I put this question to Rita Bailey, who served as director of human resources at Southwest and was with the firm for 25 years.[4]

Rita Bailey told me that Southwest's approach to being psychologically smart is embodied in its culture.[5] A key part of the culture is being financially literate about costs. Keeping costs down is a major reason Southwest's earnings trajectory is so impressive. Southwest is a very cost-conscious company. In 2002, on average, it cost Southwest about $2.90 in labor expenses to fly a passenger one mile, which was considerably lower than the cost of its competitors.

[3]See "Maverick Boss Put Jobs and Fun First," *Times of London*, June 20, 2002.
[4]Rita Bailey left Southwest Airlines to begin her own consulting firm, QVF Partners. QVF stands for quality, value, and fun.
[5]Interview, April 17, 2006.

Psychologically smart companies invest heavily in employee training so that the messages communicated within the firm take place against the backdrop of maximizing the value of the company. Southwest takes its training seriously enough to have boosted its training budget in the wake of September 11.

At the heart of its training is Southwest's University for People. The university includes a training facility that is situated in an old 40,000 square foot Dallas terminal. Southwest is based in Dallas. The company spends about $3 million per year on training.

Bailey describes the training program as the company's crown jewel, a place to come and feel inspired! Its training structure instills its culture in every newly hired employee.

Southwest does something very clever in its training program: It uses a simulation game, called Zodiac, as part of its training to help employees understand the big picture and therefore engage in effective information sharing.

I'm going to get on my soapbox for just one sentence. Properly used, simulation games are the most effective tool for building psychologically smart companies!

Okay, I hope you're ready to hear more about Zodiac. Zodiac was created by the company Paradigm Learning. Southwest uses Zodiac in its leadership-development program. Zodiac's training goals are to teach participants how to manage the sources and uses of funds at Southwest Airlines to maximize company profit. In other words, Zodiac is designed to help employees understand the big picture: where Southwest generates its revenue and where it spends its money.

The participants in Zodiac comprise Southwest employees holding a supervisor title or higher. Southwest initially used the game to train managers but then shifted its focus to supervisors. The company incorporated Zodiac into the fourth week of a four-week leadership-development plan used to train every new supervisor.

Players in Zodiac are divided into groups, each owning Zodiac Industries and each playing their own version of the game. Every group is responsible for making business decisions over four simulated years. For example, players choose between alternative ways of taking on debt and whether to spend corporate funds on research and development (R&D), manufacturing equipment, paying down debt, new management processes, quality improvement initiatives, and employee programs.[6] Significantly, players learn how to base these decisions on Zodiac Industries' financial statements. Key game variables are posted on a game board to help players see the big picture and share information about the big picture.

Zodiac takes between four and five hours to play. It kicks off a two-day training program and concludes at around 2 in the afternoon. The rest of the afternoon is titled Connections, which lasts until 4:30. Here, Southwest Airlines' game board, involving Southwest's financials, replaces the game board that was used for Zodiac Industries. In this way, training participants discuss how what they have just learned in Zodiac relates to Southwest's business.

This training helps people see how a dollar of airfare revenue is spent and how little of that dollar is left at the end of the day. This training helps people understand the difference between fixed and variable costs and how to compute breakeven points for seats filled with respect to a specific flight profitable. In other words, this training serves to help employees not only understand their specific jobs but to understand and communicate the big picture at Southwest.

The second day of the two-day leadership-development training program is called "teach-back" and is devoted to drilling down on key principles. Here, each group picks one major learning point from the game and teaches that point

[6]Interview with Travis Peterson, manager, University for People, August 18, 2006.

to the rest of the participants. Teach-back is followed up when game participants take these principles and teach them to the employees they supervise; if done properly, this means that the training spreads.

In psychologically smart companies, financially literate employees understand their company's big picture. And in understanding the big picture, they learn to appreciate their own role in that picture as well as the roles of people doing other kinds of tasks.

Getting this cross-functional perspective is important. That is why Southwest trains people in cross-functional groups who come from different areas of the company: maintenance bases, headquarters, airports, in-flight operations. If you were to look at a row of people sitting together in a training room class, you might see someone from finance sitting next to a ramp work supervisor, who in turn is sitting next to a flight attendant supervisor. Southwest finds that the dialogue generated within this mix tends to be incredibly rich. More important, the dialogue serves to generate richer communication when employees are involved in their day-to-day activities on the job.

Southwest is an ace planning organization. The managers at Denver's airport found this out firsthand when they met with Southwest's planning team to negotiate a Southwest expansion into Denver and came away with the impression that Southwest had the best planning group they had ever encountered.[7]

Planning is a key reason Southwest has managed to be a low-cost producer. In the past, when oil prices were low, Southwest engaged in some shrewd hedging activity to lock

[7] See Susan Warren, "News in Depth: Southwest Switches Its Flight Plan— Losing Lock on Low Fares Amid Higher Costs, Leaner Rivals, Budget Carrier Gets Set to Enter Expensive Denver Market," *The Wall Street Journal Europe*, November 29, 2005.

in low fuel prices. The company began to hedge its fuel expenses in 1999. In 2007, they had hedged 85 percent of their total fuel expense for the current year. In addition, they locked in below-market rates through 2010.

Southwest's hedge was extremely valuable in the second half of 2007 when the price of oil soared to nearly $100 a barrel. The average price in 2006 had been around $66 a barrel, and in 2007 it was $72 a barrel. While Delta Airlines reported a $70 million loss for the fouth quarter of 2007, Southwest reported a profit, noting that its hedging strategy had saved the firm $300 million that quarter.

Clearly, Southwest gained an important cost advantage by hedging through planning. Fuel expenses are the second most important cost factor after labor. For example, in 2005, United's fuel cost per mile was $3.32, and for Frontier Airlines, it was $2.82. In contrast, Southwest's fuel cost per mile was $1.54. The difference is important because Frontier actually had lower nonfuel operating costs than Southwest. But those lower nonfuel operating costs were not enough to overcome the fuel cost differential.

In case you might be under the illusion that cost has been Southwest's only advantage, I should point out that Southwest has a long record of superiority in many categories, such as the following: on-time arrivals, baggage handling, number of complaints, and canceled flights. Do you recognize the items in this list? You might remember the discussion from Chapter 6, when I pointed out that some of these items also appear in the bonus plan at Delta that Gerald Grinstein instituted.

In her time at Southwest, Rita Bailey thought a lot about incentives. Financially, Southwest ties financial rewards to its plan. If the company turns out to be profitable, all employees automatically share in the profits. Contributions to employee retirement accounts are made automatically. Executives at the level of vice president and above receive a bonus on top of profit sharing. Bonuses are linked to how well managers stay within their budgets. During the 1990s, Southwest added stock options to profit sharing.

Being financially literate, employees understand the goals established within their budgets and understand that their goals are tied to the company's net income. They understand that if they miss their goal, they will have to deal with a profit sharing penalty. Therefore, as the fiscal year progresses, employees keep track of where they are, where they need to be, and what they can do to affect the result.

Bailey emphasizes that Southwest's culture focuses heavily on treating people in the workforce like owners. Employees receive a constant message: "You're an owner. You're what makes the business work, so you have to understand the business. This means understanding information that is relevant to the success of the business, and includes information about the competition, and about where the money goes."

Southwest excels at sharing information. The company constantly sends messages about what it call its three Ps: pennies, planes, and people. Southwest's communications, newsletters, flyers, and message to the workforce all seek to keep the big picture on the front burner so that workers know what happened with business last year and know the current state of business going into the current year.

Southwest is a psychologically smart company that fires on all four cylinders. Do you know what this means? It means that because they're financially literate, keep score, and have a stake in the outcome, Southwest's employees are prone to ask what they can do to make the company more profitable, and they know where to go for answers.

The company thinks a lot about the challenges of communicating with people at different organizational levels. People in the company pay attention not just to the messages they send but to the messages employees receive, understand, and internalize. Rita Bailey says that this is especially the case for new employees, who are highly focused on personal issues, such as making rent and car payments, as opposed to the big picture that occupies Herb Kelleher's mind.

Among Southwest's other communication tools are The Real Deal and Knowing the Score. The Real Deal is a leader-led video that reinforces the kinds of connections at Southwest that are featured in the leadership-development program. Knowing the Score is a monthly piece that is distributed companywide and shared with all employees. Remember that knowing the score is what financial literacy is all about.

Southwest even communicates with its customers through a blog.[8] Southwest employees post articles and comments on the blog, and customers are provided with an opportunity to join a threaded online conversation about the topics presented. Figure 8.3 displays the funlike feel of the Web site and the company's overall philosophy about having fun in business.

Figure 8.3 Part of Southwest Airlines Web Site display

[8]The Web page is http://blogsouthwest.com.

The Management Illusion Is No Illusion!

I hope that by now you are persuaded that the management illusion is no illusion. I hope you are persuaded that there is significant untapped value in making a company psychologically smart. However, if you are still in need of persuading, I invite you to contrast the experiences of Southwest and United.

Before United's bankruptcy in 2002, both United and Southwest featured employee ownership. Like the employees at United, employees at Southwest also sacrificed pay for five years to build an equity stake in their company. Yet the contrast in the outcomes for those two firms is incredibly stark.

Why did Southwest thrive when United failed? The answer, I suggest, is that Southwest is a psychologically smart company, whereas United is not.

Rita Bailey strongly articulates the position that employee relations are central to running a company well. She says that at Southwest employee relations have always been healthy, even during the difficult period after September 11. She points out that the story was not the same at United, where employee relations were unhealthy. In her view, because relations at United were so poor, United didn't treat its employees like owners, and consequently, the employees didn't feel like owners, even though their equity stake in the company was high.

In a psychologically smart company, almost all the employees know the company's critical numbers. If United was psychologically smart, everyone in the organization would know that $4.60 per seat mile is too high a cost to be sustainable. Everyone in United's organization would understand what needed to be done to change the company's cost structure to make it competitive in the long run. In fact, everyone in its organization would have understood the situation long before the point of crisis was reached—and would have moved to do something about it.

In psychologically smart companies, workforce members come to hold a shared vision about the company and figure out how to work together. Bailey tells us that other major airlines were never able to learn what it takes to get people to work together. In contrast, Southwest excels at getting people to work together.

A general lesson we can all take away from the inspection incident is that nobody is immune to mistakes, even in psychologically smart companies. Southwest's maintenance crew made mistakes, they failed to share information, and the company's CEO initially missed the big picture. We are all vulnerable to mistakes. Only the overconfident believe themselves to be invulnerable. Although debiasing can mitigate bias, it is unrealistic to expect that it will eliminate bias. That is why it is so important for everyone to be vigilant about debiasing.

At the same time, like all companies, Southwest has imperfections. In 2007, the company had some negative publicity for its handling of passengers who were dressed in ways that airline staff judged to be excessively provocative. On separate occasions, two young women were asked at the gate to cover themselves up if they wished to fly. One adjusted her sweater and shirt. The second wrapped a blanket around herself for the duration of the flight. The point is that Southwest has no dress code, even though it does reserve the right to deny service.

Both women took their stories to the national media. One told her story on *The Dr. Phil Show*, where she listened to an apology sent to her by Southwest CEO Gary Kelly. The second told her story to KNBC-TV in Los Angeles.

After the first incident, Southwest's President Colleen Barrett sent an e-mail to employees reminding them that the airline has no dress code. Apparently, she didn't share the information well enough because then the second incident happened. And then, a third incident happened several weeks later when a young male passenger was told he could not board his flight wearing a T-shirt with the words MASTER BAITER emblazoned across it.

As I said, Southwest's information sharing is good but not perfect. Oh, and by the way, do you know how Southwest attendants used to dress in the 1970s? They wore hot pants. At that time, it called itself "The Love Airline"! Ironic, huh?

In early March 2008, an issue came to light that was far more serious than choice of attire. Southwest disclosed that in March 2007 it failed to conduct adequate safety checks on 46 older planes in its fleet of 520 aircraft. The planes in question were all Boeing 737s, which have a history of developing cracks in the fuselage. In 1988, a crack actually caused the skin of a Boeing 737 operated by Aloha Airlines to peel off in midflight, killing a flight attendant. This incident led the Federal Aviation Administration (FAA) to institute mandatory inspections for the 737s.

Despite all the other tasks it does well, somehow Southwest's maintenance inspection processes failed. It's not clear why this happened. Part of the reason might have been that the criteria for doing the inspections involved conflicting directives from the FAA. In this regard, the criteria determining when an inspection is due depend on a mix of factors, such as whether planes have been modified and how many hours they have been flown.

As it turned out, six Southwest aircraft had developed cracks. Some cracks were as long as four inches, although manufacturer Boeing asserts that cracks less than six inches compromise neither a 737's structural integrity nor its safety. Fortunately, no major incidents occurred. Southwest maintained its record of never having had a catastrophic crash.

On March 15, 2007, Southwest voluntarily disclosed its inspection lapse to the FAA and completed its inspections within the following ten days. During the interval, the company decided to continue flying planes that had not been inspected and repaired. Apparently, it did so with verbal permission from an FAA inspector. However, in its written communication to the FAA, Southwest indicated it was indeed in full compliance, whereas this was not so. In response, the FAA announced that it would impose a $10.2 million fine, a record amount for a safety violation.

Southwest's CEO Gary Kelly's initial reaction to the FAA's announcement was to be defensive. He argued that the FAA was being unfair and had exaggerated the flight risks in question. In doing so, he missed key psychological issues.

The first psychological issue involves Southwest's customers. They could easily have lost trust in the airline, and trust was one of Southwest's most valuable intangible assets. In this regard, most psychological studies conclude that people form inaccurate assessments about risk. Southwest's customers learned that the airline was flying passengers around the country in unsafe planes whose skins could peel off in midflight. They would not understand the complexity of the inspection criteria, nor whether a two-inch crack in a fuselage was a major problem or a minor problem. In addition, Congress announced that it was launching an investigation and would hold a hearing. Loss of trust and reputation was a bigger danger to Southwest than the FAA fine, and that was the issue that Gary Kelly needed to address.

The second psychological issue was that the FAA was embarrassed and had to act forcefully to maintain its own reputation for protecting the flying public. In March 2007 one of its inspectors allowed Southwest to fly planes that had not yet been inspected. However, the FAA's paperwork from Southwest showed that the airline was only flying planes that had been inspected and repaired. The agency did not learn the truth until a year later, when an FAA whistle blower tipped them off.

After his initial defensive reaction, Kelly realized that he needed to address the key psychological issues. He changed his approach, apologizing both to customers and to the FAA for Southwest's safety lapse. He talked openly about the need to regain the public's trust and work constructively with the FAA. He grounded 41 of Southwest's aircraft for re-inspection, placed three employees on leave, and hired an outside consultant to analyze the company's maintenance procedures. He also acknowledged that for an entire year maintenance personnel had withheld vital information from the head of maintenance and company executives.

Despite Southwest's imperfections, employees at Southwest have a shared vision. Bailey says that regardless of the tribalism and infighting that comes with the territory, Southwest employees are like warriors who band together to meet challenges. They take care of each other. They know how to put aside their differences, regardless of what is happening internally, to face external threats.

Do you know what we're talking about? We're talking about emotional intelligence. We're talking about relationships as the glue that binds.

Southwest will need these advantages going forward, as the competition heats up, and its fuel price advantages decline. In 2007, fuel prices rose dramatically. Crude oil prices went from around $60 per barrel to around $100 a barrel. But Southwest had hedged 85 percent of its fuel supply at less than $50 a barrel. The thing is that after 2007, far less of its fuel supply is hedged at below-market prices. Between 2008 and 2010, the percentage hedged declines from 45 to 17 percent. In addition, other low-cost airlines are working to compete with Southwest on service, such as providing more legroom, personal television screens, and on-time arrivals.

Southwest responds to competitive challenges through its culture. Bailey says that Southwest makes a constant effort at nurturing, aimed to let employees know how important and respected they are. According to her, this nurturing and continued reinforcement cause people to feel like owners.

Her view is that incentives involve more than money. Ownership is not just about profit sharing. Why? Because profit sharing by itself is never enough when dealing with the spectrum of human needs. Bailey emphasizes that employees need to be acknowledged as human beings. She speculates that if Southwest had profit sharing without its nurturing culture of relationships, it probably would have the same type of experience as United.

In Bailey's view, if employees have unmet psychological needs, they will seek to meet those needs through additional monetary rewards, continually asking: "How much more money can we get?" She responds that it would never be enough. Rather, it's the relationships that get employees to truly feel like owners.

As evidence for her views, Bailey points out that pay at Southwest is not especially high. Yet, in the wake of September 11, 2001, employees willingly gave $2 million back to the company through payroll deductions to ensure the stability of their employment. Why the willingness to be so generous? The answer is because Southwest employees truly feel like owners.

Ownership is more than financial ownership: It is also a state of mind. Bailey contends that if employees feel well treated, they are willing to give back. If employees are treated like manure, then the only way for them to fight back is to refuse to give back. Anyone who doubts the wisdom of this maxim might wish to ask the mechanics at United why they were unwilling to give back 7 percent to save the company from bankruptcy and their own stock from becoming worthless.

Bailey makes one last point: the need to recruit the right people. She contends that doing so is the most important part of the business because well-run companies need to be staffed by people who have an innate interest in serving others. That might be why airline attendants on Southwest flights behave like tour guides. She asserts that there are some personal characteristics that you can buy but simply cannot make.

Using Simulation Games

It's soapbox time! I am a big believer in using simulation games as a tool for building integrated business cultures. A good simulation game captures the complexity of a real business environment. And that is a good thing if you attend the school of hard knocks because in a simulated environment the mistakes are less costly than is learning everything on the job.

The rest of this chapter describes how to use simulation games to build great businesses. In great businesses, accounting, planning, incentives, and communication all work to reinforce each other. Great businesses invest in developing workforces that are financially literate. A financially literate workforce has the knowledge to develop a coherent plan. A financially literate workforce is also able to track performance against the plan. An incentivized workforce wants to track performance against the plan and then use the tracking information to take corrective action if necessary. A communicative workforce shares information vital to taking action, be it planned or corrective. The left hand cannot do its job well without knowing what the right hand is doing, and vice versa.

What simulation games do is help people learn to develop an integrated set of effective, psychologically smart processes for accounting, planning, incentives, and information sharing. And I did say "integrated," and I did say "psychologically smart." All companies engage in accounting, planning, compensation, and information sharing. The challenge is to do so in an integrated way that is psychologically smart.

In the remainder of the chapter, I will take you through a discussion of what is involved in a behavioral simulation exercise. The exercise is roughly based on how I teach my students to roll up the whole ball of wax.

I favor a simulation game that is played in groups of three to six, with five being ideal. This is not a video game played by a single player with a joystick. Players assume the roles of corporate executives who are in charge of functional areas. The roles to be played are chief executive officer (CEO), chief financial officer (CFO), chief operating officer (COO), chief officer for sales and marketing (CSM), and the chief officer for human resources (CHR).

The context for this game is the EnviroStuff example from Chapters 4 and 5 to illustrate key issues associated with financial literacy and planning. Those chapters are essentially prep work for playing the game. Chapter 6 is prep work for how to develop a compensation system. Chapter 7 is prep work for the sharing of information. Those chapters provide you with the ingredients for the recipe of how to bake a psychologically smart cake. It's now time to mix those ingredients and bake the cake.

Players play the game over a sequence of years, numbered 0 through 10. During the course of play, they make decisions about purchasing, staffing, production, pricing, inventories, and financing. What makes the game especially exciting is having enough people so that several groups can play the game at the same time.

If 20 people play the game at the same time, then four teams can compete against each other for the same customers. That really makes people's juices flow.

A competitive setting ratchets up the emotional temperature. That higher temperature is terrific for inducing the kind of mental states that are in place when real business decisions are made. Having an elevated emotional environment is ideal for learning purposes because the value of the processes is highest when players work to fight psychological biases, which is to say, debias.

In the game, different EnviroStuff companies compete for customers. They do so by submitting competitive bids to an auctioneer. The auctioneer rank orders the bids using an algorithm, which the players never see directly, and then announces the bidding outcomes. In a classroom setting, the bidding results are announced one day after the bids have been submitted. Let me tell you, the interval between submission and the announcement of the results is marked by anxiety and high tension.

Players play the EnviroStuff game using an Excel spreadsheet consisting of several worksheets. Each worksheet pertains to exactly one business function: general management, finance, sales and marketing, operations, and human resources. Each player takes responsibility for at least one major worksheet.

Figure 8.4 displays the introductory worksheet for the game, Introduction. This worksheet provides some basic information about the game. At the bottom of the screen, you can see a series of tabs. The rightmost tab is the worksheet Introduction. To its immediate left is a tab for Human Resources. Continuing left, you will see a tab for Sales and Marketing and one for Bids. The tab at the extreme left, labeled Oper Investment and Disposal, is for the operations worksheet associated with the purchase and disposition of fixed assets. Further to the left, and out of sight in Figure 8.4, is a series of tabs that pertain to other decision tasks for operations, finance, and general management.

Each simulation company uses two game files to play the game. The first file is a "live" file, in which players enter their real decisions and submit them to the auctioneer in connection with their bids. The second file is a "planning" file. The planning file is almost the same as the live file but is only used for planning purposes.

Figure 8.5 displays the tab Human Resources for the planning file. If you look at this figure, you will see simulation years across the top in row 1. The other rows contain

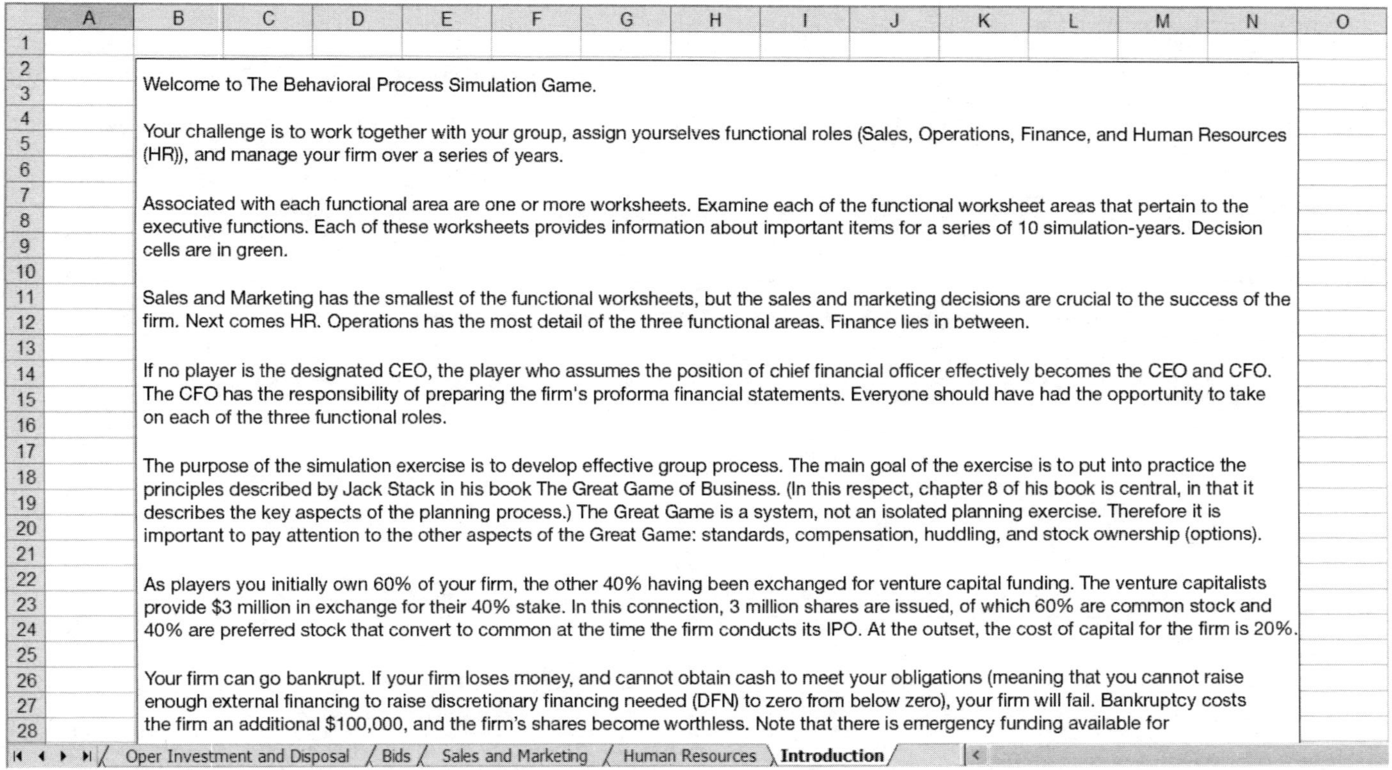

The Behavioral Process Simulation Game — spreadsheet content:

Welcome to The Behavioral Process Simulation Game.

Your challenge is to work together with your group, assign yourselves functional roles (Sales, Operations, Finance, and Human Resources (HR)), and manage your firm over a series of years.

Associated with each functional area are one or more worksheets. Examine each of the functional worksheet areas that pertain to the executive functions. Each of these worksheets provides information about important items for a series of 10 simulation-years. Decision cells are in green.

Sales and Marketing has the smallest of the functional worksheets, but the sales and marketing decisions are crucial to the success of the firm. Next comes HR. Operations has the most detail of the three functional areas. Finance lies in between.

If no player is the designated CEO, the player who assumes the position of chief financial officer effectively becomes the CEO and CFO. The CFO has the responsibility of preparing the firm's proforma financial statements. Everyone should have had the opportunity to take on each of the three functional roles.

The purpose of the simulation exercise is to develop effective group process. The main goal of the exercise is to put into practice the principles described by Jack Stack in his book The Great Game of Business. (In this respect, chapter 8 of his book is central, in that it describes the key aspects of the planning process.) The Great Game is a system, not an isolated planning exercise. Therefore it is important to pay attention to the other aspects of the Great Game: standards, compensation, huddling, and stock ownership (options).

As players you initially own 60% of your firm, the other 40% having been exchanged for venture capital funding. The venture capitalists provide $3 million in exchange for their 40% stake. In this connection, 3 million shares are issued, of which 60% are common stock and 40% are preferred stock that convert to common at the time the firm conducts its IPO. At the outset, the cost of capital for the firm is 20%.

Your firm can go bankrupt. If your firm loses money, and cannot obtain cash to meet your obligations (meaning that you cannot raise enough external financing to raise discretionary financing needed (DFN) to zero from below zero), your firm will fail. Bankruptcy costs the firm an additional $100,000, and the firm's shares become worthless. Note that there is emergency funding available for

Sheet tabs: Oper Investment and Disposal / Bids / Sales and Marketing / Human Resources / **Introduction**

Figure 8.4 Introductory worksheet for the Behavioral Process Simulation Game

289

	Year ==>		0	1	2	3	4	5	6

HR duties include the establishment of an executive stock option package and annual hiring of workers.
- Options expire after 10 years, and can be exercised at the end of year 5 on. There are 5 executives, whose compensation is spread across the members of the group, even if there are not 5 members in the actual group.
- Executive bonuses can be negative, to reflect deferred compensation. However, the sum of salary and bonus can never be negative.
- Wages and salary information appear below. Hiring and firing is done at the beginning of each year, before production decisions take place.

Executive Compensation

Finance / HR
Operations
Sales and Marketing

Setup Annual Bonus Scheme descriptively, in Text Answers.

A bonus scheme is a well-defined rule that specifies the bonus for each executive as a function of financial variables.

Annual Wages & Salaries

				1	2	3	4	5	6
Upper management				$140,000	$140,000	$140,000	$140,000	$140,000	$140,000
Manufacturing workers				$57,743	$57,743	$57,743	$57,743	$57,743	$57,743
Salespeople				$100,249	$100,249	$100,249	$100,249	$100,249	$100,249
Engineers				$80,199	$80,199	$80,199	$80,199	$80,199	$80,199
Customer support staff				$60,149	$60,149	$60,149	$60,149	$60,149	$60,149

Headcount

				1	2	3	4	5	6
Upper management				5	5	5	5	5	5
Manufacturing workers				10	0	0	0	0	0
Salespeople				1	0	0	0	0	0
Engineers				2	0	0	0	0	0
Customer support staff				2	0	0	0	0	0

Oper Investment and Disposal / Bds / Sales and Marketing \ **Human Resources** / Introduction /

Figure 8.5 Human Resources worksheet

a mix of market information and decisions. For example, the table labeled Executive Compensation records the value of annual bonuses; more on this table in the section titled Simulated Compensation.

The table for Annual Wages and Salaries provides information about the wages and salaries of the executives and for different types of employees. You don't have to worry about who these different types of employees are right now. As you can see, in Year 1, upper management salaries are $140,000. Actually, the worksheet shows $140,000 for every year, but that is only for illustrative purposes. In the planning file, players can alter the values for wages and salaries in future years to display their forecasts of how wages and salaries might change over time. In the live game file, the future values are not displayed: Only the values for the current year and past years are shown.

The table labeled Headcount records actual decisions. The number for Upper Management is set at 5, the ideal group size to play the game. The numbers for the other employee types record either planned decisions (in the planning file) or actual decisions (in the live game file). For example, Figure 8.5 indicates that the CHR plans to hire 10 manufacturing workers in Year 1.

The CSM is responsible for the worksheet Sales and Marketing, which you will find displayed in Figure 8.6. Most of the information displayed in this figure pertains to decisions that the CSM will be called upon to make. These decisions pertain to the amount spent on promotion, the deployment of the sales force across sales territories, bidding prices, and bidding quantities offered. For example, the worksheet shows the company planning to spend $50,000 on promotion and to allocate its single salesperson to Sales Territory 1 where it hopes to sell 220 units at a price of $2,200. Players find market information on which to base their decisions in the worksheet Introduction.

The following is a spreadsheet (Sales and Marketing worksheet).

	C	D	E	F	G	H	I	J
1	Year ==>		0	1	2	3	4	5
2	Sales & Marketing	Sales and Marketing worksheet						
3								
4								
5		Promotion		$50,000	$0	$0	$0	$0
6								
7		Number of Salespeople Available		1	0	0	0	0
8								
9		Salespeople (1 if assigned to territory, 0 otherwise)						
10		Salesperson in Territory 1		1	0	0	0	0
11		Salesperson in Territory 2		0	0	0	0	0
12	You compete on many dimensions: price, quality, customer support, salespeople coverage in each	Salesperson in Territory 3		0	0	0	0	0
13	territory, and promotion. Lower prices, higher	Salesperson in Territory 4		0	0	0	0	0
14	quality, greater customer support, wider sales	Salesperson in Territory 5		0	0	0	0	0
15	coverage per territory, and higher levels of	Salesperson in Territory 6		0	0	0	0	0
16	promotion all serve to increase your	Salesperson in Territory 7		0	0	0	0	0
17	competitiveness. Of course, not everyone can be	Total Salespeople Assigned		1	0	0	0	0
18	the best on every dimension. There are tradeoffs.	Feasibility Check		1	1	1	1	1
19								
20	In every year, you will place a bid with the	Price Decisions						
21	auctioneer (instructor), indicating price and	Price in Territory 1		$2,200	$0	$0	$0	$0
22	quantity offered for each territory. After all bids	Price in Territory 2		$0	$0	$0	$0	$0
23	are submitted, the auctioneer will inform you about how successful your bid has been for the	Price in Territory 3		$0	$0	$0	$0	$0
24	year. The price you charge will be the price you	Price in Territory 4		$0	$0	$0	$0	$0
25	bid. However, the volume of your sales may be	Price in Territory 5		$0	$0	$0	$0	$0
26	less than the amount of your bid. The table displaying Quantity Sold records the amount of	Price in Territory 6		$0	$0	$0	$0	$0
27	your actual bid.	Price in Territory 7		$0	$0	$0	$0	$0
28	Note that the auctioneer expects you to be able							
29	to honor your bids. If you offer to supply a higher	Quantity Offered Decisions						
30	quantity than you are capable of supplying, then	Quantity Offered in Territory 1		220	0	0	0	0
31	the auctioneer will assign a stiff penalty for	Quantity Offered in Territory 2		0	0	0	0	0
32	nonfulfillment.	Quantity Offered in Territory 3		0	0	0	0	0
33	The cells for Average Quality Offered Decisions	Quantity Offered in Territory 4		0	0	0	0	0
34	already contain a formula. The formula is correct if you ship product produced in the current year.	Quantity Offered in Territory 5		0	0	0	0	0
35	However, if you ship product produced in past years, then the average quality offered needs to	Quantity Offered in Territory 6		0	0	0	0	0
36	reflect the quality blend of what you ship.	Quantity Offered in Territory 7		0	0	0	0	0
37								

Oper Investment and Disposal / Bids \ Sales and Marketing \ Human Resources / Introduction /

Figure 8.6 Sales and Marketing worksheet

There are several worksheets pertaining to operations. The tab labeled Oper Investment and Disposal pertains to decisions about new fixed assets. Tabs further to the left than the ones displayed pertain to purchasing and production. For example, Figure 8.7 shows the worksheet Oper Production. This worksheet displays the manufacturing function, in which manufacturing workers use manufacturing machines to convert raw materials into EnviroStuff's product, enviro-generators.

Figure 8.7 displays the planned production of 224 enviro-generators. To produce these, the plan calls for the COO to assign 10 manufacturing workers to 2 manufacturing machines and use 280 units of raw material. The raw material is to be drawn from inventory, leaving 1,120 units of raw material. (A worksheet labeled Oper Purchasing, whose tab is displayed in Figure 8.7, indicates that the COO plans to purchase 1,400 units of raw material, which upon delivery will be stored in inventory.)

The CFO is responsible for several worksheets. One worksheet is labeled Finance Cash and Debt. Figure 8.8 displays this worksheet. This figure shows some of the decisions for which the CFO is responsible. These include cash management, new short-term debt, and new long-term debt. The figure shows that the company forecasts that during Year 1, it will have access to both short-term debt and long-term debt but will only use long-term debt in the amount $300,000. Also shown is $3 million in initial funding, which the company obtained from venture capitalists.

The worksheets for the CEO involve no direct decisions. Instead, the CEO focuses on summary sheets and dashboards, which effectively serve as reports. Figure 8.9 illustrates one such worksheet, labeled Summary Sheet.

Figure 8.9 shows that planned sales for Year 1 are $484,000. The figure also shows a breakdown of how the company plans to spend its money during the year. The tab

	C	D	E	F	G	H	I	J	K
	Year ==>		0	1	2	3	4	5	6
	Manufacturing Resources Available for Year								
	Summary of availability and utilization of manufacturing machine and manufacturing labor.	Manufacturing Machine Years Available		2.00	6.00	6.00	6.00	6.00	6.00
		Manufacturing Machine Years Utilized		2.00	0.00	0.00	0.00	0.00	0.00
		Manufacturing Labor Available (Person-Years)		10	0	0	0	0	0
		Labor feasibility indicator		1	1	1	1	1	1
	Manufacturing Resource Utilization								
		Manufacturing Labor (Person-Years)		10	0	0	0	0	0
	In this table, indicate how much of the manufacturing labor that you have hired you wish to use. Production of finished goods requires manufacturing machine time, raw materials, and manufacturing machine time. Raw materials are drawn from inventory. See the inventory tables below. Because material prices change over time, you need to pay attention to the year you purchased the inventory, for the purpose of computing COGS.	Units Raw Materials Currently in Inventory Purchased in Year 1		620	620	620	620	620	620
		Units Raw Materials Currently in Inventory Purchased in Year 2			0	0	0	0	0
		Units Raw Materials Currently in Inventory Purchased in Year 3				0	0	0	0
		Units Raw Materials Currently in Inventory Purchased in Year 4					0	0	0
		Units Raw Materials Currently in Inventory Purchased in Year 5						0	0
		Units Raw Materials Currently in Inventory Purchased in Year 6							0
		Units Raw Materials Currently in Inventory Purchased in Year 7							
		Units Raw Materials Currently in Inventory Purchased in Year 8							
		Units Raw Materials Currently in Inventory Purchased in Year 9							
		Units Raw Materials Currently in Inventory Purchased in Year 10							
		Total		620	620	620	620	620	620
		Raw Materials Used in Production from Inventory Year 1		280	0	0	0	0	0
		Raw Materials Used in Production from Inventory Year 2			0	0	0	0	0
		Raw Materials Used in Production from Inventory Year 3				0	0	0	0
		Raw Materials Used in Production from Inventory Year 4					0	0	0
		Raw Materials Used in Production from Inventory Year 5						0	0
		Raw Materials Used in Production from Inventory Year 6							0
		Raw Materials Used in Production from Inventory Year 7							
		Raw Materials Used in Production from Inventory Year 8							
		Raw Materials Used in Production from Inventory Year 9							
		Raw Materials Used in Production from Inventory Year 10							
		Total Raw Materials Used in Production		280	0	0	0	0	0
	Units Produced of Finished Goods			224	0	0	0	0	0

Oper Shipping / Oper Inventory / **Oper Production** / Oper Fixed Asset Resources / Oper Purchasing / C

Figure 8.7 Operations Production worksheet

		0	1	2	3	4	5	6
Year ==>		E	F	G	H	I	J	K
	Finance							
	Initial Funding	$3,000,000						
This table lists the current and past interest rates. The rate on short-term debt is tied to your recent Current Ratio, and the rate on your long-term debt is tied to your recent Total Debt Ratio and ROA. Remember that your interest rate is floating, not fixed, and future interest rates are not yet known.	**Interest Rates**							
	Treasury bill Rate (Rate on Marketable Securities)		4.4%	3.0%	3.0%	3.0%	3.0%	3.0%
	Short-term Debt		9.2%	13.0%	13.0%	13.0%	13.0%	13.0%
	Long-term Debt		7.4%	8.0%	8.0%	8.0%	8.0%	8.0%
	Cash & Marketable Securities							
In this table, you control the value of your marketable securities. You will make this decision when preparing your end-of-year financial statements.	Minimum Cash Position	$25,000	$25,000	$25,000	$25,000	$25,000	$25,000	$25,000
	Marketable Securities Held at End of Year	$2,150,000	$0	$0	$0	$0	$0	$0
	Interest Received from Marketable Securities Held		$64,500	$0	$0	$0	$0	$0
	Short-term Debt							
In this table you control your short-term debt decision for the end of each year. Note that the maximum amount you can borrow is tied to the level of your current assets.	Maximum New Borrowing Short term		$1,740,000	$450,757				
	Short-term Debt at end of Prior Year		$0	$0	$0	$0	$0	$0
	Increase in Principal Short-term Debt (Notes Payable)		$0	$0	$0	$0	$0	$0
	Automatic Repayment of Principal on Short-term Debt		$0	$0	$0	$0	$0	$0
	Net Repayment of Principal on Short-term Debt		$0	$0	$0	$0	$0	$0
	Interest Paid on Notes Payable		$0	$0	$0	$0	$0	$0
	Feasibility Check on New Short-term Borrowing		1	1	1	1	1	1
	Long-term Debt							
	Maximum Total Long-Term Debt Position		$825,000	$1,496,000	$1,037,000	$763,000	$739,000	$715,000
	Long-term Debt Position at End of Prior Year		$0	$300,000	$300,000	$300,000	$0	$0
	New Debt							
	Long term Debt from Borrowing in Year 1		$300,000	$300,000	$300,000			
	Long term Debt from Borrowing in Year 2			$0	$0	$0		
	Long term Debt from Borrowing in Year 3				$0	$0	$0	
	Long term Debt from Borrowing in Year 4					$0	$0	$0
	Long term Debt from Borrowing in Year 5						$0	$0
	Long term Debt from Borrowing in Year 6							$0

Finance New Equity and Dividend / Finance Cash and Debt / Oper Sales Summary / Oper Shipping / Op

Figure 8.8 Finance Cash and Debt worksheet

	Year ==>	0	1	2	3	4	5	6	7	8	9
		$0	$0	$0	$0	$0	$0	$0	$0	$0	$0
	Total Sales	$0	$700,000	$700,000	$700,000	$700,000	$700,000	$700,000	$700,000	$700,000	$700,000
	Total Wages & Salaries										
	Upper management (base salaries)	$0	$0	$0	$0	$0	$0	$0	$0	$0	$0
	Executive Bonuses	$0	$0	$0	$0	$0	$0	$0	$0	$0	$0
	Manufacturing workers	$0	$577,430	$0	$0	$0	$0	$0	$0	$0	$0
	Salespeople	$0	$100,249	$0	$0	$0	$0	$0	$0	$0	$0
	Engineers	$0	$160,398	$0	$0	$0	$0	$0	$0	$0	$0
	Customer support staff	$0	$120,298	$0	$0	$0	$0	$0	$0	$0	$0
	Recruiting/severance										
	Upper management	$0	$0	$0	$0	$0	$0	$0	$0	$0	$0
	Manufacturing workers	$0	$57,743	$0	$0	$0	$0	$0	$0	$0	$0
	Salespeople	$0	$10,025	$0	$0	$0	$0	$0	$0	$0	$0
	Engineers	$0	$16,040	$0	$0	$0	$0	$0	$0	$0	$0
	Customer support staff	$0	$12,030	$0	$0	$0	$0	$0	$0	$0	$0
	Total	$0	$95,838	$0	$0	$0	$0	$0	$0	$0	$0
	Promotion	$0	$50,000	$0	$0	$0	$0	$0	$0	$0	$0
	Value Materials Purchased	$0	$140,000	$0	$0	$0	$0	$0	$0	$0	$0
	Utilities on Headquarters Building	$0	$10,000	$10,000	$10,000	$10,000	$10,000	$10,000	$10,000	$10,000	$10,000
	Utilities on Operating Plant(s)	$0	$10,000	$20,000	$20,000	$20,000	$20,000	$20,000	$20,000	$20,000	$20,000
	Maintenance & Repair	$0	$11,628	$0	$0	$0	$0	$0	$0	$0	$0
	Total Capital Expenditures	$825,000	$750,000	$0	$0	$0	$0	$0	$0	$0	$0
	Total Salvage Value from Disposal	$0	$0	$0	$0	$0	$0	$0	$0	$0	$0
	Value of Inventory	$0	$743,787	$743,787	$743,787	$743,787	$743,787	$743,787	$743,787	$743,787	$743,787
	Accounts Receivable at end of Year	$0	$0	$0	$0	$0	$0	$0	$0	$0	$0
	Accounts Payable at end of Year	$0	$15,000	$0	$0	$0	$0	$0	$0	$0	$0
	Amount Factored at 80% on the $	$0	$0	$0	$0	$0	$0	$0	$0	$0	$0
	Collection Costs	$0	$0	$0	$0	$0	$0	$0	$0	$0	$0
	Cost of Stretching Payables	$0	$0	$0	$0	$0	$0	$0	$0	$0	$0

⟨ Summary Sheet ⟩ Dashboard Inputs / Finance AR and AP / Finance New Equity and Dividend / Finance ⟨

Figure 8.9 Summary Sheet worksheet

296

to the right of Summary Sheet is Dashboard Inputs. This worksheet, displayed in Figure 8.10, shows all the key planned decisions for Year 1. These worksheets allow the CEO to track activity within the company.

You have now had an overview of the simulation game. As you can see, it is quite complex. There are a lot of worksheets to manage. It can be overwhelming for a single player but is manageable for a group of five. Now that you are oriented, it's time to see how players roll up their sleeves and get to work.

Simulated Planning

Why plan? There are lots of good reasons. One reason is to engage in sensible budgeting. A second reason is to develop a coherent business strategy. A third reason is to figure out, systematically, how to execute the strategy. A fourth reason is to lay out key milestones that will let you monitor how the company is doing as the plan unfolds. A fifth reason is to have something concrete on which to base a bonus plan.

In Chapter 5, I provided an illustration of how the planning process might unfold. Typically, the planning process begins with the CEO inviting the CSM to make a sales forecast. For example, the CSM might forecast sales of $2 million for Year 1 based on available market information. He might begin by pointing out that the market for enviro-generators, while still small, is attracting a lot of attention. Based on the size of the enviro-generator market and the number of EnviroStuff firms, the CSR might suggest trying to sell 400 units at a price of $5,000 each. Notice that these numbers are higher than the corresponding numbers displayed in Figure 8.6.

Remember that forecasts are fertile ground for psychological biases such as unrealistic optimism, overconfidence, the illusion of control, and confirmation bias, all of which are especially pertinent in respect to the planning fallacy. A psychologically smart CEO would remind those present at

	A	B	C	D	E	F	G	H	I	J	K	L	M
1			Year ==>		0	1	2	3	4	5	6	7	8
2													
3													
4				HR									
5				Executive Bonuses									
6				Headcount									
7				Manufacturing workers		10							
8				Salespeople		1							
9				Engineers		2							
10				Customer support staff		2							
11													
12				Sales and Marketing									
13													
14				Promotion		$50,000							
15													
16													
17				Salespeople (1 if assigned to territory, 0 otherwise)									
18				Salesperson in Territory 1		1							
19				Salesperson in Territory 2		0							
20				Salesperson in Territory 3		0							
21				Salesperson in Territory 4		0							
22				Salesperson in Territory 5		0							
23				Salesperson in Territory 6		0							
24				Salesperson in Territory 7		0							
25													
26													
27				Price Decisions									
28				Price in Territory 1		$2,200							
29				Price in Territory 2		$0							
30				Price in Territory 3		$0							
31				Price in Territory 4		$0							
32				Price in Territory 5		$0							
33				Price in Territory 6		$0							
34				Price in Territory 7		$0							
35				Quantity Offered Decisions									
36				Quantity Offered in Territory 1		220							
37													

Summary Sheet \ **Dashboard Inputs** \ Finance AR and AP \ Finance New Equity and Dividend \ Finance (|

Figure 8.10 Dashboard Inputs worksheet

the planning meeting about these biases, perhaps even by posting a behavioral checklist, and invite others to ask questions and offer comments. Table 8.1 provides an example of what a behavioral checklist might look like.

Asking the right questions is incredibly important. Here are some examples. Is selling 400 units in Year 1 excessively optimistic? If Year 1 turns out to be an average year, is 400 a reasonable forecast? What is the evidence? If Year 1 turns out to be a bad year, what might make it so? Conversely, if Year 1 turns out to be a banner year, what would make it so? Is the CSM being overconfident? Is the CSM recognizing how much the outcome for the year will depend on luck? Is the CSM subject to the illusion of control and underestimating the extent to which factors external to the company will determine actual sales? Is $5,000 too high a price point, or could it be too low? What would happen if the forecast turned out to be too optimistic? How costly might the forecast error be? How accurate have the CSM's forecasts been in the past, whether at this company or at a different company? What would it take to produce 400 units?

The last question is best handled by the COO. And the COO might not have a ready answer. Instead, the COO might have to open up the game planning file and figure out what resources would be required to produce 400 units. In this regard, the game files do not offer the COO the option of entering a target output somewhere and reading off the resources required to produce that target. Instead, the COO has to manipulate inputs, either through trial and error or by developing an algorithm.

The COO might come back and tell the group that he sees no way to manufacture 400 units without spending a lot of money on additional fixed assets. Or the CEO might be wary of overproducing enviro-generators and getting stuck with the inventory. In the course of the dialogue, the CSM might scale back his forecast. Ultimately, the group might settle on a unit forecast of 220.

Table 8.1 Sample Behavioral Checklist

Unrealistic optimism	Are we looking at the world through rose colored glasses?
Overconfidence	Are we as good as we think we are? Are we too sure of our views? Are we underestimating risks?
Illusion of control	Are we overestimating how much control we have over the way things will turn out?
Confirmation bias	Are we downplaying information we don't want to hear, and playing up information that we do want to hear?
Planning fallacy	Do we realize that we have tended to be late and over budget in the past, but with no good reason believe that this time will be different?
Inside view	Are we too focused on the specifics of our decision task?
Outside view	Have we taken appropriate account of our past success rates?
Loss aversion	Are we being too conservative because we are extremely sensitive to the pain of loss?
Aversion to a sure loss	Are we reluctant to accept losses, instead taking chances where we have to beat the odds in order to be successful?
Anchoring bias	Are we using judgments that start with an anchor from which we make adjustments? If so, are we adjusting enough?
Availability bias	Are we placing too much weight on evidence that is in front of us, or easily recalled, but insufficient weight on information that is harder to obtain, or less easily recalled?
Hindsight bias	When we look at events in hindsight, do we mistakenly think that what actually happened was inevitable?
Narrow framing	Are we so narrowly focused that we fail to see the big picture?
Groupthink	As a group, do we play devil's advocate enough?
Information hoarding	Are we keeping valuable information from each other?

Keep in mind that there are a lot of psychological biases, and different people are prone to different biases. The CSM might be unrealistically optimistic. But he might also be loss averse. If he is especially loss averse, his forecast might be too conservative instead of too aggressive. That is one reason it is important to keep track of how well people's forecasts play out.

Oh, and by the way, the CEO might be loss averse. A CEO who is psychologically smart understands the potential for groupthink. A psychologically smart CEO will tolerate suggestions from others that she might be exhibiting some bias or another.

The COO is responsible for developing a production plan that is consistent with the sales and marketing forecast. The production plan needs to be pretty detailed. And it needs to have dollar signs attached. In other words, the COO has to tell the group not only how he thinks enviro-generators will be manufactured but also how much he forecasts it will cost. Doing so involves assessments for manufacturing headcount, raw material availability and prices, maintenance costs, and machine productivity.

The COO must also indicate what kind of fixed assets need to be in place to carry out the production plan. In other words, the COO needs to propose a capital budget as well as an operating budget. That means laying out the case for new plant and equipment.

What kind of questions might the group raise with the COO? They might probe and ask whether the COO's production plan seems reasonable. Does it call for the right number of manufacturing workers, too few, or too many? How much value does the tenth manufacturing worker contribute to the firm's profits? These are questions that the CHR might legitimately raise. The CHR might also do some experimenting with the operations worksheets to double-check the COO's replies.

How about questions pertaining to psychological biases? Machines can break down. Raw material quality can be variable. Manufacturing workers can make mistakes. Is the COO being unrealistically optimistic and overconfident in connection with the production plan?

The CFO has the responsibility of developing financial statements that reflect the planned decisions and forecasted outcomes. The CFO also has the responsibility for a wide variety of financial decisions that pertain to financing, working capital, and valuation. Ultimately, the pro forma financial statements that the CFO produces will constitute the most concrete representation of the company's plan.

If you think back to the discussion of Commercial Casework in Chapter 7, you will remember that its game plan was embodied in a spreadsheet with columns for each month. In the simulation game discussed here, the time frame is annual, not monthly. Nevertheless, the general character of multiperiod plans can be captured in the simulation game by asking players to forecast at least two years out. After all, in terms of process, a two-year forecast in the simulation game is formally very similar to an annual forecast involving two six-month periods.

The CFO also has the responsibility for assessing the impact of the financial plan on the company's value. This requires applying concepts such as net present value, free cash flow, and residual income. For this purpose, managers should forecast trends for at least four years.

Simulated Financial Standards

Standards for a company are like vital signs of health for a person. What are the company analogues for temperature, pulse, blood pressure, and respiratory rate? Profitability, cash flow, and value are good candidates. A complex simulation exercise should help players develop the habit of identifying both high-level strategic standards for the company as a whole and tactical standards for their own special functions.

By their nature, standards are quantifiable and measurable. That's why accounting is so important not just for accountants but for the entire workforce.

Think about residual income, otherwise known as economic value added. Is it a strategic standard?

Of course it is. Do you remember what economic value added measures? Most people have trouble remembering. It measures by how much net income exceeds the amount required to meet the expectations of all the company's investors.

Accountants love economic value added. They love it because of the fact that the value of a company is the sum of its book value and the present value of the future expected economic value-added stream. And book value is a balance sheet item. In a company with a financially literate workforce, everyone will understand that the way to increase a company's value over the number appearing on the balance sheet is to increase the future economic value-added stream.

Economic value added has a nice behavioral trait. It makes investors' expectations salient. If investors are expecting a rate of return of 10 percent and the company's book value is $10 million, the company has to generate at least $1 million of after-tax cash flow, including interest, before economic value added will be positive. That sets a natural standard to aim for. After all, negative economic value added means that a company's value will decline from its book value baseline.

Without question, economic value added and free cash flow are excellent standards for the CEO and the CFO. However, what about standards for those working in sales and marketing, operations, and human resources? In theory, the answer is yes. But in practice, we have to worry about issues involving line of sight. Will the workforce understand the link between their decisions and the value of their companies? For most, the link is pretty vague.

Economic value added and free cash flow are part of the simulation game. Players can learn to become comfortable with these concepts by playing the game. Notice that I said "can." If you want, you can play the game and never look at economic value added or free cash flow. In fact, unless players are encouraged to look at these items, most won't. Why not? The answer is because these concepts do not come naturally to most. For this reason, an important thing to do when playing the game is to get economic value added and free cash flow onto everyone's radar screen.

Another important thing to do is use the game to help people learn how to develop tactical standards. Jack Stack describes standards as the items that keep people awake at night. For some, it's sales volume; for others, it's cost of production. For others still, it's accounts receivable—that is, getting customers to pay for product they have already received. A standard for someone has to be something that the person can control, or should I say partly control, as most company outcomes reflect a combination of luck and skill.

Accountants can help with tactical standards just as they can help with strategic standards. Take the cost of production. In the simulation game, information on costs of production is available. The trouble is that there is so much information in the game file that most people tend to ignore it. It's not up in bright neon lights.

What has been a real surprise to me is how reluctant people are to focus attention on how much it costs to produce product, even when they are asked to do it. So much depends on it: profitability, cash flow, the value of the company. It's as if people would prefer to bury their heads in the sand and not know.

Maybe cost of production is an opaque concept. It might be tied up with how inventory is valued. For many people, valuing inventory is a mystery that they find either intimidating or boring. And for some, it's both intimidating and boring. Well, that doesn't reduce its importance. If you ignore the issue, it won't go away. So the thing to do is get an accountant to help clear up any mysteries by demystifying the concept and making the information readily available in a plain, clear way.

Figure 8.11 displays the top part of the worksheet Oper Inventory. The worksheet is loaded with numbers, although only a few are displayed in the figure. My experience has been that many players learn the hard way about the importance of this worksheet. They give it scant attention until they find themselves in a crisis, often of their own doing. For example, they might order so much raw material that their company's inventory system can't accommodate it. But if they don't track inventory, they might not know this until it's too late.

Further down the worksheet Oper Inventory, you can find information about the cost of production (see Figure 8.12). The information is embedded in the cost assigned to finished goods inventory. The value of that inventory reflects the value of the direct labor and materials that went into making the product, as well as the depreciation associated with the fixed assets used in production and other allocated overhead.

Take a look toward the bottom of Figure 8.12. You will see a section labeled Inventory Summary. The summary shows that at the end of Year 1, before the company has shipped product, it plans to hold 224 units in finished goods inventory. The summary sheet displays the value of this inventory as $686,787. On a unit basis, the sheet displays the value of the inventory further up the screen as $3,043.69. In other words, it essentially cost the company $3,044 to make one enviro-generator.

As I said earlier, some of the cost is direct materials, some is direct labor, and some is allocated overhead. It's important to know the breakdown. And for those who want to know, they can find the information in Figure 8.13.

Figure 8.13 makes clear what the biggest component of cost is: labor. Just to remind you, according to Figure 8.6, this company is planning to sell enviro-generators at a price of $2,200. That is less than the product's labor cost, let alone

		Year ==>		0	1	2	3	4	5

Description of Inventory Blocks

One finished enviro-generator occupies twice the inventory space of one unit of raw material inventory. One inventory block can hold the equivalent of 500 units of raw material. Check the Inventory Capacity Monitor below. If that monitor registers more than 100%, wastage is taking place. Remember that only at the end of the year can you make space for inventory by disposing of simulator machines and/or R&D lab equipment, or by purchasing new operating plants.

				0	1	2	3	4	5
Inventory Capacity Monitor									
		Number of Blocks Required for Inventory			3	3	3	3	3
		Percentage of Available Block Space Used for Inventory (>100% signals insufficient space)			71%	71%	71%	71%	71%
Inventory									
		Units Raw Material Inventory Purchased in Year 1			620	620	620	620	620
		Units Raw Material Inventory Purchased in Year 2				0	0	0	0
		Units Raw Material Inventory Purchased in Year 3					0	0	0
		Units Raw Material Inventory Purchased in Year 4						0	0
		Units Raw Material Inventory Purchased in Year 5							0
	This table records the items	Units Raw Material Inventory Purchased in Year 6							
	pertaining to your inventory,	Units Raw Material Inventory Purchased in Year 7							
	both raw material inventory and	Units Raw Material Inventory Purchased in Year 8							
	finished goods inventory. You	Units Raw Material Inventory Purchased in Year 9							
	will need the information in the	Units Raw Material Inventory Purchased in Year 10							
	inventory tables when shipping								
	to customers in the various sales								
	territories, and also in preparing	Value Raw Material Inventory Purchased in Year 1			$62,000	$62,000	$62,000	$62,000	$62,000
	your financial statements.	Value Raw Material Inventory Purchased in Year 2				$0	$0	$0	$0
		Value Raw Material Inventory Purchased in Year 3					$0	$0	$0
		Value Raw Material Inventory Purchased in Year 4						$0	$0
		Value Raw Material Inventory Purchased in Year 5							$0
		Value Raw Material Inventory Purchased in Year 6							
		Value Raw Material Inventory Purchased in Year 7							
		Value Raw Material Inventory Purchased in Year 8							
		Value Raw Material Inventory Purchased in Year 9							
		Value Raw Material Inventory Purchased in Year 10							
		Units Finished Goods Inventory Produced in Year 1			224	224	224	224	224
		Units Finished Goods Inventory Produced in Year 2			0	0	0	0	0

Oper Inventory / Oper Production / Oper Fixed Asset Resources / Oper Purchasing / Oper R&D / Text /

Figure 8.11 Top portion of the Operations Inventory worksheet

	Year ==>	0	1	2	3	4	5
	Unit Value Finished Goods Inventory Produced in Year 1		$3,043.69	$3,043.69	$3,043.69	$3,043.69	$3,043.69
	Unit Value Finished Goods Inventory Produced in Year 2			$0.0	$0.0	$0.0	$0.0
	Unit Value Finished Goods Inventory Produced in Year 3				$0.0	$0.0	$0.0
	Unit Value Finished Goods Inventory Produced in Year 4					$0.0	$0.0
	Unit Value Finished Goods Inventory Produced in Year 5						$0.0
	Unit Value Finished Goods Inventory Produced in Year 6						
	Unit Value Finished Goods Inventory Produced in Year 7						
	Unit Value Finished Goods Inventory Produced in Year 8						
	Unit Value Finished Goods Inventory Produced in Year 9						
	Unit Value Finished Goods Inventory Produced in Year 10						
	Quality Finished Goods Inventory Produced in Year 1		1.71	1.71	1.71	1.71	1.71
	Quality Finished Goods Inventory Produced in Year 2			1.71	1.71	1.71	1.71
	Quality Finished Goods Inventory Produced in Year 3				1.71	1.71	1.71
	Quality Finished Goods Inventory Produced in Year 4					1.71	1.71
	Quality Finished Goods Inventory Produced in Year 5						1.71
	Quality Finished Goods Inventory Produced in Year 6						
	Quality Finished Goods Inventory Produced in Year 7						
	Quality Finished Goods Inventory Produced in Year 8						
	Quality Finished Goods Inventory Produced in Year 9						
	Quality Finished Goods Inventory Produced in Year 10						
Inventory Summary							
	Units Raw Material in Inventory		620	620	620	620	620
	Value Raw Material in Inventory		$62,000	$62,000	$62,000	$62,000	$62,000
	Units Finished Goods in Inventory		224	224	224	224	224
	Value Finished Goods in Inventory		$681,787	$681,787	$681,787	$681,787	$681,787
	Value of Inventory		$743,787	$743,787	$743,787	$743,787	$743,787

Oper Inventory / Oper Production / Oper Fixed Asset Resources / Oper Purchasing / Oper R&D / Text. | <

307

Figure 8.12 Lower portion of the Operations Inventory worksheet

			Year ==>	0	1	2	3	4	5
				E	F	G	H	I	J
46									
47			Unit Value Raw Material Component of Finished Goods Inv Produced in Year 1		$125.00	$125.00	$125.00	$125.00	$125.00
48			Unit Value Raw Material Component of Finished Goods Inv Produced in Year 2			$0.00	$0.00	$0.00	$0.00
49			Unit Value Raw Material Component of Finished Goods Inv Produced in Year 3				$0.00	$0.00	$0.00
50			Unit Value Raw Material Component of Finished Goods Inv Produced in Year 4					$0.00	$0.00
51			Unit Value Raw Material Component of Finished Goods Inv Produced in Year 5						$0.00
52			Unit Value Raw Material Component of Finished Goods Inv Produced in Year 6						
53			Unit Value Raw Material Component of Finished Goods Inv Produced in Year 7						
54			Unit Value Raw Material Component of Finished Goods Inv Produced in Year 8						
55			Unit Value Raw Material Component of Finished Goods Inv Produced in Year 9						
56			Unit Value Raw Material Component of Finished Goods Inv Produced in Year 10						
57									
58			Unit Value Labor Component of Finished Goods Inventory Produced in Year 1		$2,577.81	$2,577.81	$2,577.81	$2,577.81	$2,577.81
59			Unit Value Labor Component of Finished Goods Inventory Produced in Year 2			$0.00	$0.00	$0.00	$0.00
60			Unit Value Labor Component of Finished Goods Inventory Produced in Year 3				$0.00	$0.00	$0.00
61			Unit Value Labor Component of Finished Goods Inventory Produced in Year 4					$0.00	$0.00
62			Unit Value Labor Component of Finished Goods Inventory Produced in Year 5						$0.00
63			Unit Value Labor Component of Finished Goods Inventory Produced in Year 6						
64			Unit Value Labor Component of Finished Goods Inventory Produced in Year 7						
65			Unit Value Labor Component of Finished Goods Inventory Produced in Year 8						
66			Unit Value Labor Component of Finished Goods Inventory Produced in Year 9						
67			Unit Value Labor Component of Finished Goods Inventory Produced in Year 10						
68									
69			Unit Value Allocated Overhead Component of Finished Goods Inventory Produced in Year 1		$340.88	$340.88	$340.88	$340.88	$340.88
70			Unit Value Allocated Overhead Component of Finished Goods Inventory Produced in Year 2			$0.00	$0.00	$0.00	$0.00
71			Unit Value Allocated Overhead Component of Finished Goods Inventory Produced in Year 3				$0.00	$0.00	$0.00
72			Unit Value Allocated Overhead Component of Finished Goods Inventory Produced in Year 4					$0.00	$0.00
73			Unit Value Allocated Overhead Component of Finished Goods Inventory Produced in Year 5						$0.00
74			Unit Value Allocated Overhead Component of Finished Goods Inventory Produced in Year 6						
75			Unit Value Allocated Overhead Component of Finished Goods Inventory Produced in Year 7						
76			Unit Value Allocated Overhead Component of Finished Goods Inventory Produced in Year 8						
77			Unit Value Allocated Overhead Component of Finished Goods Inventory Produced in Year 9						
78			Unit Value Allocated Overhead Component of Finished Goods Inventory Produced in Year 10						
79									
80			Unit Value Finished Goods Inventory Produced in Year 1		$3,043.69	$3,043.69	$3,043.69	$3,043.69	$3,043.69
81			Unit Value Finished Goods Inventory Produced in Year 2			$0.00	$0.00	$0.00	$0.00

|◄ ◄ ► ►|\ Oper Inventory / Oper Production / Oper Fixed Asset Resources / Oper Purchasing / Oper R&D / Text.|◄

Figure 8.13 Middle portion of the Operations Inventory worksheet

the materials and allocated overhead. Somebody had better be awake at night worrying about how much longer this can go on!

Accountants can help make companies create more value by working with people to show how their decisions affect the bottom line drivers of value like economic value added and free cash flow. Accountants can work with people to set standards, especially for costs, that are reasonable targets.

Remember, we are talking about a whole ball of wax. Planning and standards should not be independent of each other. Instead, they should be interlocking components of a well-oiled machine. In a psychologically smart company, the planning process informs the workforce about standards to shoot for. And those standards then come to be reflected in the final plan.

Simulated Compensation

The CHR takes the lead in designing a compensation system for the company's upper management. Ideally, everyone participates, especially the CEO and CFO. But the CHR has the responsibility of focusing everyone's attention on what a good compensation system does.

To be sure, a good compensation system rewards people for successful performance. But that's not all. A good compensation system structures incentives to induce people to work together to generate successful performance. A good compensation system helps people work together in a way that is psychologically smart.

Playing the simulation game well involves a lot of work, just like running a business well involves a lot of work. Some people are workaholics. Most are not. The majority need to be motivated to put in extraordinary effort. A good compensation system motivates people.

A good compensation system also focuses people on the right things by making it in their own best interests to do so. Paying attention to the value of inventory does not come naturally to most. And intrinsically, it's not all that much fun relative to life's other alternatives. Even if it's critically important to pay attention to inventory values, unless it's in-your-face salient, many people just won't do it. A good compensation system makes it salient.

A good compensation system educates people about the drivers of company value. It draws their attention to the right information and rewards them for making great use of that information.

In the section on standards, I provided an example in which the cost of labor was much higher than the sales price. This is information that needs to be flashed in neon lights so people know there's a problem. And the compensation system has to flash in neon lights that people will be rewarded for addressing the problem.

In the simulation game, there are several measures players can take to bring down labor costs. Some measures might be immediate. Others might take time. Immediate measures involve hiring fewer manufacturing workers or buying more manufacturing machines to make that labor more productive. Longer-term measures might involve investing in research and development. In this regard, the simulation game has operations tabs for R&D. Engineers can be hired to develop techniques that bring down the cost of production (see Figure 8.14).

What you can see in Figure 8.14 is that R&D activities involve both engineers and special equipment. By deploying these resources, the company can reduce its future cost of production. For example, Figure 8.14 indicates that the R&D effort in Year 1 has an expected positive impact: The same resources planned for use in Year 1 are expected to produce 141.42 percent more output in future years.

Figure 8.14 also provides information about product quality. Increasing product quality does not lower costs. It

	Year ==>		0	1	2	3	4	5	6
R&D Decisions									
R&D Equipment Available (Equipment Years)	Summary of resources available for R&D.			1,000	3,000	3,000	3,000	3,000	3,000
R&D Equipment Used (Equipment Years)				1,000	0,000	0,000	0,000	0,000	0,000
Number of Engineers				2	0	0	0	0	0
% of R&D Equipment Allocated to Research				50.0%	0.0%	0.0%	0.0%	0.0%	0.0%
% of Engineering Time Allocated to Research				50.0%	0.0%	0.0%	0.0%	0.0%	0.0%
% of R&D Equipment Allocated to Cost Reduction				50.0%	100.0%	100.0%	100.0%	100.0%	100.0%
% of Engineering Time Allocated to Cost Reduction				50.0%	100.0%	100.0%	100.0%	100.0%	100.0%
Product Quality				1.71	1.71	1.71	1.71	1.71	1.71
Improvement in Productivity (Cost Reduction)				141.42%	0.00%	0.00%	0.00%	0.00%	0.00%

There are 2 types of R&D decisions, research activities aimed at improving product quality, and development activities aimed at improving manufacturing productivity.

1. Given the number of equipment years available, decide how intensively to run each unit of R&D laboratory equipment. Full utilization is 1 unit per piece of equipment.

2. Having determined the utilization intensity of R&D equipment, allocate R&D capital and engineering-time across two functions, (1) research aimed at improving the quality of the product, and (2) cost reduction aimed at achieving improved production efficiencies. In the green cells, enter a % figure between 0% and 100% for resources devoted to research. The remaining resources are devoted to development activities that improve future productivity and lower future costs.

3. The impact of R&D investment has a random component, that is identified each year after the bid.

Note: You need to compute unit-weighted average quality when submitting bid, if you supply finished product with differential quality.

Oper Inventory / Oper Production / Oper Fixed Asset Resources / Oper Purchasing \ Oper R&D / Text |

Figure 8.14 R&D Operations worksheet

raises costs. However, offering higher quality might provide the company with an opportunity to raise its prices.

In Chapter 6, you read about general guidelines for developing bonus plans and employee stock ownership plans. Those guidelines apply to playing the simulation game. An annual bonus plan should have at least two targets: one associated with the income statement and one associated with the balance sheet.

The bonus-plan variables do not have to be same from year to year. If, in some year, the biggest threat to a company comes from its labor costs, then labor costs might be identified as an income statement target for the bonus plan. But labor costs might only be an issue in some years. In other years, quality might be the issue, with the income statement manifestation of quality coming through sales revenue. In those years, the bonus plan might target a mix of revenues and quality.

As for the balance sheet, if the company has inadvertently built up its inventories, then the CHR might recommend using inventory levels as the balance sheet target.

These examples are just that—examples: things to think about. Whether or not they are worth doing depends on how the compensation system is structured. The law of unintended consequences is a psychological law. Compensation systems are effective to the extent that they increase a company's value.

A company's value does not just depend on next year's economic value added or free cash flows. It depends on the whole stream of numbers for expected future economic value added and free cash flow. It is possible to take actions that make next year look good but the years after that terrible. Unnecessary cost cutting is an example. Therefore, somebody in the company needs to be engaged in long-term planning to identify spillover effects from one year to another. This is an important reason to have a stock ownership component as part of compensation. However, just making stock available will not automatically induce people to maximize the value of the company. The workforce needs to understand how their decisions affect that value.

In seeking to identify sensible variables on which to base a bonus plan, does it sound like we are talking about standards? The answer is yes. And this should come as no surprise. We are talking about a whole ball of wax here. Standards are the key vital signs of company health. It's extremely important to put those on everyone's radar screen. A bonus plan should heighten the attention focused on key standards. A bonus plan should make standards salient. And of course, a bonus plan should reward the workforce for the successful achievement of those standards.

Simulated Information Sharing

Time is a limited resource. Time is valuable. Sharing information takes time. What should the people in a company be talking about to each other?

Remember that, psychologically, people are not predisposed to share information. If anything, people are predisposed to hoard information. So, a well-functioning simulation game will induce people to share relevant information in a structured, systematic, open manner.

What should be the items that go on the front burner? What should be the items that go on the back burner?

What goes on the front burner is the company's plan, described in large part by the company's financials. Communication takes place throughout the simulation game. However, the simulation game specifically sets aside time for players to engage in an SRC-type huddle to share information. That time occurs every simulation game year, after the bidding results are announced. To see where the huddle comes in chronologically, let me describe the structure of a simulation game year.

Simulation game years are divided into three phases: the period before players submit bids, the moment they submit bids, and the period after they receive the results of their bids. Before they bid, a group faces the task of hiring employees, purchasing raw materials, engaging in production, and preparing the bid for the year. After receiving the results of their bids, their tasks are to ship product, engage in investment and disposal of fixed assets, raise money for financing, prepare financial statements, and revise their rolling year plan, including compensation policies for managers. The next year does not begin until all players have closed out the previous year.

Players need to be sure not to engage in crossover activities. For example, they should not purchase inventory after submitting their bids. They should not purchase or dispose of fixed assets before they have submitted their bids.

Most of the activity described in the last two paragraphs is accomplished in the live game file. This file is where real decisions are recorded. This file records the actual bids submitted to the auctioneer. This file gets updated by the auctioneer to reflect the outcome of the bidding process as well as to note unforeseen random events that affect the firm's profitability.

The planning file is an internal document. It is not submitted as part of the bid, although it might get submitted to be checked for quality of effort. The planning file is a locus for developing a rolling year plan. In the last part of the year, before making decisions about purchasing new capital equipment, new financing, bonus-plan parameters, and so on, players work to revise their prior plans. They do this because their decisions at the end of the year will affect their company in successive years. One reason to do planning is to ascertain what the future impact of current decisions will be.

For the sake of discussion, suppose that at the end of Year 1, the players develop a two-year plan involving Years 2 and 3. At the end of Year 2, the bidding results for Year 2 will have been announced. That will allow many of the variables in the Year 2 financial statements to be finalized, particularly in the income statement. The actual income statement numbers for Year 2 can be compared against the Year 2 plan numbers that were forecast at the end of Year 1.

The players huddle in Year 2 when they engage in a pre-liminary revised forecast for Year 3 and compare their revised Year 3 forecast with their previous Year 3 forecast that was put together at the end of Year 1. In doing so, players take responsibility for particular items. The CSM takes responsibility for the sales forecast. The COO takes responsibility for COGS and R&D. The CHR takes responsibility for SG&A. The CFO takes responsibility for interest and other income.

The comparison of the revised forecast for Year 3 against the Year 1 forecast of Year 3 is designed to focus attention on what new has happened. When I teach the EnviroStuff simulation game, I encourage players to make short presentations to each other to justify their new forecasts. The idea is to institutionalize the sharing of relevant information.

When I teach the EnviroStuff simulation game, I encourage players to engage in a quick percent of sales exercise, along the lines described in Chapter 5. The idea is to institutionalize the sharing of relevant information.

The basis for the quick pro forma exercise is a worksheet which is pre-programmed with key formulas, but features particular blank cells that players fill in. These blank cells pertain to such items as the Year 3 sales forecast, various percent of sales ratios, and so on. The CEO assigns responsibility for each of the blank cells to the various players. Players then simulate a huddle whereby they meet and report their first pass suggestions for populating the blank cells. The CFO then does what Francine did in Chapter 5, namely proposing financial decisions that would make the pro forma Year 3 balance sheet come into balance.

The huddle is the first step in formulating the next phase of a rolling plan, to cover Year 3, Year 4, and perhaps more. Based on the huddle, players make decisions about new capital equipment purchases. If those purchases require external financing, the revised rolling plan will have to feature the nature of that financing. The players must make their Year 3 capital budgeting decisions and financing decisions before they close out their Year 3 financials. And they do this in their live game file.

In theory, players revise their rolling plan, close out their financials, and simply transfer the decisions from their plan to their live game files to submit their bids for the next year. In practice, it often works this way, but not always.

The simulation game has a beneficial side effect. Players become very adroit with financial statements. The combination of planning, setting standards, developing a compensation system, and sharing information focuses their attention on financial statements like a laser beam. Accounting becomes the language of communication. It ceases to be a foreign language for most. And it puts profitability, cash flow, and value on the group's radar screen, front and center!

The Secret Is Out

If there is a secret to building a psychologically smart company, I hope I have shared it.

Psychologically smart companies recognize human vulnerabilities. They institutionalize procedures for addressing unrealistic optimism, overconfidence, the illusion of control, and confirmation bias. They understand emotional intelligence and the importance of relationships.

Psychologically smart companies use smart heuristics to address human vulnerabilities, especially the susceptibility to the planning fallacy, the fear of accounting, naiveté about incentives, and the reluctance to share information. Moreover, smart heuristics focus on the basics: accounting, planning, incentives, and information sharing.

Most importantly, psychologically smart companies incorporate the basics in a fully integrated manner. They are not content with half measures. Their corporate cultures feature the whole ball of wax.

INDEX